ON EAGLE'S WINGS

A TRUE STORY OF FAITH AND LOVE
IN THE WAKE OF TRAGEDY

ON EAGLE'S WINGS

Senator Bob Giuda

FRANKLIN GREEN
PUBLISHING

On Eagle's Wings:
A Story of Faith and Love in the Wake of Tragedy

Copyright © 2023 by Bob Giuda

All rights reserved. No part of this publication may be reproduced, stored in a retrieval system, or transmitted in any form by any means, electronic, mechanical, photocopy, recording, or otherwise, without the prior permission of the publisher, except as provided by USA copyright law.

No patent liability is assumed with respect to the use of the information contained herein. Although every precaution has been taken in the preparation of this book, the publisher and author assume no responsibility for errors or omissions. Neither is any liability assumed for damages resulting from the use of the information contained herein.

Published by Franklin Green Publishing

Print ISBN: 9781936487509

Cover and Interior Design by Bill Kersey, KerseyGraphics
Editor: Mary Sanford

I dedicate this book to God, the Author of All Life, and to the most precious gifts He has bestowed upon me: His Son Jesus Christ; my beautiful wife Christine; our three amazing children Joseph, Lauren, and Stephanie; and our grandsons, Hunter and Braden. I'm also profoundly grateful to the many friends who have prayed for us and supported us along the way. And finally, no words can suffice to express my undying gratitude to the men and women who, day and night, tirelessly care for Christine and for the many among us unable to care for themselves, often under daunting conditions and never adequately compensated for their calling. Your work is truly God's work. Thank you, all of you, for showing me the way.

Contents

FOREWORD 9

CHAPTER 1: THE DAY THE MUSIC DIED. 11

CHAPTER 2: SHARING THE FEAR 15

CHAPTER 3: BEGINNINGS 19

CHAPTER 4: CRITICAL CARE 25

CHAPTER 5: BOY MEETS GIRL, OR
            "WHAT WERE YOU THINKING?" 29

CHAPTER 6: IT'S ABOUT THE RIDE. 35

CHAPTER 7: WHIDBEY MAGIC 41

Chapter 8: The Volcano 47

Chapter 9: The Weekend That
          Clinched the Deal 53

Chapter 10: About Landing
          on Aircraft Carriers 57

Chapter 11: In Memory of Three Friends 61

Chapter 12: Threads 67

Chapter 13: Strays and Wounded 71

Chapter 14: Transition 75

Chapter 15: Kids 81

Chapter 16: The Thread of Faith in Our Lives 87

Chapter 17: Go Your Way—
            Your Faith Has Saved You............ 95

Chapter 18: The Rest of the Story 99

The Posts................................. 101

Epilogue 403

Foreword

February 18, 2018, was no different from any other day. I prayed the Rosary with my loving wife, Christine, just before first light—one hand holding the beads and the other resting on her forehead as I quietly recited the prayers. It's a sacred time, this early morning awakening, and as I was praying, the RN on duty quietly came into the room to make sure Chrissy was OK, to refill the nutrition and water supplies for her feeding apparatus, and to check the gastric tube that has fed her since the day she was stricken. As he was leaving, he turned to me and said, "You know, I really hope you write that book."

He was right, and though that comment was made several years ago, the idea of writing a book eventually became an imperative. Intuition told me it was important to share the spiritual road my family has traveled. Christine always listened to the keen voice of her intuition, and it never steered her wrong—or me.

This book provides some vignettes of important events in our lives, and it also contains the entire compilation of four years of Facebook posts I published since the journey began. They include personal musings and observations about life and death, sin and forgiveness, hope and despair, uncertainty and purpose, love and family, and above all, faith. It's not so much

FOREWORD

my gift to you as it is Chrissy's gift to us. It's her legacy to a world desperately in need of inspiration and a renewal of faith.

I wrote this book to try to make sense of the spiritual, emotional, and physical turmoil that rocked us in the aftermath of an inexplicable tragedy. It shares with you my battle to use misfortune for God's purposes, because when all is said and done, life is really all about finding our way to Heaven. It starts with God, and it ends with God—the Alpha and the Omega, the beginning and the end.

Our quest to turn this tragedy to God's purposes began in earnest when my wife's out-of-the-blue catastrophic brain aneurysm shattered our lives. The very next day, I began writing Facebook posts to keep family and friends apprised on Chrissy's condition. But the posts quickly became much more than just updates. As you read them, you will feel the desolation and joy, the anger and peace, and the horror and beauty that we experience when tragedy befalls us. Every chapter and every post has a message; some will have more meaning for you than others. I hope each one brings you closer to our Lord and Savior.

My prayer is that this book takes you places you've never been before, emotionally and spiritually. I hope you'll learn to pray more perfectly, live more fully, and love more deeply as a result of reading it. And most importantly, I hope that you will know the infinite love Almighty God has for you, and His desire to bring you to eternal joy and glory in His presence in Heaven.

In faith,
Bob and Christine Giuda

CHAPTER 1

The Day the Music Died

THE HANDWRITTEN MESSAGE FROM MY ASSISTANT WAS TERSE: *Senator, your wife has fallen. Your daughter called and wants you to call her ASAP.*

He had knocked on the closed door of the senate conference room on the third floor of the New Hampshire State House. It was 1:18 p.m. on January 18, 2017. As a newly elected state senator, I was keenly interested in the caucus discussion, as we were getting acquainted with our newly formed NH State Senate colleagues and beginning the discussion of our legislative priorities. But suddenly the importance of the caucus evaporated. Something had happened to my wife, and that was all that mattered. I excused myself and called home. My daughter's voice was filled with fear as she explained what had happened. "Mom was in the kitchen, and she suddenly grabbed the back of her head, yelled 'Ow! Ow! Ow!' and knelt down on the floor. I told her to go to your recliner and rest, which she did. But when I looked a couple of minutes later to see how she was doing, she wasn't there. I ran into the dining room, and she was lying on the floor in the foyer to the master bedroom, arms at her sides as she had apparently tried to get to the bedroom to lie down. It seems she had realized something was very wrong and laid down rather than risking a fall. Dad, I'm scared, and I don't know what to do."

Christine, my wife, was in good health, and everything my daughter said screamed out "Stroke!" I returned to the conference room, apologized for the interruption, explained the situation, and asked the senate president for a state police escort to my home. Ten minutes later, I was headed up I-93 at 120 miles per hour. All I could say was, "Please, God, let her be okay." The sixty-five-mile drive seemed to take forever, but at last I arrived home, slammed the car into park, and ran into the house. A lifelong friend came racing up the hill after he saw me speeding through town with my emergency lights flashing. He was the just-retired fire chief for our small, rural New England town nestled in the shadow of 6,812-foot Mt. Moosealuke, in the western reaches of the White Mountains.

After what seemed like an eternity, the ambulance arrived and the EMTs came into the house. While I was racing home, I had called my next-door neighbor and asked him to come down to our house to help my daughter. Together, they had lifted Christine up off the floor and moved her onto our bed. When I arrived, she was lying on her back, unresponsive, with occasional tremors and spasms shaking her right arm. Her eyes were open but unseeing, and she began to vomit. I quickly turned her on her side, clearing her mouth and protecting her airway to make sure she didn't inhale vomit into her lungs. The EMTs, unaware of the critical importance of time in dealing with brain injuries, were fumbling around trying to take her vital signs. My friend, the former fire chief, recognized the gravity of the situation. He said, "Guys, she's in bad shape; just scoop her up and go." They brought in the gurney, strapped her in, rolled it out of the house and into the ambulance, and headed for the nearest hospital, twenty minutes away. Lights and siren provided grim affirmation of her perilous condition. I drove right behind them in my car, refusing to let Chris out of my sight.

My heart sank when another ambulance came speeding up the road in the opposite direction with lights and siren blaring, did a U-turn, and stopped on the shoulder. Our ambulance pulled up behind it, and a paramedic from the other unit ran to Chrissy's ambulance. I since learned that EMTs can only do so much, and this rendezvous meant that the severity of Chris's condition was such that she needed the higher-level skills of a paramedic and couldn't wait to get to the hospital. I was scared, my mind racing as I watched Chrissy fighting for her life. The only thing I could do was pray, and I prayed every prayer I knew—the Lord's Prayer, Apostle's Creed, Hail Mary, Glory Be, Memorare, Hail Holy Queen, and Prayer to St. Michael. When I ran out of prayers that I knew, I made up new ones, begging God to spare her life.

We arrived at the hospital, and they took her in for an MRI. After what seemed like a very long time, the doctor came to the waiting room, looking grim. "It's bad," he said. "She's had an aneurysm rupture, and the damage is devastating. She needs to get to Dartmouth Hitchcock as quickly as possible. The weather is too poor for the DHART medevac helicopter, so we've reassigned the DHART critical care ground ambulance to take her by road." Fortuitously, the DHART critical care ground unit had been sent to this hospital for non-emergency transport of another patient, but it was reassigned to us because Chris was in critical condition.

It was wet, rainy, and dark, and it took almost two hours to get to Dartmouth Hitchcock Medical Center in Lebanon,

New Hampshire. The ambulance crew rushed her inside, and after several hours of emergency surgery, the neurosurgeon and the ICU team came out to brief us. Their faces were somber, the look you always see on TV when things aren't going well. "Mr. Giuda, Christine has a ruptured aneurysm of the anterior communicating artery in her brain. There's a significant amount of blood in the brain's ventricles. Because of the hours of severe excess pressure on her brain, she has suffered extensive brain damage. We've relieved the pressure with a shunt, but your wife is in extremely critical condition." The unasked question hung in the air. "We can't say for sure, but we're giving her a ten percent chance of surviving. If she does survive, it's highly unlikely that she'll ever again be able to function in any way that will remotely resemble a normal life."

My mind screamed, "Wait a minute. This is Dartmouth Hitchcock; you people do miracles here. What do you mean, *a ten percent chance of survival?* What do you mean, *unable to function ever again?* We're one month from our retirement, and everything we've worked for during our thirty-five-year marriage is right in front of us. This can't be. Not Chrissy. Not now. We're going to beat this. We *have to* beat this."

When they finally allowed us into her room in the Critical Care Unit (CCU), she looked like she was asleep. And in one sense, she was. The scenario was everything you see in the movies: machines and monitors and tubes and IVs, and all the associated beeps, hisses, and clicks that signaled that death was not far away.

CHAPTER 2

Sharing the Fear

The day Christine was stricken, I began to share her condition on Facebook with the many friends and acquaintances we've gained over the years. It was the first of many posts, every one of which is found in this book. Those posts became a catharsis for me, an outlet for the fear, anger, and bewilderment that had overtaken my life and our world. They became an almost daily event, and as prayer groups and friends picked up on her desperate condition, these posts eventually circulated around the world. For me, they quickly became much more than status updates on Chris's condition. They became my way of trying to transform a devastating tragedy to fit God's purposes, sharing my thoughts on faith, family, love, marriage, and life. The overwhelming "emotional adrenaline" generated in response to the devastation visited on Christine drove me to write these posts. I fought with every ounce of strength to avoid asking the question we all want answered: "Why her?"

Life is like a tapestry, and during this life we only get to see its back, with loose ends and vague shapes and unclear designs. The complete beauty of the front is reserved for us to see only after we leave this life and head off into eternity. I do know that "Why?" will never be answered, and pursuing that question leads us away from what God wants us to be. I believe the only way to deal with tragedy is to care for the stricken and to turn what has happened to God's purposes.

I consider myself to be the scribe who wrote these posts, not the author who generated them. God is most effective during times of tragedy. He is a source of solace and encouragement, comfort, and guidance if we have "eyes to see and ears to hear."

Here's the first Facebook post I wrote, on the day the love of my life was stricken:

. . . .

January 18th, 2017—Day 1

Dear Friends,

I wish I were bringing good news, but such is not the case. This afternoon, my wife Christine suffered a massive sub-arachnoid hemorrhage caused by a brain aneurism which ruptured while she was at home. Stephanie (one of our identical twin daughters) discovered her lying on the floor very shortly after it happened, and she was taken first to Speare Hospital, where they stabilized her, and then immediately transported to Dartmouth Hitchcock Medical Center. Unfortunately, the DHART helicopter was unable to make an airlift because of bad weather, so their ground critical transport ambulance made the trip in two hours.

Christine is in a coma and on a ventilator, and the neurosurgeons and vascular surgeons have done all they can do. They inserted a drain to relieve the pressure on her brain, and she is stable but in extremely critical condition.

All our children and their spouses are either already with me at DHMC or will be here by 10 AM Thursday.

I'm asking for you to join us in praying together for my life partner, my best friend, the mother of our children, and the person who truly is "the wind beneath my wings."

Thank you so much for your prayers.

Bob

. . . .

And thus began the journey.

CHAPTER 3

Beginnings

I MADE UP MY MIND TO BE A PILOT AT THE AGE OF TWELVE, WHEN I got my first ride in a small airplane at Sky Manor Airport in central western New Jersey. Long story short, that ride "set the hook," and I decided to make flying my life's professional ambition. After finishing high school, I attended and graduated from the U.S. Naval Academy and opted to serve as a United States Marine Corps pilot. After I completed the Basic School at Quantico, Virginia, I completed navy flight training in Pensacola, Florida. After serving on board (and flying on and off) the *USS Midway* (CV-41, the navy's designation for an aircraft carrier whose keel was laid in 1941), I found myself on orders to serve as a naval flight instructor in the EA-6B Prowler, then the world's only carrier-based tactical electronic warfare aircraft. I was assigned to VAQ-129, the Prowler Fleet Replacement Squadron (FRS), formerly called the Replacement Air Group (RAG), based at Naval Air Station (NAS) Whidbey Island, Washington. It was a billet highly coveted by Marine electronic warfare pilots, but getting assigned to that billet required qualification as an Air Wing Landing Signals Officer (LSO). That meant spending hundreds of extra hours and several years both ashore and at sea on aircraft carriers to gain the Air Wing LSO designation. Because carrier duty was something most Marines avoided like the plague, I was the only one who put in the time to get qualified to train others in the dangerous challenge of landing high speed jets aboard America's aircraft carriers day and night. Though the LSO assignment was intended to be filled by a major, I was the only pilot available with the LSO qualification, and Headquarters Marine Corps (HQMC) gave me the nod as a first lieutenant, two ranks junior to the recommended major's rank. I arrived at NAS Whidbey Island, north of Seattle, Washington, in mid-August of 1979.

As the oldest of eight children, Christine became her mother's helper, taking care of her younger siblings. They were a blue-collar family, hard-working, close knit, and salt-of-the-earth, descended from solid stock who built the Northwest's timber industry. Her mom's grandparents had come from Poland, and her dad's grandparents from Sweden. Because money was tight and the family was large, all the children worked from an early age, among other things picking string beans and other vegetables alongside their mother at truck farms around Eugene, Oregon. She graduated from Sacred Heart School of Nursing in Eugene with her RN certificate and answered the call of duty by joining the Navy as a Registered Nurse. She attended Officer Indoctrination School (OIS) in Newport, Rhode Island. For her first assignment on active duty, she was stationed at Oak Knoll Naval Hospital in Oakland, California. While there, she cared for many of the wounded sailors and Marines returning from the Vietnam War.

After completing her active-duty Navy commitment, Chrissy went to work full time as a Registered Nurse at

BEGINNINGS

Children's Hospital in Seattle—a place of breathtaking miracles and crushing tragedies. Children's hospitals work tirelessly to save the lives of youngsters who are gravely ill or severely injured. One of her patients, Matthew, had been struck by a car driven by a drunk driver and terribly injured. After several months, he eventually died from those injuries. Until the day she was stricken, Chrissy wept every time we spoke of him, because of the love she felt for him. That's who she is.

Because her Navy commitment included four years of reserve duty as a nurse after leaving active duty, she was assigned to the Naval Hospital at Whidbey Island, Washington. One weekend each month, she would travel from her apartment in Seattle to Whidbey Island to complete her required duties. When a posting came open for a civil service nurse at the naval hospital, she applied and was hired. She moved to Whidbey Island and took an apartment there, providing medical care for sailors and Marines five days a week as a civil service nurse and one weekend each month as a Navy Reserve nurse. It was the perfect setup—in more ways than one.

Caring for others, particularly as a registered nurse, was Christine's calling, according to every person who ever knew her. She was the person to whom those in need instinctively turned, because of her love of people and her caring spirit. She was also the person that injured animals somehow always found, because they could somehow sense her love and compassion. She was unabashed in her love of pets, and when fate brought us together, she owned a cat named Daisy (more about her later) and a Keeshond named Jonathan.

. . . . . .

January 19th, 2017 — Day 2

Dear Friends,

Chrissy remains in a coma, and the doctors are telling us that based on statistics in these types of cases, we should expect little or no improvement (ever) because of the extent of the damage caused by the hemorrhage. With complete respect for their skills and knowledge, we also know there is a greater Doctor who performed many miracles during His earthy ministry, and that miracles continue to happen to this day because of His love for us and His power over death. We remain quietly resolute in our faith.

We're keeping round-the-clock presence with Chris at DHMC, holding her hands, talking to her, and praying over her. We've asked for a second opinion of her condition to provide more certainty, and we are meeting again today in conference with medical and palliative specialists, our Pastor, and the entire family to discuss options and possibilities. However, we (the family) are of one mind in that we will not yet be making any decisions with permanent consequences.

We're reviewing her living will - something everyone should have before you ever have to face this situation - to be certain of her wishes and to reinforce and clarify the decisions she wanted made about her life if she were ever unable to make them herself. Living will or not, who really expects to find themselves in this situation? We live life, we love life, and too often we never stop to consider how precious and fragile our lives really are...

Chrissy is breathing almost completely on her own, and we are seeing some occasional movements of her head and her lips, stretching-type movements of her entire body, and an occasional squeeze of her fingers. We have no way of knowing whether these are conscious muscle movements or merely reflexive contractions, but on several occasions, her finger squeezes and lip movements seem to have come in response to something we've asked or said. By far the hardest part of our work is waiting to allow time for her body to begin to wage the fight to reverse the damage to her brain. Though it seems like a lifetime, it has only been 36 hours since she was stricken. And amid a world consumed by pursuit of instant gratification, we know that for right now, waiting, watching, and praying are what we must do. And fear and tears notwithstanding, we do it with quiet and complete confidence in the Lord our God.

At 8:30 this morning, the doctors will perform surgery to repair the aneurysm that caused the hemorrhage. Unless this is fixed, the prognosis is certain, and we will lose her. If it is repaired, we open up the medical possibility that she could recover. I'm asking each of you to pray for the success of this operation for an hour, starting at 8:30. We know the power of prayer, and we need this operation to succeed to even allow for the possibility of a medical reversal. We thank you - every one of you - for your continuing support, your prayers, and the love you have shown as we continue our journey of faith with our wonderful, beautiful lady, your friend, my wife, and my children's mother, our Christine.

Bob

CHAPTER 4

Critical Care

The Critical Care Unit waiting room at Dartmouth Hitchcock Medical Center in Hanover became my home for the next five weeks. The joke was that I had signed a lease agreement with the hospital. I ate there, slept there, and prayed there. I only went home three times during that five-week stay. My daughters shuttled clean clothes from home to the hospital. On Thursdays, I left the hospital only long enough to attend senate sessions in Concord so I could vote on proposed legislation. I'm forever grateful to Senate President Chuck Morse and my colleagues in the state senate for their understanding and compassion as I dealt with the devastating consequences of Christine's condition.

Chris was truly at death's door. She was intubated, on a ventilator, and unable to see, speak, move, or eat—barely clinging to life. A later surgery replaced the temporary shunt relieving the fluid pressure on her brain with a permanent shunt. Intercranial pressure, or ICP, became the barometer by which we measured her chances of survival. After several days, her medical team surgically installed a feeding tube (called a *g-tube*) directly into her stomach, through which she would be "fed," since her swallowing reflexes were so badly damaged and they didn't want to risk her choking.

You learn a lot during a medical crisis. We secrete a lot of saliva, and swallowing it is an involuntary reflex that most of us don't even realize we have. Chris's reflex was severely impacted by the damage to her brain, and she faced the constant threat of inhaling these secretions and either suffocating or developing pneumonia. It was a constant battle, and though I stood at her side, in truth I was a helpless spectator who could only watch and pray as she fought for her life.

The care she received from the CCU nurses and her neurosurgical team was incredible. I called a Naval Academy classmate who had gone on to become a renowned neurosurgeon and asked him if Dartmouth Hitchcock was appropriate for her condition and whether I should consider moving her to a better hospital. His words were concise: "Leave her right there. They're one of the best in the world." That settled the question, and we began the agonizing wait to see whether medical science was in consonance with God's will.

. . . . . .

January 20th, 2017—Day 3

"...and it was evening and morning, the third day..."

This popped into my head as I began to write this update. And in a way, it's so very appropriate, as our lives and our personal world are being re-created.

So, yesterday's operation to repair the aneurysm was successful, and for this we are grateful. The neurovascular surgical team "coiled" the aneurysm in a procedure that lasted about 1-1/2 hours. It will enable the medical team to adjust blood pressure, heart rate and other medical factors to maximize the possibility of survival and recovery.

The doctors' prognosis remains unchanged: 10% chance that Chrissy will survive, and if she does, at this point, she will only have basic brain stem activity. Dark though this assessment may be, we are receiving accounts of people who have suffered similar devastating brain injuries that have not only survived, but are back leading normal, productive lives. We're gathering information from the families of these survivors with the help of family and friends, and developing a sense of possibilities based on asking specific, detailed questions about medical aspects of Chrissy's situation. We greet each day with optimism even as we deal with our immediate harsh reality.

I want to share a personal thought with you. Last Wednesday, the day she suffered her aneurysm, as I walked out to the garage to leave for the Senate (Concord), I backed the car out and suddenly realized that I hadn't said good-bye to Chris, Stephanie and Hunter like I always do. I got out of the car, walked back into the house, called them together in the living room (as I always do) and gave them each a kiss and a hug, and told them each individually, "I love you."

The last words I heard from my beautiful wife were, "I love you too, Robert." Those words stay with me every second of every day, because they may be the last words I ever hear her say. So when you are caught up (or bogged down) in the humdrum drone of everyday life, and you step out that door away from those you love, please take those few seconds to show and tell them that you love them. Please do it, because you may never have another chance.

Life has downshifted into slow motion, as the centerpiece of our lives and our home lies stricken and we discover the myriad of things that we never noticed because they always got done, and now they're not. Our home seems empty, no longer a home but a house, and we wander about trying to put some semblance of order back into our lives. We haven't been home for more than 2 hours every day since Chrissy arrived at DHMC, and we thank the friends who prepare meals, care for our pets, and watch our home as we stand by our wonderful Mom and wife. We will rebuild our lives to include whatever reality we have to deal with. We'll do it with love for our Lord, for one another, and for each of you who have taken time to pray for Chrissy and for us.

Please, please, please continue your prayers, as we are now in a place where we need the grace of God to boost the efforts of those who labor to bring her back to us.

Bob

CHAPTER 5

Boy Meets Girl, or "What Were You Thinking?"

WE MET LATE ON A FRIDAY AFTERNOON, SEPTEMBER 14, 1979, AT the Back East Deli in Oak Harbor, Washington. (Oak Harbor is the host community for Naval Air Station Whidbey Island.) The deli was the "hangout" for active duty and reserve military personnel. Most were Naval Aviators or Naval Flight Officers (weapons system operators), but there was always a smattering of doctors, nurses, Judge Advocates General (military lawyers), and other military specialties, as well as a few brave civilians who dared to venture into our aviator mecca.

The persona of the pilots who fly on and off America's aircraft carriers day and night around the world would later be immortalized by Tom Cruise in the epic film *Top Gun*. Much of that characterization was true, and many of us carried an air of cocky invincibility with us. We had to, because flying on and off ships day and night, in good weather and bad, required us to believe we were the best jet jockeys on the planet. There was no room for doubt or error, and I was no different.

When I met the love of my life, I was wearing a white t-shirt, jeans, and Docksiders (no socks, of course), sitting alone at a strategic corner table from which I could observe everyone who came into the deli. I had ordered a meatball sub and a root beer for dinner, and I consumed it with gusto. I finished the sub, got up from my table, and went to the restroom to wash my hands. On the way back to my seat, I passed by a table with two ladies, one of whom asked me, "So how was the meatball sub?"

"It was outstanding!" I replied, seizing the opportunity to engage a member of the opposite sex. Maneuvering for the kill, I asked her, "So what brings you here today?"

"We're Navy Reserve nurses here for our drill weekend. What about you?"

With just the right amount of swagger, I replied, "I'm a Marine Corps instructor pilot with the Prowler RAG."

The other gal at the table rolled her eyes, waited a few seconds, and then commented, "Well, that's two strikes against you: you're a Marine *and* you're a pilot." Her name was Mary, and as I would soon discover, she was divorced from—you guessed it—a Marine pilot. Chris gave Mary "the look." I laughed, sat down at the table, and we began the conversation that would change the rest of our lives.

It didn't take too long for Mary to figure out that she wasn't the object of my attention. I began the somewhat delicate process by which I hoped to make it clear that I was only interested in the better-looking and much-more-sociable Christine. How to separate two members of the opposite sex in a social setting is a problem that has plagued men since the dawn of time. But on this Friday night, failure was not an option. Chris and I danced a few times to some disco music (all the rage at the time), and my clear interest in her (and my courteous lack of interest in her companion) soon produced the desired result: Mary left and headed back to the base.

Chris's quick smile and her happy disposition were magnetic, though I was honor bound not to show too much interest. You see, control is a Marine Corps thing, and it's doubly important as a Marine Corps pilot. We can't not be in control! And as the only Marine Corps instructor pilot on the base, I had to uphold the honor of the Corps by appearing to be appropriately nonchalant, walking a fine line between being a Marine and maintaining the interest of this cute potential conquest.

After several more dances and a few drinks, I suggested that we go somewhere else, and she said, smiling, "Sure—why don't we head over to my apartment?" At this point, you couldn't exactly characterize my thoughts as virtuous. Little did I know that Chris—and God—were playing me like a fiddle.

I got in my car, followed her pale blue Mustang (with white vinyl top) to her housing complex and parked in an open space. She motioned me to follow her up the stairs, opened the door to her apartment, and invited me in.

Christine had inherited her grandmother's large, mainly-green-with-woven-maroon-threads Victorian style couch. It was a sturdy piece of furniture, with ornate wooden legs and trim around the armrests. It was situated in the middle of her living room with a coffee table in front, and a brick fireplace complete with spark screen and fireplace utensils on the opposite living room wall. As we entered the apartment, we picked up our conversation where we'd left off at the Back East Deli. Ultimately, to my delight, we wound up sitting on the couch side-by-side. After a time, as our conversation continued, I reached up and rested my arm on the back of the couch behind her.

Suddenly, a furry black and white flash came streaking out of the kitchen. It jumped up on the back of the couch past the end of my extended arm, arched its back, and let out a hiss that rivaled the sound of a venting brake cylinder on a steam locomotive. There was no mistaking the message: "Don't even think about it!"

This was my introduction to Daisy. My arm beat a slow, careful retreat from the back of the couch back to my lap, and Daisy stayed on the back of the couch guarding Christine. Her arched back, frazzled fur, angrily switching tail, and occasional hissing snarl made it clear that no funny business would be happening this night. We now had a very effective chaperone—a role that Chris laughingly told me the cat assumed with every guy that had ever been in her apartment!

Given the imminent threat of my bodily harm from our chaperone, Chris suggested that we sit on the floor and continue our conversation. In the interest of self-preservation, I agreed. We sat on opposite sides of the coffee table in front of the couch, and for the next six hours, until sunrise, we shared our life stories, family histories, and everything about ourselves that was appropriate for a first encounter.

I left shortly after sunup, drove back to my room at the Bachelor Officers Quarters (BOQ) on base, and went to bed, having been outfoxed by an irritable cat.

Later, I found out that Chris called her mother and told her she had met the man she was going to marry.

. . . . . .

January 22nd, 2017—Day 5
Sunday morning, the Lord's Day...

BOY MEETS GIRL, OR "WHAT WERE YOU THINKING?"

Not much changed last night, as we're past the first 3 days and really just stabilizing Chrissy's condition. We hope to begin the healing process soon. We see some good signs, and some not so good, but overall, Chris is holding her own. This is not an exact science, and so some of the medical procedures are proactive, and others reactive. We will be going to Mass here at the DHMC Chapel at 11:00am, and invite any of you who might have time or the inclination, to come as well. We have now reached the limit of what man can do. Chrissy's life and future are now completely in God's hands, and in His time we will know what is to be. And because of this, I ask you to continue your prayers and positive thoughts.

I had a phone call from a close friend, Hillary Seeger, last night in the early evening hours. She shared that at the Governor's Inaugural Ball, the attendees were made aware of Chrissy's situation and held a moment of silent prayer for her and for us. Let me share with you that in our very small, and sometimes dark corner of the universe, with fear and worry our constant companions, words cannot express what an incredible boost it was to know that people had, for a moment, consciously made us a part of their lives in prayer. I think there's a lesson there. When you see someone - anyone - including strangers who are suffering or struggling, stop for just a moment and offer them a prayer and some encouragement. That's how we change the world - one person at a time. Thank you, Hillary Seeger, and Gov. Sununu, and Sen. Morse, for your public expression of care and concern for one small family and one beautiful lady.

I sense that we are now engaging in a battle of time as Chrissy is past the initial few days of her trauma. We saw an actual CT scan of her brain yesterday, and the damage is unquestionably severe. We have access to some of the world's leading neurovascular surgeons, neurologists, and other specialists, and they are not optimistic about her long-term prospects. But we remain resolute in our faith, and firm in our conviction to allow Chris the time she needs to begin, and to complete, her healing.

Your prayers continue to lift us up, and we believe without reservation that your prayers are bringing to God's attention a wonderful human being who is the center of our family, the foundation of our home, and the core of our earthly existence. Please continue to pray for her, that she will be restored to full health and wellness.

Thank you, and God bless you, every one.

Bob & Christine, Joseph & Naomi, Lauren & Derry, and Stephanie & Hunter

CHAPTER 6

It's About the Ride

CHRISSY AND I HAD EXCHANGED PHONE NUMBERS (NO CELLphones back then), and the week after we met, I decided to ask her out. She accepted, and that Friday afternoon, I knocked on the door of her apartment. She opened the door with a beautiful smile, and we walked to the parking lot and stopped next to a shiny black Harley Davidson chopper. "Wow," she said, "nice bike!"

Now, a Marine pilot must maintain a certain image, and at the time, that image meant owning a motorcycle suitable for the persona of a fighter pilot. I had owned several bikes, and in early 1977, before finishing flight school, I had sold my Kawasaki 500 and bought a 1973 1200 cc Harley Davidson FLH Police Special from the Pensacola (Florida) police department. But riding a bulky, green and white police "hog" didn't convey the right image, so I had it chopped, raked, and tricked out with "Fat Bob" gas tanks, a wide-glide front end, chrome forks, and a king-queen seat. It was akin to something a Hell's Angel would be proud to own.

I had stored the motorcycle during my Far East assignment aboard the aircraft carrier *USS Midway*. When I returned to the states and received the coveted orders to Whidbey Island, I was allowed thirty days of military leave, ten days for travel, and four days to find quarters and check in. I rode the Harley from Marine Corps Air Station Cherry Point, North Carolina, up the east coast to New Hampshire, visiting family along the way. I spent a week at our then-family home in Chichester, where I had some modifications made to the bike, and then, in the style of Peter Fonda in the movie *Easy Rider,* rode my chopper across the entire United States to my new assignment at Whidbey Island.

I learned a lot about our country's geography during that trip. In fact, I learned more than I ever wanted to. I learned that the most enjoyable part of the trip was riding on back roads through the rolling hills of Wisconsin. I managed to make it to the legendary annual Sturgis motorcycle rally in the Black Hills of South Dakota. I learned that it could snow during the summer, as I was snowed on riding through the Teton Mountains of Wyoming on August 7, 1979.

I also learned that Washington, not Alaska, is our nation's largest state. You might ask why. The answer is because after riding for thirty-one days and arriving at the Idaho/Washington border, I thought I was almost to Whidbey Island. However, nine hours later, tired and soaked to the bone from a summer rainstorm, Whidbey Island was still nowhere in sight. And I was so ready to be there.

So back to our first date.

Standing next to the Harley with this petite Navy nurse, I reached over, took one of the helmets, and tried to hand it to her. She looked at me and asked, "What's this for?" I answered, "If you're going to ride a motorcycle, you have to wear a helmet." She looked at me as if I had two heads, swallowed, and donned the helmet. I put mine on as well, kick-started the bike, motioned for her to get on, and we roared out of the parking lot on our first real date.

For the second time since we'd met, she had trusted me with her life. It was to set the pattern for our life together. Her trust was implicit and complete. It had to do with her upbringing, her attitude toward life, and her faith in God. And I was always the beneficiary of that trust. I couldn't have achieved anything I've done without her trust in me and her boundless love for me and our family.

. . . . . .

January 23rd, 2017—Day 6
So, today we have no change to Chrissy's medical outlook. Last night did bring some difficulties. In watching the amazing team at DHMC address them, I continue to be grateful that we are blessed to live in a nation with access to such an incredible level and standard of care. I'm not a medical person, so the analogy that follows is one befitting my layman's understanding of the myriad complexities of the human body. Laughter is absolutely permitted. :-)

The neurovascular surgeons and neurosurgeons are "driving the treatment bus" because Chrissy's injury is to her brain. They are focused on the injury and the consequences to the brain, which in turn affect most if not all of the functions of the rest of our bodies. But there's a lot of non-brain body that has to continue to function through all of this. That's the function of the ICU doctors and nurses, who are doing everything possible to make sure that the actions of the neuro-team are coordinated safely with the many functions of the rest of the body required to keep Chris alive and give her a chance at recovery. Picture a dozen water bottles, all of different sizes and shapes, interconnected in various combinations by hoses of differing diameters, and valves of different types. Sometimes a water bottle springs a leak, or a line gets a kink, or some other system problem arises. So when they address that particular problem, it affects every other bottle and line in the system in some way. Simply stated, they are doing an extraordinary job of keeping all the bottles full, and all the lines working.

Last night at around 2:30am, Chrissy's blood pressure plummeted, and the team had to work quickly and accurately to get it back under control. If her BP goes below a preset level, some bad things start to happen, beginning with a loss of blood circulation to her brain, which in turn causes some very bad things to happen. By changing medications and doses, they brought her BP back to where it needs to be, and her numbers are now back in line. The bottles are all full, and the lines are all intact.

It is easy to criticize Big Pharma, and in some cases there are things about their business practices that need to be addressed. But let me tell you, when someone you love is in danger, and the Docs can simply reach out and make a change to a very complex medication on the spot, you appreciate the science and technology, the Research and Development, and the availability of the complex chemistry needed to save her - right off the shelf in the ICU.

Things are stable early this morning, and we greet the new day with optimism and faith. I thought about my choice of words ("greet the new day with optimism and faith") before typing them. I almost said, "face another day of challenges in our struggle." But isn't that what every human being does, every day of our lives? So instead of "facing" the day, we are "greeting" the day as a gift, and reminding ourselves that we should each follow that ancient maxim, "Carpe diem" - "Seize the day." It's all about the attitude with which we awaken each morning, and which we choose to "wear" into the world around us.

And that brings me to my final thought. Many years ago, one of my sisters-in-law embroidered a saying on a beautiful piece of cloth. All it said was, "What you are is God's gift to you. What you become is your gift to God." Words to live by...

Please keep Chrissy's name on your lips and in your hearts in prayer. Thank you for the love and faith you continue to share with me, with our children, and with the beautiful Love of My Life.

Bob

CHAPTER 7

Whidbey Magic

WHIDBEY ISLAND WAS A MAGICAL PLACE OF MISTY MORNINGS, spectacular sunsets, and bucolic tranquility. Its beauty was supplemented by the relationships we had with our military friends, many of whom went on to stellar careers in the Navy and Marine Corps. We had friends who had been POWs in Vietnam, friends who had served as naval attaches to exotic places around the world, and of course, there was the cadre of Naval Aviators (pilots) and Naval Flight Officers (NFOs, who operated the planes' weapons systems) for the dozen or so A-6 and EA-6B squadrons that were based at the Naval Air Station.

While we were there, we rode the Harley, walked the beaches, stood atop the cliffs overlooking the spectacular vista of Puget Sound and the distant Olympic Peninsula, and slowly built the foundation of our future life together. We went to church, attended squadron parties, went to the movies, and dined at the Officer's Club and other fabulous restaurants around the island. It was truly a magical time.

While we were stationed there, the movie *An Officer and a Gentleman* was filmed at the base. It was about an aspiring and rebellious Naval officer candidate (Richard Gere) and his love interest (Deborah Winger), and it depicted the rigors of Aviation Officer Candidate School (AOCS). Interestingly, all the Marine extras in the movie were students of mine in the EA-6B FRS, VAQ-129.

On the afternoon of Friday, February 22, 1980—the day after my twenty-eighth birthday—the Commanding Officer of the Air Wing at Whidbey Island ordered all officers to a Safety Standdown at the Officers Club. These standdowns were generally reserved for discussing issues related to flight safety, but this one was for something entirely different: we were given the afternoon off to watch the U.S. Olympic hockey team play the Russians. That legendary contest became the basis of the movie *Miracle on Ice.* Given that every one of the squadrons based at Whidbey Island was directly engaged on the front lines of the Cold War, the U.S. team's upset victory had a symbolism much, much greater than the game itself. And I suppose, given the amount of alcohol consumed during the game and the subsequent victory party, one could argue that the standdown actually *was* safety related.

Chris and I met at the club and watched the game together. I remember eating three dozen raw clams and drinking a commensurate amount of Molson Canadian beer. When I woke up the next morning, in my bed and fully clothed, I had no idea how I'd gotten back to my room the night before. Around noon, Chris called to say the decorations in my room were in serious need of help, and did I need any Alka Seltzer or Excedrin?

The U.S. Olympic hockey team celebration was the first time people became aware that Chrissy and I were more than "just friends."

January 24th, 2017 — Day 7

Tuesday morning - icy roads, so be careful out there...

I met with the neurosurgical team this morning, and not much has changed relative to Chrissy's neurological status. But...

SHE BLINKED HER RIGHT EYE. Once yesterday when Joseph was with her, and once this morning when I went in to pray our morning Rosary. Starbursts of joy and exhilaration over two blinks of an eye. Do we ever really SEE our incredible good fortune in the amazing normalcy of life? Should we maybe learn to feel and share the joy of just being alive?

So that's the good news. But there's also some worrisome news. In the first 4 days after a severe brain injury, all efforts are focused on finding and maintaining "normal" in the body functions while treating the brain. From days 5 - 21, four serious risks present themselves, among others: vasospasms, infection, fever, and pneumonia.

Vasospasms are spasms of the arteries in the brain (and maybe the entire body, but I'm not sure) produced because the ventricles in the brain do NOT like blood in the cerebro-spinal fluid (CSF.) So the arteries begin contractions - spasms - which greatly raise the risk of stroke. The neuro-team can assess whether vasospasms are occurring by using ultrasound imagery of the brain. Yesterday, they ran the ultrasound scans, and this morning the team shared that there is no evidence of vasospasm. While we are happy, we also know that this risk remains for another 15 days.

Infection is self-explanatory. Remembering that hospitals are where sick people go, we know (and the staff openly admits) that the risk of infection in hospitals is significant. So the ICU team (remember - they're taking care of the body as the neuro-team deals with the brain injury) runs cultures on blood and various body fluids to look for signs of infection. So here's our first bit of not good news: Chrissy's white blood count is elevated. Why is this concerning? Because when our bodies detect infection, they fight it with white blood cells. So Chris is on a "wide spectrum" antibiotic for now, until they can determine whether there actually is an infection, and exactly what kind it is. Then, if there is, they'll target it with much more potent antibiotics designed for that particular problem.

Fever for purposes of brain aneurysm is defined as a mean body temperature above 38 degrees Centigrade for two days. Chrissy's temp hadn't been a concern, but yesterday it was a bit higher than normal, and this morning it is higher still. It could be the result of infection, or of damage to the "thermostat" in her brain that regulates body temperature. We don't know. But fever has a significant negative effect on outcomes. Yesterday the ICU team used a couple of icepacks to reverse the slightly elevated temperature. I don't know what today will bring, but we are concerned.

Pneumonia is a buildup of fluid in the lungs. It can be caused by aspiration (inhaling) of fluids into the lungs. Chrissy vomited several times while we had her laying on our bed before the ambulance arrived. We had kept her on her side, and I kept cleaning out her mouth to prevent her from inhaling anything. Right now her breathing is fast but ok, but they are suctioning fluid out of her lungs - more than normal. Again, we don't know, but we will find out today the results of a chest x-ray they took yesterday.

So, our emotional roller coaster continues - ups and downs, exhilaration and despondency, day after day, within a framework of constant uncertainty. That said, we continue to read of numerous aneurysm survivors who are now leading normal lives, whose symptoms were identical to Chrissy's.

The way we deal with the unending uncertainty and emotional extremes is with prayer. We know that God's love is infinite, constant, perpetual, and unconditional. And we're depending on His love, asking Him in our prayers for a full and complete recovery for Christine. I know that your prayers are lifting us up, and all I can do is to humbly ask you not to stop, not to give up, not to believe that your prayers and ours don't matter. Because they do. A wonderful lady who gave to everyone she ever met, every day of her life, needs us now.

Jesus himself told us, "Seek and ye shall find. Ask, and ye shall receive. Knock, and it shall be opened to you." And we are doing exactly that.

Bob

CHAPTER 8

The Volcano

NEW INSTRUCTORS TO THE PROWLER TRAINING SQUADRON (VAQ-129) were required to complete an IUT (Instructor Under Training) syllabus, which required qualifying in the various aspects of flying the aircraft and operating its weapon systems. During one of the training flights with a newly arrived instructor, we flew a "round robin" through the Pacific Northwest to familiarize him with the borders and topography of the operating area, which included Washington, Oregon, Idaho, and the coastal waters of the Pacific Ocean.

On Sunday, May 18, 1980, the world witnessed the eruption of Mount St. Helens. It was a spectacular event that forever altered the landscape of the Pacific Northwest, including the operating area for our training flights. The following week, I conducted a flight that included an approach (Hi Tacan 28R) into Portland International Airport, located southwest of the mountain.

Words are utterly insufficient to describe the aerial view of the volcano and surrounding area. The devastation was a clear proclamation of the insignificance of man when nature chooses to display her power. This is something with which professional pilots are intimately familiar because of the impact of weather on flight operations.

As an example, I once piloted a Douglas A-4F SuperFox Skyhawk attack aircraft on a cross-country flight from Naval Air Station (NAS) Miramar in San Diego, California, to NAS Dallas, Texas (closed in 1998). It was a perfect day to fly: clear skies, no turbulence, no precipitation, and, according to the Navy weather forecaster (we affectionately called them *weather-guessers*) who briefed my flight, no inclement weather along my route of flight. However, flying over Tucumcari, New Mexico, at thirty-five thousand feet, I had to deviate around a single, massive unforecasted thunderstorm that towered far above my altitude. It was the only thunderstorm in sight over the entire desert Southwest.

Thunderstorms are deadly because of the tremendous forces within them: violent 200-mph up and down drafts, windshear, hail, icing, and torrential rains that can actually cause a jet engine to "flame out." I radioed a nearby Flight Service Station, which was equipped with a height-finding radar, and asked the FAA specialist if he could determine the height of the thunderstorm. A few seconds later, he reported that the top of the storm was at 77,000 feet—almost twice the maximum altitude I could reach with my military fighter. The power of Mother Nature is truly awesome—and dangerous.

But back to Mount St. Helens. Chris was born and raised in Eugene, Oregon. Since her mom and dad still lived there, at some point I was going to have to meet them. That happened during the early spring of 1980. Her father was a wonderful man, a World War II veteran of the war in the Pacific. He had been with McArthur's forces when they recaptured the Philippines from the Japanese. He never spoke about what he saw, and I never asked. As a Naval Academy graduate and Marine, I knew about the Japanese treatment of POWs and the horrifying brutality and sadism they visited on the troops that were captured.

Christine and I were beginning to talk about getting serious. That meant traveling from Whidbey Island to Eugene to make my case to her mom, dad, and seven younger siblings. We regularly made the five and a half hour, 345-mile trip using I-5 from Mt. Vernon, Washington, to Eugene, leaving Whidbey Friday night and returning on Sunday afternoon. The highlight of the trip was always her mom's Sunday dinner, served around noon. It was almost an unspoken obligation, a weekly event that brought the family together and reinforced the bonds they had forged growing up. These dinners were wonderful occasions, and they added to my growing sense that this Navy nurse was going to become a major part of my life. They gave me insights into the bedrock values that had made her who she was, and that would one day become the foundational values for our family as well.

The eruption of Mount St. Helens had deposited millions of tons of volcanic ash on and around I-5, the major north-south interstate highway on the West Coast. The highway crews had cleared it off the highway and created huge ash mounds alongside the road. Whenever there was any wind, it would create a huge ash cloud for miles, and we had to drive in fog-like conditions for about half an hour. The ash would clog the engine's air filter, so that we had to change it both going to and coming back from Eugene. We also had to wash the car in Eugene and back home on Whidbey Island because of the corrosive effect of volcanic ash on paint. But we persevered, refusing to allow our growing attraction to be outdone by a mere volcano.

. . . . . .

January 25th, 2017 — Day 8

This morning I awakened at 4:00am, with a renewed sense of purpose and a much clearer view of the path ahead. The past week has been one of emotional carnage for our family, as we each struggled to put Chrissy's ailment into context. As we flailed, supporting one another, scared of what the future could mean for Chrissy and for us, we were supported by countless prayers from friends and loved ones, and from thousands of people we have never even met. My faith has been incredibly bolstered, and this morning I actually physically feel the power of your prayers for us as we seek God's healing love for Christine. I'm reminded of a certain Marine Corps General who, after one of the bloodiest battles in the Pacific, made the statement, "To those who understand, no explanation is necessary. To those who do not, no explanation is possible." That is absolutely the case here.

Yesterday was not an easy day. Problem after problem kept arising, but the nurses (phenomenal) and doctors (amazing) managed to avert disaster. Blood pressure was the most significant issue for most of the day. The problem is that the medication they're giving her to prevent vasospasm (absolutely necessary) causes her BP to drop precipitously - and I do mean precipitously, as in from 140/80 to 70/30 in about 30 seconds. Not good. So they've cut the dosage in half, and are administering it twice as often, and this has the problem under control.

This morning, I got to Chrissy's room about a half hour earlier than normal, and found her resting as well as I've seen since she's been at DHMC. All her physiological parameters are within limits, her temperature is back down to almost normal, her breathing is steady and unlabored, and the look on her face is one of peace and comfort. Your prayers are working. Even the doctors admit that other than reacting to stressors impacting

Chrissy's physical progress, this is out of our hands. I frequently harken to Hebrews 11:1: "Now faith is the substance of things hoped for, the evidence of things unseen." And I believe without a shred of doubt that we are seeing that evidence firsthand.

Below is a text I sent to our children this morning, as we were granted the privilege of another sunrise...

"Today we start our journey out of the desert and towards the Promised Land of Mom's complete recovery. We are to be, after God, her next best source of positive attitude, energy, and love. We are Mom's reason for living. She must now become ours, until she is whole again and we can rebalance to that joyful reality. I love you all more than words can convey.

Yesterday is done. It is a new day."

This situation has challenged me to rethink many things. And while I can't say which is more important - sometimes it varies day to day - we need to take a really careful look at not "whether," but HOW we love the important people in our lives. In our busy lives, it is dangerously easy to allow our relationships to slowly become routine. We begin taking people and gifts for granted. So I asked myself, "What can I do to keep that from happening?" And the answer came like a bolt of lightning. When we marry, we promise in a very special way, before God and man, to love, honor and cherish our spouse. If we truly understand the full meaning and implications of that promise, we must know that loving a spouse can never be routine, or ordinary, or unremarkable. We must love them SPECTACULARLY, every minute of every day of our lives.

Chrissy's road, if God allows her to remain with us, is going to be long and arduous. I will be part of that road, as will our children and the rest of the family. But so will you, because just as your prayers have brought her to this point, she, and I, and our family will need your continued prayers all the way to the end of the journey, wherever it may take us.

Please pray as you love: spectacularly.

God bless each and every one of you with His love and mercy.

Bob

CHAPTER 9

The Weekend That Clinched the Deal

CHRISTINE'S CLOSEST AND BEST FRIEND, JO MARIE HORTON, WAS also a Navy nurse. They had met during Navy nurse Officer Indoctrination School at the Navy base in Newport, Rhode Island, and had served together at Oak Knoll Naval Hospital in Oakland, California. They have remained the closest of friends for nearly fifty years. Jo Marie sang our wedding song ("Longer," by Jon Fogelberg) and also visited Christine's family in Eugene from time to time, sometimes with us and sometimes on her own.

One weekend in the early winter of 1979–80, Jo Marie and Chris invited me and 1st Lt. Tom Mushyn, a Marine student ECMO (Electronic Countermeasures Officer) to Seattle for dinner. After completing our respective flight and ground assignments that Friday afternoon, we drove to Seattle in my car (a dark green 1979 Datsun B210.) I parked, and we headed up the stairs to Jo's apartment to pick up our dates. Little did we know that a culinary ambush was waiting for us!

We knocked on the apartment door, and Chris opened it, giving me a hug and inviting us inside. Tom and I had thought we were going to go out for dinner, but we were seriously misinformed. Chris and Jo had prepared dinner in the apartment, and what a dinner it was: homemade antipasto salad, lasagna, manicotti, meatballs, sausage, spaghetti, Italian bread, spumoni, tiramisu, cannoli, and other assorted pastries. They topped off the dinner with my absolute favorite dessert: coconut custard pie. There were also several bottles of red and white wine from the world-famous Chateau Ste. Michelle vineyards in Washington. Some months later, Chris and I visited the winery on a summer evening dinner train ride along the beautiful coastline of Puget Sound.

Every bit of that incredible meal was made from scratch. There was enough left over to feed a squad of Marines. Not only did we enjoy Italian food for dinner on Friday night, we ate Italian for breakfast, lunch, and dinner on Saturday. And then we ate Italian before and after church on Sunday morning. And then—you guessed it—we had Italian for Sunday dinner.

When Tom and I drove back to Whidbey Island very early Monday morning, my little Datsun B210 was loaded with leftovers from the incredible weekend smorgasbord. Later, I learned that they had conspired, as only Navy nurses can, when they seek to capture the heart of a Marine.

. . . . . .

January 26th, 2017 — Day 9

My mind was quiet this morning, and I realized that "quiet" is God's way to "restoreth my soul." It is during these quiet times that God often whispers to us.

Yesterday was a good day. Chris opened her eyes several times in response to loud questions. Tiny signs, but signs nonetheless. There is a "but."

Sometime between the time the ambulance left our home and our arrival at DHMC, Chris bit almost completely through her tongue. We're pretty sure it was during a spasm caused by the injury to her brain. It is serious, and we need to pray that God keeps infection from setting in, and that He strengthens her to enable the Ear, Nose and Throat team to perform necessary surgery to repair the incision. At this point, they cannot, and judging from her reflex reactions to anything touching her mouth, she is suffering a great deal of pain from this injury.

The neurosurgeons performed their standard tests this morning, as they do every morning. That's how they assess whether Chrissy is improving, slipping, or maintaining the status quo. Her neurological status remains unchanged: in a coma, with basic brain stem activity. Except that she opened her eyes. :-)

God does things that doctors cannot. As one of the neurosurgeons said, "If I was able to prognosticate, I would be at a table in Las Vegas, not in a hospital." Bottom line is that no one really knows what will be, except the Father.

So - in summary, Chris spent a very restful night, and nothing has changed.

Or maybe I should say, Chris spent a very restful night, "but" nothing has changed.

There is a profound difference, as I read the two words.

The first speaks to me of acceptance and going about our business as usual. The second speaks to an expectation that something will change because we believe it. And we have that expectation because the entire world is praying for Chrissy. (Thank you to Ms. Eunice Sumary, who sent a message yesterday from Arusha, Tanzania, East Africa, where she gathered family and friends together to pray for a full and complete recovery. She is absolutely certain that it will happen. Do we share her level of conviction and belief?)

As we (and you) continue our prayers throughout each day, and as I lead my family forward on this new chapter of our journey, we believe that Chris will be healed. Any less faith introduces doubt that the same Lord who stilled the weeping of the family of Lazarus by bringing him back to life, and who cleansed lepers, healed cripples, and cured hemorrhages, will bring Christine back to full health. Is our faith strong enough to believe - not that this CAN happen, but that it WILL happen?

BELIEVE.

Thank you for loving us and keeping us in your prayers.

Bob

CHAPTER 10

About Landing on Aircraft Carriers

THE FLIGHT DECK OF AN AIRCRAFT CARRIER IS THE MOST dangerous work environment in the world. The hazards are many, and lethal: walking into a propeller, blown overboard by jet blast, sucked down a jet engine intake, crushed by a jet blast deflector, run over by a taxiing aircraft, hit by an aircraft tug, sliced in half by an arresting gear cable—you get the idea.

Landing a high-performance jet fighter on an aircraft carrier at night is the most challenging pilot undertaking in aviation. Naval Aviators learning to fly carrier-based aircraft receive intense training, with every single practice and actual carrier landing observed, analyzed, and recorded permanently in their flight qualification records. The job of training and evaluating the carrier landing performance of these pilots is assigned to a special cadre of Naval Aviators known as "Landing Signals Officers" (LSOs). Their job is to prevent aircraft accidents during carrier landings by carefully watching the aircraft's speed, position, attitude, and lineup and listening to the sound of its engine(s) as it approaches the stern of the ship. If the pilot's approach doesn't meet the stringent parameters for safely landing on the ship, the LSO will "wave off" the aircraft, and the pilot will go around for another attempt.

During practice ashore, and during actual carrier operations aboard ship, LSOs stand on "the platform," right next to the runway (ashore) or the angled flight deck (aboard ship) on which the jets land when the carrier is underway. This puts them in the best possible position to observe and evaluate each approach, and to order a wave-off if the pilot and aircraft aren't conforming to the very demanding parameters for a safe arrested landing (known as a *trap*.)

LSOs are affectionately (and sometimes not so affectionately) called Paddles, a nickname left over from the early days of naval aviation when they actually held large ping-pong type paddles in their hands. They moved the paddles in specific patterns to signal actions required by the pilot flying the approach (add power, reduce power, adjust glide path or lineup, etc.) Though the hand-held paddles have long been relegated to museums, the name Paddles remains an active term in navy jargon.

Becoming an LSO is not easy. Volunteer carrier pilots, who are selected because they excel at flying around the ship, spend hundreds of hours over several years, in addition to their regular duties ashore and aboard ship. They observe and grade thousands of "passes" (approaches) under the direct supervision of specially designated senior LSOs. They also receive classroom instruction in the highly technical geometry of carrier approaches, the engineering technology of catapults and arresting gear, individual aircraft flight and engine characteristics, and the psychology of communication in high stress environments.

After completing the required training aboard the aircraft carrier *USS Midway* (CV-41), I received the coveted designation of Air Wing LSO, qualified to observe and evaluate day and night approaches for every fixed-wing aircraft type aboard the carrier. Those aircraft included the F-4 Phantom II, A-6 Intruder, A-7 Corsair II, E-2 Hawkeye, S-2 Tracker, C-2 Greyhound, RF-8 Crusader, and A-3 Skywarrior.

Shortly afterward, I received orders to report to Naval Air Station Whidbey Island for an exchange tour as a Familiarization/Navigation instructor pilot and FRS LSO for the EA-6B Prowler Fleet Replacement Squadron. It was during this assignment that I met the petite Navy nurse who would one day become my wife.

. . . . . .

January 27th, 2017 — Day 10
Yesterday was a good day, some ups, some downs, as Chrissy continues in a coma and the doctors try to gradually wean her off some of the numerous medications and IVs she is receiving. It's a slow process, as they continue to work hard to get her back to her normal physical state. The Ear/Nose/Throat doctor said her tongue won't be a problem, but that they'll have to wait until she's in a better neurological state before they risk anesthesia for that operation. She slept well ...through the night, and she remains stable this morning. She has developed pneumonia, but the ICU doctors assure us it is eminently treatable and should present no problems going forward. Equally or more important (and worrisome) is that there's been no change in her neurological status, though we do sporadically see her eyes open and her toes move. We do not know what these mean. In fact, right now we do not know anything about what is happening to the precious lady who makes our house a home, who brings each day new life, who is the most giving person I ever met.

We united around a rallying cry to deal with this crisis: BELIEVE. Coming up with that was a critical first step, because we needed something to focus on, something to unite us. But after a while, my mind began to question what it means to "believe." Believe what? Believe who? Questions like this have been swirling around in my head since Chris was stricken. Will she survive? Will she recover? To what degree? Will she be blind? Will I ever hear her beautiful voice again? I WANT TO KNOW. And in my "not knowing," frustration and anxiety began to build. And it suddenly dawned on me that frustration and anxiety are the antithesis of "BELIEVE."

I've spent most of my adult life thinking I had some semblance of control over our future. Until now. I want certainty, and I want control. And because I don't have either, a new piece has appeared on my chessboard: doubt.

As I reflected on this during our morning Rosary, a most amazing thing happened: the swirling questions stopped, and a word just popped up into my head. That word is now the battle cry for the next segment of our journey. I share it with you because you will one day likely experience a similar journey, and maybe this will help guide your steps. That word is simply this:

SURRENDER.

We surrender not to the dark clouds of despair lurking nearby, but to the unfathomable and infinite will of God.

Thanks for your continued love and prayers.

Bob

CHAPTER 11

In Memory of Three Friends

Before ever landing aboard a carrier, Navy and Marine Corps pilots make several hundred practice landings on land. Every approach ("pass") is evaluated by the LSOs responsible for training them to land aboard ship. These land-based practice sessions are known as Field Carrier Landing Practices (FCLPs). During initial training, pilots only qualify to land aboard the ship during daylight hours in a training aircraft. After getting their Wings, they're sent to a different training squadron to become fully qualified in a combat aircraft. It's here that they begin the intense training necessary to perform night carrier landings—the most challenging evolution in aviation.

Marine Corps 1st Lt. Tom Mushyn, an EA-6B student Electronic Countermeasures Officer (ECMO), was not only a student. Because he was a Marine, we had struck up a friendship as he was progressing through the training syllabus. During his tenure as a student, as my interest in Christine was beginning to manifest itself, he similarly took an interest in her best friend, Jo Marie Horton, also a Navy Reserve nurse (see Chapter 9: The Weekend That Clinched the Deal).

To fully understand the incident I'm about to share, it's important to understand a bit about the Grumman EA-6B Prowler. The Prowler is a four-place aircraft designed specifically for tactical electronic warfare. Its mission is to protect airborne strike aircraft from the sophisticated weapons in today's battle space by jamming enemy radar detection and missile guidance systems. The aircraft has two cockpits, each with a gold-plated canopy. The gold plating protects the crew members from the massive amounts of electronic radiation emitted by the external wing-mounted jammers. The two crewmembers in each cockpit sit side-by-side in independent ejection seats: with the pilot in the left front seat, and the Mission Commander, an ECMO, in the right front seat. The two ECMOs in the rear cockpit operate the aircraft's sophisticated electronic jamming and surveillance weapons suite. Because several critical circuit breakers (CBs) are mounted on a panel accessible only from either of the two rear seats anytime a Prowler is flying, at least one of the two rear seats must be occupied by an ECMO. For FCLPs, the back seat ECMO was jokingly referred to as the "CB rider."

On February 26, 1980, as I was training four student pilots for carrier qualification ("CarQuals"), I scheduled a practice session ("bounce period") of night FCLPs (Field Carrier Landing Practices). As an LSO, because I needed some carrier landings to maintain my own qualifications, I was also flying, and a different LSO, LCdr. Tom "Whizzer" White, was "waving" us (grading our approaches from the LSO platform).

My crew consisted of me as pilot, Lt. Dave Lauck in the right front seat, and Lt. Bill Luti as my "CB rider." In one of the four other Prowlers flying that night was pilot Lt. (jg) Bill Readman, and ECMOs LCdr. Dick Smith and Marine 1st Lt. Tom Mushyn.

IN MEMORY OF THREE FRIENDS

Mushyn and Luti had been in the academic building ("Prowler U") studying when a PA announcement was made that two CB riders were needed for a night FCLP session. Before they came to the ready room, they flipped a coin to see who would fly in which airplane. Luti won the toss and opted to fly with me.

The night was clear, and the air was smooth, and all was going well. Suddenly, the aircraft ahead of me, with Tom in the back as the CB rider, pitched sharply nose-down and started a sudden rapid descent toward the water off the end of the runway. I keyed my microphone and yelled, "POWER! POWER! POWER! DON'T SETTLE!" I watched in horror as the aircraft continued straight down and plunged into the dark, frigid waters of Puget Sound.

When a ship is steaming in salt water at night, the turbulence produced by the movement of the hull through the water causes a chemical reaction that leaves a phosphorescent yellow-green trail in its wake. When the ill-fated Prowler struck the water, it had a similar effect, and the phosphorescent planform of that Prowler in the waters of Puget Sound is forever etched in my memory.

As the senior pilot in the landing pattern, I immediately radioed the other three aircraft to focus on flying their aircraft and to make sure they landed safely. I remained aloft as "On Scene Commander" until the SAR (Search and Rescue) helicopter arrived and began the rescue effort. I landed my Prowler, taxied to the apron, shut down, and ran with my two ECMOs to the squadron ready room. By the time we got there, the SAR crew had radioed the terrible news: there were no survivors. The ready room, normally abuzz with conversation, was punctuated by silence as we realized that we had just lost three of our own.

Christine was on duty at the naval hospital that evening. When the Search and Rescue helicopter radioed the ER team at the hospital that there were no survivors, the news flashed through the hospital with lightning speed. Chris knew I was flying, but because the squadron couldn't release the names of the crew until after their next of kin had been notified, she had no way of knowing whether or not I was among them. The hospital staff knew that she and I were dating, and they waited alongside her with dread for confirmation of the names of those killed in the crash.

Cellphones didn't exist back then, and both the squadron and hospital telephone lines were jammed. I knew Chris would be terrified that I might be one of the crash victims, so I raced out of the ready room, still in my flight suit, and drove the half mile to the hospital. I entered through the emergency room sliding doors, and the ER team, still on standby, wordlessly pointed me toward one of the ER stalls.

I pushed aside the curtain, and Chrissy was standing there alone, head down, eyes closed, fists clenched tightly to her chest. She later told me she was praying.

I quietly said, "Chrissy." Her eyes flew open, and as she ran into my open arms, weeping, her tears of relief added to my growing sense that God had destined me to share my life with this beautiful diminutive Navy nurse that I'd met because of a meatball sub.

(Thirty-nine years later, in 2019, I would run into retired Navy Captain Bill Luti back in New Hampshire. He related the story of the fateful coin toss that saved his life. I checked my logbook and confirmed that we had in fact flown together that night.)

This wouldn't be the only time I would meet Chrissy at the naval hospital with news of a tragedy.

. . . . . .

January 28th, 2017 — Day 11

Good (Saturday) morning to all!

We are seeing gradual and (finally) specific improvements in Chrissy's condition as we enter Day 11 of her odyssey.

She would whack me upside the head (and I believe she will one day) if she knew I was sharing this next information. While it probably does approach the threshold of "TMI," I am thrilled to make a triumphal proclamation that she delivered quite abundantly on a bodily function that most of us routinely perform each morning - her first since the aneurysm. I haven't yet spoken with the neuro-team about what this means, but to me it's yet another sign that physiologically, things are slowly returning to normal.

AND, as of last night, it was determined that she no longer needs medication to stabilize her blood pressure, so it has been discontinued. Again - small things that point in a direction. And while we are not privileged to know the future, our family continues to pray with you constantly that Chrissy's health will be fully and completely restored. BELIEVE.

Neurologically, things remain status quo, though in the course of each day, we notice small things that the doctors don't see while "making rounds" once each day. For example, Chrissy's face is quite sensitive, and this morning when I wiped the corner of her mouth with a wet surgical napkin, she turned her head away. It was a deliberate response to an external stimulus. It was not a reflex. :-)

We continue to receive visitors, who sit with Chris when the RNs say it's ok - which is most of the time. A harpist visited her yesterday (daughter Lauren learned to play the harp), and she seemed to rest easier while the harpist was playing her beautiful music.

Chrissy's Mom (age 86) and next-younger sister (Chris is the oldest of 8) arrived late last night from Oregon, and are in visiting her as I'm writing this. One day, I will share with you why this is a matter of major spiritual significance. But I'm not quite ready, as it's intensely personal and will serve a better purpose addressed on its own merits.

These small items all point to a slow, subtle change for the better. I have felt the power of your prayers for her and for us - at times physically picking me up when I'm tired or weary. Her life is in God's hands, and your prayers are making a difference.

Profuse thanks to all who continue to post their thoughts as we reinforce the fabric of our faith. Your support is truly transformative, as so much of our lives is dictated by our outlook, and I read every one of your thoughts every day. Much as I would like to reply to each of you, sheer force of numbers only allows me to thank you "en masse" for the strength you bring to us. And so I do - from the very bottom of my heart and soul - thank you for helping us continue this journey.

One final thought I thought I'd share with you: I have come to find both strength and relevance in reading Psalms. If you have time, I invite you to sit down, read Psalm 27, and then spend a few minutes reflecting on it. May you love and pray SPECTACULARLY as you go about this day. God bless you.

Bob

CHAPTER 12

Threads

I HAVE COME TO BELIEVE THAT THE ENTIRETY OF MY LIFE, EVERY decision, event, achievement, and failure, was intended to deliver me to the Back East Deli in Oak Harbor, Washington, on Friday night, September 14, 1979. I don't believe in predestination, but the fact that a Marine pilot from New Hampshire met a Navy nurse from Oregon on a small island off the coast of Washington was certainly extraordinary—as was everything about this petite, blue-eyed nurse who brought joy into the lives of everyone she ever met. Her blue eyes were (and still are) amazing. Sometimes they're as pale blue as the summer sky; at other times they're as blue as the turquoise stones in Navajo jewelry from the desert Southwest. Chrissy's quick smile gave a warm welcome to everyone she met, and her innate care and compassion somehow always managed to attract injured and stray dogs, cats, and Marines.

As time progressed and we began to get serious, our conversations started to focus on values, family, and those things that build the foundation of a life together. I am certain that being of the same religious denomination and practicing our faith together was an essential component of our marriage. I know that having a common and active faith life helped us weather the storms of life that tested us over the years.

I've also learned over the years that when you return to a place that holds wonderful memories, it's never as good as it was when you lived there. But that doesn't mean we shouldn't revisit places that became landmarks in our lives. There is joy to be found in remembering and reminiscing.

So it was that on our twenty-fifth anniversary, in June of 1996, Chris and I returned to Whidbey Island for a walk down memory lane. It was a beautiful sunny day, and we were staying at the venerable Camlin Hotel in downtown Seattle. We took our rental car and rode the Mukilteo Ferry across from the mainland to the southern tip of Whidbey Island. We visited the place where I had proposed to her, Portofino's Restaurant in Coupeville. The restaurant had long since closed and been replaced by another business, but that didn't diminish the wonderful memory of me on bended knee asking her to marry me, her beaming smile as she said, "Yes!" and the subsequent rousing applause from the patrons as I gave her the ring.

We continued driving northward toward the Naval Air Station, passing many of the places—restaurants, beaches, and parks—we had visited during the wonderful years of our courtship. We decided to visit the Back East Deli, where we had met twenty-seven years before. The town of Oak Harbor had changed so much that it took us half an hour to locate it. It, too, had changed in the ensuing years, from a restaurant and social gathering place to a printing shop. I parked the car outside and went inside. Chrissy stayed in the car.

The downstairs was much changed, and what had been the bar was now a counter, with cash register, displays, and other print shop paraphernalia. No one was behind the counter, but there was a small sign next to a bell that read, "Ring for Service." I followed the instructions and from upstairs, a man's voice answered and said, "I'll be right down." Shortly after, he arrived at the counter.

I introduced myself and shared my reason for visiting his shop, telling him that Chris and I were retracing our past and that we had first met at the then–Back East Deli in September 1979 when I was a Marine pilot instructor and she a Navy nurse.

He looked at me, chuckled, and said, "You probably don't remember me, but I remember you. I'm the guy that brought the meatball sub to your table..."

Our lives are threads in the fabric of God's creation, and sometimes He gives us a peek at His handiwork. All I can say is that we miss the incredible riches of life if we don't take the time to "set a spell" and look for those threads. They're there if we have eyes to see and ears to hear.

. . . . . .

January 29th, 2017 – Day 12

Sunday - the Lord's Day. A day of new beginnings and amazing grace. I can not wait to go to Mass. I need the grace. I need God.

We always have someone at the hospital with Chris, and last night it was our son Joseph standing watch. He texted me this morning, after praying the Rosary with his Mom, that things are the same. Except that Chris is "sustaining/regulating her potassium levels better today." :-) She continues to improve physiologically, one day at a time, one parameter at a time.

Yesterday, we had another sign that Chris is stirring within the coma. Our RN injected some medication into her abdomen, and Chris opened her eyes fully and blinked. When the nurse shined a light into her eyes, it seems she didn't like it, and closed them almost all the way. So we continue to see small signs that her brain is beginning to recover from the "devastating" (doctor's words) effects of the aneurysm. I ask you, and I thank you, for continuing to pray with us. Chrissy needs you. We need you.

Last night, I went home and stayed the night for the first time. In fact, I'm writing this from my living room recliner. My children came with me, strong yet gentle with their loving care, and for that I'm thankful beyond words. But the reality is that the real reason to COME home is Chrissy. And she's not here.

I walked into the house, and... Silence. Stillness. I walked around as if it were the first time I'd ever seen the place. And in many ways, it was. Except it wasn't the things that are there that you notice; it's what's MISSING. She's not here.

Looking around, I realized there's a lesson in the silence. Chris isn't here, but there are vestiges of her everywhere - pictures, cards, love notes, flowers - small gifts and trinkets. Small, you think, until you realize that they are a window into her soul, and a reflection of what she believes and what she wants you not to look at, but to SEE. Eternity lies within those trinkets.

So, as I begin this new day, I ask you: do you really SEE what your loved ones are trying to show you? Do you give them dedicated time and complete attention when they "show you their soul" in the hundred little things they do for you? Do you look, and SEE, even when they are not watching?

God gives us the chance to do so, every day of our lives. I challenge you: don't just look. SEE. See the tiny bits of love that fill the silence. And thank God and your spouse, SPECTACULARLY, for the gift of each other, and the gift of faith, every single day of your life.

Bob

CHAPTER 13

Strays and Wounded

FROM HER EARLIEST DAYS, CHRISSY WAS A CAREGIVER. HER MOM greatly relied upon her to care for her seven younger siblings and help out around the house. Her selflessness was born of this, and it carried through every day of her life.

Throughout her life, she befriended the less fortunate, regardless of station, finances, appearance, or any of the worldly metrics we use to avoid those with whom we would rather not be seen. Lana Nelson was one such person. Christine met her as a nursing student classmate, a quiet person of humble background and very modest means who purchased her clothes at thrift stores. She drove an old car and suffered from poor self-esteem during her entire life. Lana married after attaining her RN degree, but her marriage broke up after the birth of her son. As a single mother, she spent the rest of her life struggling with severe bouts of depression. Chrissy kept in close touch with Lana from nursing school until Chris was stricken—a period of forty years—helping her battle her depression. Chrissy flew from New Hampshire to Oregon on numerous occasions when the severity of Lana's depression warranted it, and she stayed with her until the episode passed.

My youngest brother lived with us for several years. He'd had a troubled upbringing. Our parents divorced when he was six, and our mother was killed in an auto accident when he was nine. After our mother's death, my brother lived with friends and family members, ultimately winding up with Chris and me until he turned eighteen and enlisted in the Marines.

Additionally, my dad lived with us during his long convalescence from quintuple bypass heart surgery until shortly before his death. At that time, I was away flying my trips as a United Airlines pilot, which meant that Chrissy did all this while raising our three children.

Her love played equally to the four-legged friends that somehow always managed to find their way into our lives. While living in Lakewood, Washington, Chrissy had decided she wanted another cat. I, however, was not of the same mindset. Within two weeks of her sharing her wish for a cat, I found a stray jet-black kitten sitting atop the woodpile in our back yard, yowling for all it was worth. I picked it up and brought it into the house to show Chris. Knowing her nature, I stated authoritatively that the kitten's name was "No," because we were not going to add it to our already existing menagerie of two cats and a dog. I issued an edict that we would keep it until I had a chance to take it to the local animal shelter. She smiled, named the cat Fonzie, and he lived happily with us for the next six years until he went to kitty cat heaven.

Jesus said, "In as much as you do it for one of the least of these, my brothers, you do it for Me" (Matthew 25:40). I'm not sure if He meant for this to apply to our four-legged friends, but Chrissy never left it to chance.

January 30th, 2017 — Day 13

Monday morning, the world awakens after its weekend respite, and business begins again as usual. Or does it?

Chrissy slept well last night, with little change yesterday in her physiological and neurological conditions. The doctors continue to make small adjustments the many IVs and medications she is receiving to sustain her body as her brain seeks its way. Patience is the watchword, as we await God's handiwork.

This morning a conference will take place. It is the initial step in determining the direction our journey may take given Chrissy's medical and neurological status. I spent much of yesterday, after Mass at DHMC with the family, internally wrestling with possibilities. Unknowns and "What if?s" raced around inside my head. They consumed me, so that by day's end, I was spiritually, physically and emotionally exhausted. I had forgotten about BELIEVE and SURRENDER.

Then, just after midnight, as I prayed at Chrissy's bedside, she opened her eyes slightly and looked at me. I don't know what she saw, or if she saw anything at all. But it struck me, tired as I was, that God was also looking at me to see if I had made any progress towards becoming what He expects me to be for her, and for you.

Throughout life, I've endured tests of intellect, endurance, strength, and mental toughness - as a Naval Academy Midshipman, a Marine Corps officer, Naval aviator, FBI Agent, airline pilot and political candidate. Each of these endeavors tests your will and makes you grow beyond anything you've ever done before. But they all pale in comparison to the epic journey on which we are embarked today.

I believe that everything we do in life is preparing us for something yet to come. It has literally been "the story of my life." And in truth, if we BELIEVE, we know that this life itself is actually preparation for the life that is to come. We who are praying for Chrissy's healing must believe in that next life, else why would we be praying?

No matter how complicated or difficult the circumstances in which we find ourselves, whether tragedy, temptation, or tribulation, we have to get back to the basics: BELIEVE. SURRENDER. SEE.

And GROW.

It's no coincidence that I'm suddenly not tired any more. I thank God for the precious gift of my wife and the inspiration her love for me has become. I thank Him for each of you, praying on her behalf for a full and complete recovery.

I thank God for this new day and the love of my wife, my family, and you. And I am renewed by the continuing inspiration to GROW: through Him, and with Him, and in Him.

Have a SPECTACULAR day.

Bob

CHAPTER 14

Transition

In April 1981, I made the decision to resign my regular commission in the Marines and join the active Marine Corps Reserves as a pilot. With no thought of what I would do for civilian employment, I woke up one morning and decided I didn't want to make the Marine Corps a career. We sold our home on Whidbey Island and rented a house there for a couple of months. We wanted to move to Eugene so Chrissy could be near her family. She was working full time as a civil service RN at the naval hospital on Whidbey and one weekend each month there as a Navy Reserve nurse.

Two months after we were married, on a Sunday morning while Chris was working at the naval hospital, I received a phone call from Chris's brother Bob. Their father, John, had died suddenly. John didn't attend church that day, and when the family arrived back home, they found him on the floor, not breathing and with no pulse. He was gone. I told Bob I would deliver the news to Christine.

I called the duty officer at the naval hospital, explained what had happened, and asked if I could come and tell her the sad news. They were wonderfully accommodating, and a few minutes later, I arrived at the hospital. Word had spread quickly, but at my request, no one had said anything to Christine. The staff pointed me toward an empty room and let me know it was there if we needed it.

Chrissy was walking down the hallway when she saw me. She broke into her beautiful smile, we hugged, and after some small talk, I walked her to the empty room and kissed her. We were still newlyweds, and the joy of our wedding was still fresh in our hearts and minds.

And then I told her.

Among her seven siblings, Chris was the only who had joined the military, and her father had been very proud of her, as he had served in the army in the Pacific during World War II as part of MacArthur's return to the Philippines. He never talked about the horrific things he saw—POWs that had been beaten, tortured, and starved by their Japanese captors. As it happened, his death was caused by an undetected heart condition from malaria he had contracted while liberating the Philippines with General MacArthur. Chrissy was no stranger to the ravages of war, as her first tour as a Navy nurse had been at Oak Knoll Naval Hospital, where she had cared for casualties from Vietnam.

At our wedding, when her dad had walked her down the aisle and given her hand to me, he'd told me, "She's yours now. Take good care of her." Little did I know that just two months later, I would have to tell her that the biggest hero in her life, her dad, was gone. His words at the altar, in retrospect, seemed almost prophetic. And the truth is that looking back over the years, I realize I could have done a much better job as the new hero in her life.

TRANSITION

A month later, we made the move to Oregon and went back to school using our GI Bill benefits. The economic climate in Oregon at that time (the early 1980s) was dismal. The unemployment rate was 28 percent, and meaningful jobs were scarce to nonexistent. One day, while venting my frustration at not finding work, I told Chrissy I was beginning to feel like a has-been.

In her own beautiful way, as she always did, she replied softly, "Robert, better a has-been than a never-was. God will provide." That was vintage Chrissy, always finding the bright side of things, always there to support and love and encourage. When my own father died, I had to make arrangements for his funeral and burial. Doing so was all the more stressful because my three younger brothers had been estranged from him for years. Amid the barrage of paperwork, phone calls, family dynamics, and legalities, Chris was ever present, quietly doing what she always did: taking care of our family and supporting me with her quiet strength and wisdom. Whenever I needed something, it was suddenly there. She spent her entire life nurturing and caring for others—as the oldest of eight children, a Navy nurse, a civilian nurse, a wife, a mother, and an active member of our church.

Thank you, God, for bringing her to me.

· · · · · ·

February 1, 2017 — Day 14

"This is the day the Lord has made. Let us rejoice and be glad in it."

We continue our journey today with the good news that three tests performed on Chrissy all came out the way we needed them to.

The first is a "duplex ultrasound," in which a very skilled technician scans her brain for any signs of vasospasm. The duplex is administered on Monday, Wednesday and Friday, takes almost an hour, and the results are reported at the following day's neuro-team morning rounds. So as ...of yesterday, Chrissy is free of any signs of vasospasm (a reaction of the brain to blood in her CSF - cerebro-spinal fluid - in which the blood vessels of the brain spasm, usually resulting in stroke.)

The second test was a lab culture taken to see if Chris may have been infected by a "super-bacteria" that is extremely resistant to most antibiotics. The lab report came back negative for any sign of intestinal or alimentary canal infection, so no more "precautions" because that concern was unfounded.

The third piece of good news is that the results of tests performed on Chris to check for any sign of blood clots in her legs came back negative. This concern arises when someone has been bedridden for a long period of time with a hemorrhage injury.

I'm hard pressed to think of a time when I've been so happy to have heard "No" three times. :-)

Her pneumonia is largely cleared up, and so we welcome another day of "no news is good news." There will probably be many more such days, as there is no way of knowing how long until her brain has re-engineered itself to deal with the consequences of her injury. But that is in God's hands, and we continue to pray for her full and complete recovery.

As I was praying with Chris this morning, thinking back over 35 years as husband and wife, it occurred to me that even though we are united in the sacrament of marriage, she really doesn't belong to me. She belongs to God, who gifted me with her presence in my life. She is His precious treasure, created for His purposes and not for mine.

This means that I am God's purpose for her, and she is God's purpose for me.

Let that sink in. God had our purpose planned before we were even created. And if we view marriage as a sacrament, as something uniquely holy, shared with the one person created by God to complete us, how can we be anything but incredulous at God's infinite goodness?

Do we really, truly understand that God created the person we are within the sacrament of marriage to complete us and to help perfect us for eternity? Do we give this truth the credence it deserves?

The next time someone asks you if you think you're God's gift to mankind, smile and answer them, "No, just to my spouse." And act accordingly.

May God bless you SPECTACULARLY this day,

Bob

CHAPTER 15

Kids

CHRISSY AND I BOTH WANTED CHILDREN. IN JULY 1983, TWO years after we married, our first, Joseph, arrived. We had already relocated to Eugene, Oregon, Chrissy's birthplace and where most of her family resided. We were both going to school on the GI Bill, and I was flying with the Marine Corps Reserves. After we learned that she was pregnant, Chris opted to have a natural delivery.

Joseph's arrival wasn't easy; Chris was in labor for nineteen hours before he came into the world. I dutifully stayed with her, occasionally slipping out to the waiting area to grab a snack or a quick nap. Sometime around the seventeenth hour, as I was standing next to her bed and giving her ice chips from a paper cup, she looked up at me and said, "I love you, Bob." She then proceeded to vomit all over my trousers and shoes. I'm not often at a loss for words, but that was one of the few times in my life that I was completely incapable of speech. Sometimes people show their love in the most amazing ways.

Just short of three years later, we learned that Chrissy was pregnant again. We were now living in the suburbs of Denver,

Colorado, where I'd been assigned as a new first-office Special Agent of the FBI. The work was interesting and the hours irregular, so I wasn't able to go with Chris to all her prenatal doctor's appointments. In preparation for the birth of our second child, we took Lamaze classes. Chris was so impressed with the Lamaze method that she became a certified Lamaze instructor and helped many parents prepare for childbirth. Among them were John Elway, Hall of Fame quarterback for the Denver Broncos, and his then-wife, Janet.

Near the end of her first trimester, I came home, walked in the door, and went over to give her a kiss and hug. Much to my surprise, when I kissed her, she burst into tears. I immediately asked, "Chrissy, what's wrong?" I knew she'd had an appointment with her OB/GYN that morning, and because she was crying, I was afraid I was going to hear some bad news about the pregnancy.

Instead, what she said through her tears was, "It's twins. We're going to have twins." I laughed with delight and maybe a hint of hysteria, sat down next to her, took both her hands in mine, looked into her beautiful blue eyes, and said, "Think of all the extra fun we're gonna have!"

The remainder of the pregnancy required her to be very careful, both because she was thirty-nine and because she was carrying twins. When her water broke, I drove us to the hospital. The labor and delivery team had Chris lay down on her back and put fetal heart monitors on each of the babies. As her labor progressed, one of the twins' heart rates—normally around 150 beats per minute—slowed dangerously to 45. Chrissy (who had worked labor and delivery during her career as a nurse) told the charge nurse she needed lie on her side rather than on her back. The nurse ignored her and instead went to the interphone on the wall. She hit the "Crash" button, came over to me, and in a voice akin to that of a Marine Corps drill instructor, said, "YOU have to leave NOW." She took my arm and there was no doubt in my mind about whether or not I was leaving that room.

Chris managed to roll onto her left side, causing the fetal heartbeat returned to normal. Because of that moment of panic, however, I wasn't there when our twin girls (Lauren and Stephanie) were born, but no matter. God blessed us with two little cherubs in perfect health who have enriched—and sometimes challenged—our lives in ways we never imagined.

Not long after the twins were born, one of Chrissy's sisters gave us a gift, a framed needlepoint that hangs on a wall in our home to this day. It says, "Children are God's proof that the world should go on."

Truer words were never spoken.

. . . . . .

February 2, 2017 — Day 15

Today is Day 15. For some reason, the song, "Sixteen Candles" by The Four Seasons popped into my head. Chrissy and I love that song. :-)

Mid-morning yesterday, while I was gazing at her face, she coughed up some phlegm. It's difficult to watch her cough, as there's no sound because the ventilator tube bypasses her vocal cords. I called the nurse in to suction her mouth, and as she did so,

Chris opened her eyes wide open for about 30 seconds, and then she blinked.

It was the longest period of time with her eyes wide open since the aneurysm burst - A-Day - January 18th. I moved my hand in front of her face, hoping to see some sign of cognition, but her eyes didn't track, and it didn't appear that she was seeing anything.

But I saw something. I saw yet another sign that God is at work, doing what doctors cannot. It's one more tiny sign, one more reason to stay the course as Chrissy continues to defy the odds.

We continue to be buoyed by your prayers. If you have any doubts about whether those prayers are working, please know that we would not be where we are today without them. Chris continues to beat overwhelming odds, and we continue to effectively repel a relentless onslaught of doubt, guilt, worry and self-pity because you are praying with and for us. Without your prayers, it was a virtual medical certainty that Chris would not be here, and we would not be in this fight. But Chris IS here, against tremendous odds, and our faith remains strong and our resolve unwavering. Thank you, "seventy times seven."

We've been reading and putting into practice everything we can find about recovering from aneurysms and severe brain injury. We've brought in a Crucifix, pictures and cards from home to decorate her hospital room. We constantly speak to her, and read to her from her favorite books - among which is The Chronicles of Narnia. How many times she read them to the kids before bedtime, or during the day when they were small. For those who don't know, you might consider reading them, and sharing them with your kids. The series was written by C. S. Lewis, and is an allegory on the life and death of Christ. Interestingly, it is very relevant to both children and adults.

Night before last, we sat in one of the conference rooms attached to the Critical Care Waiting Room and recorded stories about our family vacation in Maui (Hawaii) for Chrissy's birthday last June. We play this for her every few hours because there is solid scientific proof that it stimulates brain activity in brain-injured patients. We also play some classical piano music, and some of her favorite pop music artists (Neal Diamond and Abba, among others). We'll be doing more recordings, as they will remind Chris of the many wonderful times and places we enjoyed as a family, and contribute to a quicker recovery.

The twice-delayed (dreaded?) medical/palliative care/case manager conference is happening today at 3pm at DHMC. While not completely certain, we think it will involve a discussion of Chrissy's current status, including presenting future options to consider. Please say a special prayer at 3pm, as we begin to assess alternatives. We fully believe that God will show us the way if we give Him the time to work.

I leave you with the following prayer, shared with me by a now-deceased missionary priest from the Oblates of St. Francis de Sales many years ago. It has helped me beat down the demons of fear and worry which can sap our strength and attack our faith. It is my gift to you today.

PEACE

Do not fear what tomorrow may bring.
The same everlasting Father, who cares for you today,
Will take care of you tomorrow and every day.
Either He will shield you from pain and suffering,
Or He will give you unfailing strength to bear them.
Be at peace, then,
And put aside all anxious thoughts and imaginations.
(To which I add a knowing "Amen.")

Bob

CHAPTER 16

The Thread of Faith in Our Lives

During our Plebe (freshman) Year at the Naval Academy, I and half a dozen fellow Catholics in my company decided to go to Mass every day during Lent. So it was that on Good Friday of 1972, we enjoyed a powerful sermon given by one of the Navy Chaplains assigned to the Academy, Father (Commander) Bob Ecker.

His sermons were unique in that he spoke in the first person, actually taking the role of one of the actual characters in the Gospel reading. On this particular Good Friday, he took on the persona of Pontius Pilate and cleverly led us through the thought process by which we rationalize committing sin. "I had to get rid of that Jesus. He's become quite a problem because he speaks of being a king, and Herod isn't happy about someone else proclaiming themselves king. Crowds are starting to follow him, and Rome doesn't want more insurgent problems in Israel. Not only that, but for me to keep my job, I need the cooperation of the Sanhedrin, Chief Priest, Scribes, and Pharisees to help keep order in the region, and they want this Jesus guy gone too."

Father Ecker's manner of presenting the essence of his message was unique and extremely effective.

My faith hasn't always been as strong as it should be, waxing and waning over the years. I allowed events and circumstances to distract—and, sadly at times, to divert—me from living as a faithful Christian. Being a single Marine Corps second lieutenant in flight school was an invitation to trouble, as the deadly combination of achievement, ego, and bravado led me away from Jesus Christ. I imagine that many have followed such a course; hopefully, most find their way back into God's fold before standing before Jesus in judgment.

A couple of years later, I was at sea aboard the *USS Midway* somewhere in the Pacific or Indian Ocean. I was in my flight gear, walking down a passageway to man up for a night mission, when I ran into a tall Navy captain wearing chaplain's insignia and a Roman collar (the sign of a Catholic priest). I stepped aside so he could pass, as was military protocol, and said, "Good evening, Father." He looked at me and said, "Hi! Going or coming?"

I answered, "Going!"

"Be safe!" he said. "I'll say a prayer for you at Mass this evening."

I returned safely from the mission, and I never gave another thought to that brief encounter with a senior Navy chaplain in a dimly lit passageway on the other side of the world.

After completing that tour of duty, I received my orders to report for instructor duty at Whidbey Island and returned to "the fold," renewing the active practice of my Catholic faith. I met, courted, and married Christine, and we were blessed with three beautiful children.

THE THREAD OF FAITH IN OUR LIVES

Fast forward to late 1985. We were living in Broomfield, Colorado (a suburb northwest of Denver), and I was employed flying a corporate jet for a private company in Boulder.

On Christmas Eve, while watching TV on a layover, I found a channel that was carrying Midnight Mass at St. Patrick's Cathedral in New York City. As I watched the beautiful celebration, I was astonished to recognize the priest celebrating the Mass. It was the Navy chaplain I had encountered at sea on the *USS Midway* eight years before! His sermon reflected on why God, in the person of Jesus Christ, had chosen to enter the world in such a humble state—a helpless infant in a stable under a cold, starlit sky—when He had all the power and glory of the universe at his command. That sermon etched itself in my memory, just as Chaplain Ecker's homily at the Naval Academy had done in 1972.

The name of that priest was John Cardinal O'Connor, Archbishop of New York.

After our chance meeting halfway around the world, he rose to become Chief of Chaplains for the US Navy, retiring as a rear admiral. He then served as auxiliary bishop to Terence Cardinal Cooke of New York, was subsequently appointed Bishop of Scranton, Pennsylvania, and then shortly thereafter, installed as Archbishop of New York, and elevated to Cardinal of the Church by Pope John Paul II.

Fast forward again, to spring of 2000. We had moved several times due to my employment with United Airlines, and we were living in New Hampshire, flying out of New York City. While watching the evening news, I learned that Cardinal O'Connor had contracted brain cancer and was dying. This hit me particularly hard, and I decided to write him a letter thanking him for his life of service to Christ. In that letter, I mentioned our long-ago meeting aboard the *USS Midway* and his sermon that I had watched several years later about Jesus coming in such a humble manner, and I thanked him for the prayers he had said that had ultimately led me back to Christ.

Imagine my surprise when I received a reply several weeks later, written by his niece, who was caring for him during his final days. I hold that letter as one of my most treasured possessions.

But the story doesn't end there.

Seventeen years later, after Christine was stricken (January 18, 2017), I began writing the posts that are the purpose of this book. On Good Friday that year, I wrote a post in which I recounted Chaplain Ecker's sermon as Pontius Pilate at the Naval Academy on Good Friday in 1972. Several days later, I received a Facebook message from an Academy classmate (whom I've never met) sharing that Father Ecker was now ninety-two years old and fulfilling three ministries in San Diego, California. As part of his message, he provided the priest's contact information.

A week later, on Easter Friday, I called Father Ecker. After several rings, he answered, "Hi, Bob!" I have to believe that it was caller ID that let him know who was calling. We exchanged pleasantries, and I shared with him the lifetime of events that had led me to make this call, recounting his 1972 sermon as Pontius Pilate, the chance meeting with Chaplain O'Connor at sea years ago, my return to Christ, marriage, children, Christine being stricken—in essence my whole life story since graduation from the Naval Academy. I shared with him the very same story I've shared with you in this chapter, including my letter to Cardinal O'Connor as he lay dying, and the fact that I had actually received a response, though written by the Cardinal's niece.

And now, I share what Father Bob Ecker, a retired Navy chaplain with whom I'd had absolutely no contact for forty-five years, told me: "I know about that letter, Bob. You see, because he was too weak to speak, I dictated it for him."

I titled this chapter "The Thread of Faith in Our Lives" because this story showed me that God works to save us, often through what appear to be "chance meetings" with others. He is ever-present, even when we abandon Him and reject his love for us. And I'm willing to bet that if you look back over the years, you too will find a "thread of faith" woven through the tapestry of your life.

God never abandons us; it is we who abandon Him. And yet, He is always waiting with open arms to welcome us back whenever we decide to renounce sin, acknowledge Him as our Lord and Savior, and "take up your cross and follow Me."

Please don't keep Him waiting; eternity is a very long time.

. . . . . .

February 3, 2017 — Day 16

"...My help comes from the Lord, who made Heaven and Earth..." (Psalm 121)

As I sit in the Critical Care Waiting Room, I am with a family whose father just passed away during emergency surgery. As they cry, I am praying for them, that God will bring solace and guidance to face the sadness of the coming days, and that they will experience the love of God amid the desolation of their loss.

My friends, constancy is so critical in life. It enables us to build foundations of trust - in God, in our families, our friendships, our congregations, our world. It provides a steady rhythm to our days. Constancy in prayer builds faith. And constancy in faith builds the foundation and framework upon and within which we can better accept and understand why things happen in our lives.

And yesterday, things happened.

At around 9:30am, our neurologist stopped in to do an evaluation of Chrissy's condition. He "knuckled" her sternum to stimulate her, clapped his hands sharply, and said very loudly, "Christine, open your eyes."

And she did.

After her eyes closed, he did it again. And guess what?

She did. Again.

She remains in a coma, but yesterday for the first time, a woman who was not expected to survive, responded directly to a human voice. What better testimony to the power of prayer, and the value of constancy? How can my family and I ever thank you for the constancy of your faith and prayers?

Then, the 3pm conference. Words cannot express the incredible knowledge, compassion and understanding of the team of doctors, nurses and staff that provided us formation, guidance and questions framed to help us move the process of her healing forward. The result is that, based on our decision, Chris is going to remain here at DHMC to continue treatment and observation as she continues her battle.

Last night the doctors clamped off the drain that was inserted the day she arrived here, to relieve the pressure on her brain from the blood that escaped through the aneurysm. They need to see if her brain can manage ICP - Inter Cranial Pressure - on its own, or if they'll have to install a permanent internal shunt to deal with it. We do not yet have an answer.

We also made the decision to perform a tracheostomy, to remove the breathing tube and replace it with a "valve" in her trachea so she doesn't have the breathing tube irritating her throat and interfering with her mouth. We also opted to put in a "peg" - a device that will enable her to be fed directly into her stomach through her abdomen. While this all sounds gruesome, it is actually good, as the risk of infection is substantially decreased, and her comfort increased as a result. Those operations are expected to take place this afternoon.

The exhilaration we felt when we learned that Chris had opened her eyes on command was wonderful. Though it is a very small step, and though she is still critical, we believe, we surrender, we see and we continue to grow, as the woman who captured my heart 37 years ago remains with us because of your love, your prayers and the mercy of our God.

Praise be to the Father, and the Son, and the Holy Spirit.

Bob

CHAPTER 17

Go Your Way—Your Faith Has Saved You

A FRIEND ONCE SHARED THIS THOUGHT WITH ME: "NO MATTER where I go, there I am."

It's a simple phrase suggesting that the circumstances in which I find myself are the product of my own decisions and actions. It's especially relevant in our world today, where accepting responsibility for the choices we make is increasingly rare. Victimhood and entitlement are displacing responsibility and sacrifice in our culture. Underlying this deadly transformation is our societal loss of respect for God as the author of life, and for every human being as a unique creation with a God-given purpose for their existence.

We were granted free will to make choices in this life that will ultimately determine our eternal destiny. We all fail, and we all fall, and because of the sacrifice of Jesus Christ at Calvary, we were given the ability to repent, atone, and find our way to Heaven. We will all face tragedy and temptations that attempt to lure us away from Godliness. Thus the ability to differentiate between good and evil, right and wrong, Godly and ungodly, is critical to living happy, healthy, productive lives. Ultimately, that's what God wants for each of us. Our ability to live such lives depends on the strength of our faith and our commitment to Jesus Christ.

There are things that have happened since Christine was stricken that defy scientific explanation but are completely understandable with faith. She has come home three times, making her presence known with the unquestionable scent of her favorite perfume, even as she lay bedridden over one hundred miles away. She always came at exactly the right time to defuse difficult family situations. That's who she was and is: a dedicated wife, loving mother, and the heart and soul of our family.

I don't know why you chose to read this book, but I do know that what's written in its pages can change your life. Each of these messages was written as I navigated the fear, anguish, desperation, and anger that challenged my faith. I believe these words were heaven-sent and meant to be shared with you. There aren't any more "stories" preceding the posts; but from this point on, the posts *are* the story.

Please know that our individual prayers, and the prayers of others, are critical when rebuilding our lives after transgression or tragedy. Many people all over the world offered prayers for Christine and our family. There were days when I could actually feel the power of those prayers, and I'm certain that Chrissy felt this as well.

In the end, out of chaos and devastation came order and purpose. I knew that if my faith was to survive, I had to turn this tragedy to God's purposes. That's why this book exists.

Believe.

Surrender.

See.

Grow.

Witness.

Rejoice.

I hope you will seek the thread of faith that's woven into your existence. It's there if you look hard enough. And when you find it, my prayer is that you will follow it for the remainder of your life.

God is waiting.

. . . . . .

CHAPTER 18

The Rest of the Story

THE REMAINING PAGES OF THIS BOOK CONTAIN THE MESSAGES I posted on Facebook in the days, months, and years after Christine was stricken. They are our gift to you, thoughts born of devastating tragedy, words that we hope will help you grow closer to God. I still re-read them from time to time, often gaining new insights into how I can live a better life.

If a single word in this book brings you to a closer relationship with the Almighty God, you will have helped me accomplish the mission I took on in the aftermath of tragedy: turning what happened to achieving God's purpose for your life, and for the world.

May the road rise up to meet you,
May the wind be always at your back,
May the sun shine warm upon your face,
May the rains fall soft upon your fields,
And, until we meet again,
May God hold you in the hollow of His hand.

—Bob and Christine Giuda, October 25, 2022

The Posts

February 4, 2017
> *"...Then they cry out to the Lord in their trouble,*
> *and He brings them out of their distresses.*
> *He calms the storm, so that its waves are still.*
> *Then they are glad because they are quiet;*
> *so He guides them to their desired haven..."*
> **(Psalm 107)**

Yesterday was a "guardedly" good day. We made some progress, and we had some "side steps." I don't consider side steps to be setbacks. I think you'll see what I mean.

The clamp on Chris' CSF (Cerebro-Spinal Fluid) drain line was released last night (a "time out") after about 24 hours, as her ICP (Inter Cranial Pressure) was increasingly unstable, and creeping higher than the neurosurgeons like. They'll clamp the line again soon to again test whether Chrissy's brain can handle the CSF it produces every day without a drain. The concern is hydrocephalus - fluid on the brain - that causes pressure and destroys tissue. If her brain can't dispose of the daily excess fluid, the neurosurgeons will install a permanent "shunt" - an internal line from her brain to her stomach to drain her excess CSF.

It's important to note that the clamp test often takes several attempts before it produces acceptable results.

The teams of doctors working on Chrissy coordinate regularly, and yesterday they decided to postpone the tracheostomy and g-tube ("peg") operations because of the unstable ICP. As I said in my initial remarks, we don't see this as a setback, we see it as a side step, as these operations will take place when the ICP issue is resolved.

Every hour or so, the nurses take and record Chrissy's temperature using an oral thermometer, and Chris just hates it. Coma or not, she clenches her jaw, and will move her head just a bit from side to side to avoid the probe. Sometimes, her eyes will open for a few seconds. So yesterday evening, while Lauren and I were standing beside the bed, the nurse took Chrissy's temperature. She had her normal reaction...

Except that both her eyes stayed open. :-)

We spoke to her for about 3 minutes, her eyes fully open, her right eye looking directly at us and her mouth intermittently opening and closing as if trying to speak.

Your prayers are the "boat" carrying Chrissy towards her "desired haven," and God is "calming the storm" and providing wind for her sails.

Thank you for helping us on our voyage. We love you.
Bob

. . . .

February 5, 2017

"Give ear to my words, O Lord; give heed to my groaning. Hearken to the sound of my cry, my King and my God, for to thee do I pray." (Psalm 5)

Yesterday, Chrissy seemed restless, as her BP and ICP finally restabilized after the 24-hour clamp test on her CSF drain line. This morning (3am) she is resting very quietly, and all her "numbers" are where they should be. Sometimes it's easy to forget that she's still in critical condition, as we take encouragement from the several small gains she has made. But the sights and sounds of her Critical Care room are a disquieting reminder that she is literally poised at the door to God's Kingdom.

Over the past 18 days, with Chrissy's small victories, I found myself starting to anticipate more and greater improvements. Yesterday brought this into sharp focus, as she "regrouped" without any noticeable gains. I learned very abruptly that anticipation begets expectations that may not to be in line with God's plans for her or for us. When expectations aren't met, we become susceptible to doubt born of disappointment. These human emotions can poison our faith. And they can affect our health.

As we pray fervently and constantly that God will continue healing Christine, are we developing expectations of Him? Or is our trust in God and His infinite mercy based on total submission to His will, regardless of outcomes? When we "ask, seek and knock," should we be expecting His answer to be the answer we want?

These questions drive to the core of our spiritual lives. When intertwined with the volcanic emotions associated with life and death, they create intense spiritual challenges that can either strengthen our faith, or undermine it.

"Now faith is the substance of things hoped for, the evidence of things unseen." (Hebrews 11:1)

Do we truly believe in God's awesome power? While soldiers defeated in battle can surrender their arms and still look for ways to resist and escape, we do not have that luxury when dealing in matters of faith. Our surrender must be total, complete and unconditional.

And so today, as we offer our prayers of hope, let us not be weakened by expectations. Let us

pray as Jesus prayed in the Garden of Gethsemane, "Father, if you are willing, take this cup from me; yet not my will, but thine be done."

Thank you for your prayers, and for the love you continue to bring to Chrissy and to us.

Bob

. . . .

February 6, 2017

*"...He leads me in paths of righteousness,
for His name's sake..." (Psalm 23)*

Yesterday was peaceful, and Chrissy continued resting. In the words of the young (brilliant) neurosurgeon during rounds at 6am yesterday morning, "Now, what she needs is time..."

"Good numbers," we say to each other at the bedside "changing of the guard", meaning that all her physiological parameters are where they should be. She opens her eyes infrequently, occasionally, sometimes when she hears a voice, always when receiving the "mouth care" she clearly detests, sometimes when we adjust the position of her head on the pillow. Ever so gently, God's hand is touching her. What an incredible privilege to see it happening...

Today (Monday), three days after the (unsuccessful) clamp test, Chris is scheduled to receive her tracheostomy and g-tube - "trake" and "peg" in medical jargon. These will do away with the ventilator and feeding tubes in her mouth and down her throat, reducing both irritation and the threat of infection. Once these procedures are complete and the doctors are certain no problems arise from them, they will resume the clamp test to determine whether Chris will need the shunt.

Gazing out my bedroom window this morning, I realized it had snowed last night, just enough to blanket our world in a fresh coat of white - clean, unblemished and perfect. It then struck me that on this new day (thank you, God), my feet will leave tracks in that new-fallen snow. And my actions will leave tracks on the lives of those whose lives I touch.

The path I walk today will leave footprints on the lives of every person I meet.

God gives us "new snow" in our "yard" every day of our lives. And every day, we leave tracks in that new snow. Hopefully, our tracks are footprints of kindness, respect, compassion and faith. But too often, they are not. We can become entangled in worldly endeavors that leave tracks which don't reflect God's will or His love. We should never forget that every encounter with another human being is an opportunity to share the Word of God by virtue of how we treat them.

At home, at work, in the grocery store, in the hospital, at the doctor's office, driving the car - every single day of our lives, God provides us "new snow" - another chance to leave tracks that lead others to Christ. Tread gently, for we never know that we won't be the presence of God to a soul in search of Him.

As your prayers continue, my life is changing. You raise Chrissy up to our God, and you shine light in the darkness when our hearts are heavy burdened. I thank you for the grace you bring to us on our new journey. Be SPECTACULAR today. :-)

Bob

February 7, 2017

*"I will sing of thy steadfast love, O Lord, for ever;
with my mouth I will proclaim thy faithfulness
to all generations. For they steadfast love
was established forever, thy faithfulness
is firm as the heavens." (Psalm 89)*

Chris is resting as peacefully as I've seen on this journey. When I went in to pray the Rosary, I took her right hand and said, "Good morning, Mrs. G. I love you." Her right eye opened and she looked at me and moved her mouth several times. As I prayed with her, she went back to sleep. I have no idea whether her movements were a response, or just happened to occur as reflex actions at that precise moment. But I know what I believe. :-)

The "trake" and "peg" did not happen yesterday after all. "Monday mornings" also happen in hospitals, and there was simply no time available in the operating room suites for our procedures. The doctors had considered performing them in her room, but decided that they wanted all the equipment and capabilities of a full operating room available for exigencies, so they postponed her surgeries to 7:30AM today.

This morning as I prayed the Rosary with Chrissy, I felt a strong pull to focus on the Cross. While amazingly simple, it proclaims contradiction. With its 2 pieces at right angles, its very shape is a contradiction. Made of wood, it will nevertheless last through all eternity. Used to kill, it opened our gateway to eternal life. A public symbol of ignominy, it is the abiding symbol of God's love and majesty. It brought the end of the Old Law, and began God's New Covenant.

Just as the Cross presents contradictions that can and should challenge us to grow our faith, life presents contradictions that can erode it. Christians are called to challenge the world's moral contradictions, and there are many. Not least among them are contradictions between the laws of man and the Laws of God.

We must search our lives to find the contradictions between "our way" and God's way; between the laws of man and the Laws of God; between what the world says is right, and what our faith tells us. Doing so will afflict our comfort, bedevil our opinions, and confound our thinking.

It will also change the footprints we leave in the fresh morning snows of each new God-given day.

Believe. Surrender. See. Grow.

And be SPECTACULAR again today. :-)

Bob

. . . .

February 8, 2017

"For God alone my soul waits in silence; from Him comes my salvation. He only is my rock and my salvation, my fortress. I shall not be greatly moved." (Psalm 62)

Today, Christine sleeps free of the once needed but cumbersome and ungainly breathing and feeding tubes and supporting paraphernalia that only yesterday crowded her beautiful face. She is so much more comfortable, and looks so much more the Chrissy we know and love. Both surgeries yesterday went perfectly, with no complications.

"Good numbers" this morning, as her healing continues. The ICU team reports that both the tracheostomy and the stomach tube look good, and the Neuro-team this morning relayed that Chrissy passed her "SBT" (Breathing Test), and that at some point today, they'll try taking her off the ventilator for good, because she is able to breathe on her own. :-)

But amid the joy of these victories, we begin to wrestle with two of the longer-term logistical concerns of our journey.

First is the immutable fact that Chrissy, our wife and mother, is no longer part of the everyday activities of our lives. On several levels, my mind and heart are rejecting this, because we do not want to have to move ahead without her. But we must, and we will. We are gradually, reluctantly taking on the tasks she did so routinely every day, hating this evolving new normal, this necessary filling of the gaping void created by her physical absence from our everyday lives. Though ever-present in our thoughts and prayers, she is, for an indeterminate period of time, absent from our home and our everyday activities. We're being forced to acknowledge this, whether or not we want to accept it.

Second is the challenge of whether we can continue to maintain our round-the-clock presence at the hospital. Difficult as it may be, we have to acknowledge that this may not be sustainable, and we may have to begin leaving the most important person in our lives alone for some part of each day.

We struggle with a nagging sense of guilt that we were not all that we should have been for her; cannot be all that we need to be for her; cannot do everything that our sense of duty calls us to do for her; cannot maintain the ideal standard of loving care we feel obligated to provide for her. Deep down, we know that we're going to have to change our own expectations of what we should be, to incorporate the reality of being what we can be, for our beloved wife and mother.

And so, mindful of our humanity...

We stand, firm in our faith. We BELIEVE.
We stand, humble in our hope. We SURRENDER.
We stand, following God's word. We SEE.
We stand, embracing God's will. We GROW.

We pray that God answers our petition for Chrissy's complete recovery, in the name of Him who is the author of all life, the God of Abraham and Isaac, the Alpha and the Omega.

Bob

. . . . . .

February 9, 2017

> *"Praise is due to thee, O God in Zion. And to thee shall vows be performed, O thou who hearest prayer!" (Psalm 65)*

Yesterday morning, we took another small step forward. "Look ma, no ventilator!" Chris is breathing completely on her own. She has been initiating her breathing on her own since A-Day, but now it's real. We can see it. More good numbers this morning, and the Neuro-team is discussing taking her off Nimotapine (sp?) - the medicine to prevent vasospasm. Now in Day 22, we are past the Day 5 - Day 21 "danger zone," and the risk of vasospasm is now almost zero. They also want to do another clamp test on her CSF drain line to see if her brain can manage its daily CSF production internally so they can remove the drain. If not, they'll eventually have to put in a shunt (internal drain line) to drain the CSF into her stomach.

As I awakened this morning, I caught a reflection from my right pinkie finger, reminding me that I'm wearing both our Wedding

Bands. Very early on, we had to remove Chrissy's jewelry from her fingers due to swelling, so I chose to wear her ring for her. It has never once been taken off since I had the honor of placing that slender ring of gold on her finger on June 27, 1981. It is an incredible symbol, and makes an incredible statement. It represents our sacred commitment to each another and to our marriage. And I look forward to the day I can place this beautiful, simple, powerful symbol of our lifetime commitment onto her left ring finger again. :-)

I've noticed over the years that more than a few married men don't wear their wedding bands. Some years ago, as I was thinking about our Wedding Day, and our vows, and the reason we even have weddings, I wondered why anyone would ever not wear their Wedding Band...

I believe that there are 4 "constituencies" at a wedding: bride, groom, guests, and God. Each of these parties is essential to completing the sacrament. When the minister announces, "I now pronounce you man and wife," something miraculous happens: bride and groom become one. And they do so, sworn under oath before Almighty God, in the presence of friends and family as witnesses.

When we attend a wedding, we are not just there to celebrate, we are there to WITNESS a sacred union, as parties to their shared promise of fidelity.

We place Wedding Bands on our hands to publicly proclaim to the world that we are united in marriage. But somewhere along the way, if a man chooses not to wear that band, he conceals, intentionally or not, the existence of his sacred union to the woman he has chosen as his sacramental companion for life. Unwittingly or not, the absence of a Wedding Band makes a statement. It sends a signal to those who do not know he is married. It invites others to tempt him into violating his marriage vows.

Have you ever seen a married woman without her Wedding Band?

Men - do we honor our wives and our marriages as we should? Do we wear our Wedding Bands, not only to proclaim our love for our wives, but also as a public proclamation of our belief in, and commitment to the institution of marriage?

Today, I'm wearing two Wedding Bands. One is on loan from the girl who stole my heart 38 years ago, and made it official on a beautiful June day in 1981. I'm her WITNESS, and God's WITNESS, that she's still the one person in the world who makes me complete, just like that delicate circle of gold around my finger.

And so today, another word becomes part of the journey, as we pray for our Christine - daughter, wife and mother.

BELIEVE.
SURRENDER.
SEE.
GROW.
WITNESS.

Thanks for your love and your prayers. God is at work here because of them.

Bob

. . . . . .

February 10, 2017

"May God be gracious to us and bless us and make His face to shine upon us, that thy way may be known upon Earth, thy saving power to all nations. Let the peoples praise Thee, O God, let all the peoples praise Thee!" (Psalm 67)

Yesterday, only a few hours after beginning the clamp test on the CSF drain line, the doctors stopped it. It became apparent that Chrissy's brain isn't managing the extra fluid she produces each day, and her ICP (Inter Cranial Pressure) increased past an acceptable level. Today, we'll probably be discussing a permanent shunt to relieve her ICP. So, good numbers except for the short time when her ICP was elevated. She rests quietly in the care of a great team at DHMC — and in God's care as well, lifted up every minute of every day by your prayers.

Wednesday night, sheer exhaustion - physical, emotional and psychological - finally took their toll, and our family fractured. While spending the night with Chris, I received a phone call from home from children under terrible duress. I drove home in the snowstorm Thursday morning to bring healing to our home.

The choice to leave Chrissy alone for the first time since January 18th was one I didn't want to make. So on the spur of the moment, I spoke aloud and shared my concerns with her - still in the coma - and it came to me that were our roles reversed, and I laying in that bed, she would do what she's always done - put her family first. So, difficult though it was, I left her bedside Thursday morning to do as she would do. Some would say she spent last night alone for the first time - but I know better. Your prayers and God's angels are with her. And I know she's good with that.

Thursday morning very early, before heading home, I called a friend whose faith is a shining beacon in a sometimes-dark world, and out of thin air, in a 10-minute window which only God could have made available at that time of day, he shared with me the following verse, which became the bookends of our family discussion and prayer:

THE POSTS

"The steadfast love of the Lord never ceases, His mercies never come to an end; they are new every morning; great is Thy faithfulness." (Lamentations 3:22-23)

I drove home wondering what I would find.

When I walked into the house, there were 5 individual people in various states of emotional shock, amid quiet born of anger and pain. Everyone had built walls to deal with the stresses of the past 22 days, and the consequences finally came home to roost. Our home was in dire need of healing and rest.

After about an hour, we sat down together and talked for almost 2 hours. We then prayed, and spent the entire rest of the day in a quiet, pensive home where I could see God at work. I prayed, and we prayed, for strength and solidarity, for peace and comfort, for God's healing touch. It was a very quiet day, and we each spent much of it alone with our thoughts. Sleep caught up with us, and all was quiet.

When I awakened this morning, it was still dark. I opened my eyes, and the first thing that came to mind was the verse from Lamentations. I took the time to think about what it really means, and how it relates to our changing family dynamics. Then I rose to face the new day.

God gives us a new chance to embrace His mercy every single day of our lives.

Think about that. Another chance to attain salvation every time we open our eyes. Another chance to accept His mercy and faithfulness.

Please don't waste that chance, because we know not the day nor the hour.

God's mercy be with you, and His peace be upon you.

Bob

February 11, 2017

> *"...Be angry, but sin not; commune with your own hearts on your beds and be silent. Offer right sacrifices, and put your trust in the Lord." (Psalm 4)*

Yesterday we headed back to DHMC. Chrissy's numbers weren't perfect, but they were within acceptable limits. There's really nothing much to report beyond that. I believe we're beginning a phase of our journey that can stiffen our resolve, strengthen our faith, and anneal our love for each another. It's really all up to us.

We met with the Palliative Care doctors yesterday, allowing us to focus on some things we need to do - and not do. We're starting to organize our lives for the long road ahead, with no idea where it will lead us, or what Chrissy's future holds. One of the hardest things to deal with is not knowing if any or all of her conscious mind is trapped inside the inert figure laying in the hospital bed. We just don't know, and we can't fix it. Period. All we can do is pray, and wait. We're troubled by the prospect of going on with our lives as our wife and mother lies helpless in a bed 47 miles away from her home.

Every day we deal with the entire spectrum of human emotion - anger, joy, fear, sorrow, confusion, frustration, love, irritation, discouragement, joy, and everything else. We're forced to deal with a reality none of us wants. And we have to deal with it one-on-one, face-to-face with God. "Group think" doesn't work here.

This morning when I grabbed my Bible, it opened to Psalm 4. I don't believe it was an accident, given the events of the past couple of days. God tells us there that it's OK to be angry, so long as it doesn't lead us to sin. He tells us to use our anger as a reason to "offer right sacrifices" (pray) and put our trust in the Lord. Put another way, how we deal with our anger can bring us closer to God. Or it can take us farther away from Him...

The tongue is an organ, intended to proclaim the glory of God and our love of His plan for salvation. But because we are human, it is also very capable of inciting war; of sowing discord; of promoting division; of inflaming passions. And unlike nuclear weapons which have a "destruct" button to stop them in midflight if launched in error, words launched from our tongues in anger always reach their intended destination. Once fired, they are going straight to the target, every time. Whether launched out of habit or with intent, we bear the moral consequences of every word that ever crosses our lips. It's probably a good idea to re-read that last sentence a couple of times or more.

Some wise person once said that the human tongue is the most difficult thing on Earth to tame. I have to agree. As with every other part of our body, it is a wonderful instrument if used for God's purposes. Used otherwise, there literally may be hell to pay.

Jesus said to love the Lord with our whole heart, our whole mind, our whole soul, and our whole strength, and to love our neighbors as ourselves. Being ever mindful of what we say, and how we say it, is one really good way to do both. Used for God's purposes, our words can bring peace, unity and grace to those we love, and, yes, to those we do not.

Today, "May the road rise up to meet you... :-)
Bob

. . . . . .

February 12. 2017

> "O give thanks to the Lord, call on his name, make known his deeds among the peoples! Sing to him, sing praises to him, tell of all his wonderful works! Glory in his holy name; let the heart of those who seek the Lord rejoice!" (Ps. 105)

Sunday morning... As I entered Chrissy's room in the predawn darkness, her beautiful face was the perfect picture of peace.

While praying our daily Rosary aloud with her in the quiet stillness of the predawn darkness, I thought of another Sunday morning 2000 years ago, when Mary, mother of Jesus, went to the tomb of her crucified Son. She saw the stone rolled back. She entered the tomb. She saw the death shroud. She saw an angel.

Try to put this into context. Imagine what a mother would feel witnessing the unjust crucifixion of her innocent child, his broken body laid in a cave sealed by a huge stone. Imagine coming to the tomb in the predawn darkness several days later and finding the stone rolled back. Imagine finding an angel sitting in the tomb, announcing that "He is not here. He is risen as He said."

In today's world, we communicate at the speed of light, and probe the deepest recesses of our oceans; we map the human genome and explore the farthest corners of the galaxy. Technology continues to make the impossible possible. Technological advancements have brought us a quality of life that was unimaginable only a few decades ago.

As these advancements become commonplace, we begin to accept them as "ordinary." Just as with an addictive drug, we build a level of immunity to the "incredibleness" of everyday things, as they meld into the "noise level" of life.

I believe that "amazement" is a critical part of faith. We are utterly incapable of understanding the infinite power of God. Yet in today's world, if a person expresses true amazement, it is often considered a sign of naivete or ignorance. After all, if we do so, we are admitting that something is beyond our understanding; beyond our capability; beyond belief...

What would I have done, as a disciple or an uninformed passerby at Jesus' tomb? Would I have doubted? Would I have been skeptical? Would I have found every worldly reason to guffaw and trivialize the most significant event in human history because I just didn't think it could possibly happen?

Or would I have been amazed?

Today I am amazed by the incredible gift of life. I am amazed by the incredible love of God. I am amazed by a beautiful woman who continues to enrich my life as we sit together contemplating the power of God and the mysteries of life and death. And I am so thankful that God has given us this opportunity to be together in this way.

Our God is an awesome God. :-)

Bob

. . . . . .

February 13, 2017

"The heavens are telling the glory of God; and the firmament proclaims His handiwork..." (Psalm 19)

Yesterday, after 25 days in the Critical Care Unit, Chrissy graduated. :-)

Because her physical condition no longer requires the level of attention provided by the Critical Care Unit, while I was at Mass,

Chris was moved to the "NSCU" - pronounced "NisCue" - the Neurosciences Special Care Unit. It is the Neurosurgery Center for DHMC. And amazing things happen there.

Sometime later this week, she'll undergo surgery installing the permanent internal shunt to drain her excess CSF. Last night they had to revert to a heated humidifier from the unheated one she initially was using here in NSCU. The humidifier provides water vapor into the trake so her throat doesn't dry out. The heated unit has very significantly reduced her coughing.

While I was sitting with her last night, Chrissy opened both her eyes spontaneously, and looked directly at me, focused and with cognition. I spoke to her for about 20 seconds, explaining where we were and that so many were praying for her, and that I loved her and was walking with her wherever this road might lead us. Then she closed her eyes and lapsed back into unconsciousness. But for 20 seconds, she was here. I know it. I saw it.

If you ever doubt the power of prayer, I will tell you that the most important person in the world to me is alive today because of it. I will tell you that she is slowly coming back to us because we believe in it. And I will thank you every day of my life for the constancy of your prayers, the steadfastness of your love, and your unwavering faith in the power of Almighty God.

Oh - and it snowed last night. :-)

A few days ago, I was at home folding some laundry. I'd seen Chris doing it hundreds of times, and I'd never given it much thought. Only this time, because she isn't home (yet) to do it, I did think about it. And I suddenly realized the thousands of opportunities that doing household chores had provided for us to share time together, every day for the past 35 years. With more than a little regret, I realized that I had never looked upon doing ordinary things as being extraordinary opportunities to be together.

When we're "with" someone, are we really WITH them? Do we give them the fullness of attention they deserve? Are we talking at, to, or WITH them?

The distractions of the world and the realities of life rob us of time. As we walk our journey on Earth with those we love, it might be fitting to ask ourselves, "In the course of our family life, how much time do we spend apart, together?"

"This is the day the Lord has made. Let us rejoice and be glad in it."

Please drive carefully. Chris needs you. And I need you.

Bob

· · · · · ·

February 14, 2017

> *"Those who trust in the Lord are like Mount Zion, which cannot be moved, but abides for ever. As the mountains are round about Jerusalem, so the Lord is round about His people, from this time forth and for evermore." (Psalm 125)*

Last night was again restful for Chris, as we adjust to the still-wonderful quality of her care, at a reduced level. Though the critical stage is over, we balk because the resources devoted to her care are being reduced, and more quickly than we like. Yesterday, the inflatable plastic "bulb" that is part of her internal trake hardware was deflated, allowing her to start breathing partially through her throat, and partially through the trake. The objective is to see if the trake can be removed sooner. We worry that her oral secretions could drain down into her bronchia, with the potential for infection. Last night I fell asleep in her room with that on my mind, but when I awakened this morning, all seems ok. Chris is breathing just fine, though the occasional gurgles of the trake are (and will always be) a bit unnerving. The doctors and therapists steer a course that I am reluctant to steer on my own, though I know it's necessary. I think it is human nature in these circumstances to prefer the safety of the status quo over the risk of "pushing the envelope" and risking her life. But that's what's needed, and that's where we're going. God has this, not us.

We're also faced now - as in right now - with having to select an appropriate care facility for Chris. Bringing her home is not an option because of the level of medical and physical care she needs. And because of the severity of her condition, our choices are few. And for a while, they will not be nearby.

The woman we love, our wife and mother, our friend and companion, our joy and our solace, will be leaving an incredibly competent "home" where we know and participate every day in her care.

We now face the terrifying reality of moving her to a place where she knows no one, is unable to speak or act for herself, and is totally and completely dependent on strangers for every single aspect of her life. Everything. And we will be very limited in our ability to get there.

I am afraid. I can't begin to imagine what she must be feeling. If ever ANYONE didn't deserve this, it is Chris.

I've always believed, and the events in my life have borne out, that everything we do in life prepares us for something that we will face. And as Christians, we know and believe that this life, in its entirely, is preparation for the life that is to come, promised by the Father, through the sacrifice of His Son, with the inspiration of the Holy Spirit.

We have, by sheer necessity of self-survival, avoided thinking about what we are facing post-hospitalization. Until now. Because now we have nowhere to go, no place to escape to, nowhere to run.

Except straight into the open arms of Jesus.

I have talked the talk. And now I am going to walk the walk. Because God will show me the way. And your prayers will continue to bring the grace and courage for us to make this trek. Your prayers provide sustenance for Chris, for me, and for my family. I am totally dependent. On God. And on you.

I want you to promise me something. I want you to promise that sometime today, you will walk over to every member of your family, unexpectedly wrap your arms around them, kiss them, and tell them you love them. Because you can, and because you should. After all, it is the Feast of St. Valentine. :-)

I wish you the fullness of God's love, and the love of your spouse and family this day, and every day of your life.

Bob

. . . . . .

February 15, 2017

> *"My God, my God, why hast thou forsaken me? Why art thou so far from helping me, from the words of my groaning? O my God, I cry by day, but thou dost not answer; and by night, but find no rest." (Psalm 22)*

Good numbers yesterday. The trake is doing well (though Chrissy's oral secretions continue to be significant, and the resulting sounds disconcerting.) Her breathing is a bit fast, but she's getting plenty of oxygen in her blood.

Early in the afternoon, we held the second conference of participants in Chrissy's care. Not fun. Reality check with subtle but clear pressure reflecting the financial dance between insurance companies, hospitals, patients, and families. Our system of emergent care is outstanding. But the transition process out of the hospital requires knowing the rules of the game. Navigating this process requires an ally (Thank you, Bob and Carolyn) who knows the business, because there are certain pieces of information (that hospitals and insurance companies won't tell you unless you ask) which have a significant impact on what happens and when, and on your ability to advocate and get the best care for your loved one. If you "go along to get along" out of fear or ignorance, your loved one will be at risk. Not "may." Will. Stay tuned.

Each of the last 2 days, Chris has "gotten out of bed" and sat in the recliner in her room. She's unable to do so herself, but the nurse and aide work together using a mechanical hoist and sling to get her out of the bed and into the chair for a few hours, twice a day. Chris can't do it without them. She needs their help.

Read that again: She can't do it without them. She needs their help.

Walking back to Chrissy's room yesterday afternoon, I passed a woman in sweat pants and a comfortable multi-colored shirt. She was sitting in a chair, with an IV shunt with multiple ports in both her arms. I glanced at her, and our eyes met briefly. They appeared empty and resigned. Her face was the picture of weariness.

I walked about 50 feet past her, and that little inner voice whispered, "In as much as you do it for one of the least of these, my brethren, you do it for me."

I turned around, walked back to her, held out my hand, palm up, and asked, without another word, "Shall we pray?" She nodded, took my hand, and we prayed right there in the main passageway, as people went about their lives, immersed in their own worlds, unaware of the despair in their midst. She never said a word. She just needed to pray, and someone to help her.

A person of faith once told me, many years ago, "Christ came to comfort the afflicted, and to afflict the comfortable."

Are we "comfortable" in our faith? Do we live our lives in our spiritual "safe space?" Or do we stretch out our hand to strangers, the way that God stretched out His hand to us? He didn't have to. He chose to. So can we.

How many people do we pass each day that need the gentle touch of Christ in their lives? How many times have we had the chance to be Christ to someone, but didn't want to leave our comfort zone? How many times has fear of rejection kept us from doing what God would have us do?

I found a tiny bit of peace yesterday. Someone was looking for God's love, and found it in me. The Holy Spirit prompts us more often than we recognize. If we listen and follow that prompting, our lives are richer, the world is better, and the grace we gain in taking that small step brings peace that the world cannot give.

Let's live our faith. Let's be Christ to someone we don't know. Surprise a stranger and share what we know: the saving power of prayer, and the infinite love of Almighty God.

Be CHRISTIAN. Today. :-)

Bob

· · · · · ·

February 17, 2017

"I will give thanks to the Lord with my whole heart; I will tell of all they wondrous deeds. I will be glad and exult in thee, I will sing praise to thy name, O Most High."

Yesterday, Chrissy was back in surgery as planned, as the neurosurgeons removed her "EVD" - extra ventricular drain" - and installed the permanent internal shunt that will drain excess fluid from her brain into her abdomen for the rest of her life. In a few days we'll know whether she can be moved from DHMC. Right now, we're worried because her neurological posturing - the rigid extension of her arms, elbows locked, wrists pulled back - has returned as bad or worse than when she initially was admitted. We think it is a natural consequence of the surgery. The EVD was in place for about 2 weeks longer than usual; so between removing it and installing the permanent internal shunt (new hole drilled through her skull, new line placed into her brain), we think the new surgical trauma is the cause of her posturing. Time will tell.

I apologize for not posting an update yesterday. Lack of time and sheer exhaustion took their toll. I worked until 3:45AM yesterday morning drafting a letter to DHMC dealing with issues centered around Case Managers, decision-making authority and communications. Dealing with DHMC and their "Discharge Planning" process, as we navigate the coming transfer to another facility, has not been easy. As with so many (most?) of life's problems, poor communications - meaning failure to send or receive the message correctly, if at all - is a major issue.

A number of different forces intersect as insurance, medical, administrative, and facility qualifications, availability and acceptability have to line up in the discharge process. if a family doesn't advocate - as in knock-down, drag-out insistence on incorporating family and patient rights and issues into the process - the needs of the patient and family can be trampled in the interaction of the enormous institutions that operate our health care system. These institutions, dealing with millions of people, thousands of hospitals, and hundreds of nursing homes, sometimes lose sight of the humanity of the individual and the legitimate needs of the family in the crush and complexity of making the health care "machine" function. I was exhausted from fighting the system for the last two days. But if total exhaustion is what it takes to bring the outcome we seek - not just statistical success - then I will spend every day of my life exhausted in the fight for Chrissy's life and future.

We continue to work extra-hard to get out in front of the many things we're facing in the coming weeks. Faith has enabled me to accept our situation, and to recharge my batteries every night after the dealing with the sometimes-overwhelming issues of the day. I thank God for the many opportunities He gives to touch the lives of those we've met because of Chrissy's condition. There are times when my shoulders droop under the weight of our burden. But it's at those exact times that I stop, look up to Heaven, and remind myself, as I've told so many others over the years, that no matter how ominous and terrifying the storm, there is ALWAYS sunshine above the clouds.

Our faith is what enables us to see that sunshine, even during the darkest of nights. Our hope enables us to grow in its warmth, even during the coldest of days. And our love is what enables us to share God's light and His warmth, even as we traverse the journey of life.

Be SPECTACULAR today. Walk in faith. Live in hope. And bring God's love to someone. Go ahead. I dare you. :-)

Bob

THE POSTS

. . . . . .

February 18, 2017

"...I believe that I shall see the goodness of the Lord in the land of the living! Wait for the Lord; be strong and let your heart take courage; yea, wait for the Lord." (Psalm 27)

Yesterday, Chris was convalescing from her Thursday surgery. Her arms are once again limp and limber, and she has "good numbers." Fever and infection are now the major threats to her recovery, now and going forward. And the neurologists finally told us that they consider Chris to be in a vegetative state, but not a "persistent" vegetative state.

Were it not for our faith, I would resign myself to accepting this as the status quo going forward. However, while fully aware of her condition, we believe in the power of prayer to effectuate outcomes that defy science, medicine and human understanding. And there is ample evidence to support this, specifically with her type of affliction.

Hebrews 11:1 tells us, "Now faith is the substance of things hoped for, the evidence of things unseen." But in the case of brain aneurysms, there is actually evidence of "things seen." :-)

Tomorrow, I operate my last flight as a United Airlines Captain. The law says I must retire at 65, and the date is not subject to change. It is known. It is certain.

Chris and I were able to plan carefully for our retirement, because we had exact knowledge of when it would take place. We could plan and execute based on that certainty.

Question: If we knew the exact date and time of our death, would we live our lives any differently? If we knew that tomorrow, at exactly 6:43PM, God would fetch us home, would our priorities be the same? Or would we be making sure our souls were spotless and that we were ready to meet God?

And ask yourself today, and every day: Am I living my life in such a way that I'm ready for that special date and time that only God knows?

Several years ago, I captained a flight from Beijing, China, to Dulles Airport in Virginia. While waiting to catch a commuter flight home, I struck up a conversation with a modestly dressed gentleman waiting for the same flight. As it turned out, he was the owner of "Hobby Lobby," a global network of stores that sell hobby and craft items. He is a billionaire, but you would never know it. He was effused with humility.

Our discussion migrated to the topic of faith, and its role in our lives. He shared with me something that I have carried with me every day of my life since that meeting. I now share it with you...

"Everything in this world is either temporal (of this world), or it is eternal (of God's kingdom.) And there are only two things that are eternal: God's Word, and your soul." He built his business empire, and he lives his life within that premise. And his manner, his demeanor, his appearance and the entirety of his persona reflect it. Faith is truly the foundation of everything he does.

We deal constantly with the heartbreak of seeing Chris motionless and silent. We want to see her as we round the corner into the kitchen. We ache to hear the voice that was the central nervous system of our home. We ponder and question and challenge and rail and reject and rebel and hate this thing that was thrust upon her, and upon us.

Beware these emotions. They are temptations - tools of the slathering wolves of doubt, discouragement and despair hell-bent on eviscerating our faith and devouring our souls. Because we are human, we experience and accept them. But we must deal with them just as Jesus did during His 40 days in the desert: Pray, and pray, and pray some more. Prayer will keep those wolves at bay.

Let every day of our lives reflect God's light and His love. And thank you for your prayers. We need them. We need you.

Bob

. . . . . .

February 19, 2017

> *Whoever dwells in the shelter of the Most High*
> *will rest in the shadow of the Almighty.*
> *I will say of the Lord, "He is my refuge and my fortress,*
> *my God, in whom I trust." (Psalm 91)*

This is a special day for Chris and me. After this day, I'll be able to stay by her side for the rest of our lives. For over 40 years, I've been privileged to climb into the sky and share the realm of angels and eagles.

Today, that comes to an end, and a new chapter of our story begins.

Over the course of my career, I've been privileged to see every single day things that many never see in a lifetime. I've seen incredible sunrises and sunsets, volcanoes erupting, the eye of the hurricane, comets and shooting stars, the powerful vastness of the seas below and the humbling magnificence of star-split skies above.

All of this ultimately brings a sense of wonderment and awe at the magnificence of God's creation. Through the years, though flying became routine, it never became ordinary. I remember looking up into the sky as a young boy, marveling at the contrails and the noise and the speed and the technology of those incredible flying machines.

I always wanted to fly, and that meant spending a lot of time away. I got to live my dream because of a woman in whose trust and care I was able to leave the enormous responsibilities of home and family, time after time, year after year, without ever having to worry. Ever. Not once.

I have walked the treacherous sands of ego and self-importance, sometimes failing to distinguish between pride and satisfaction, power and authority, self-importance and leadership. I've survived threats, emergencies and malfunctions that are the consequence of 24,000 hours aloft. And I learned about people, and how important it is to recognize that we are none of us perfect, that we all bleed red, and that we are all of us on a journey in a world filled as much with the potential to cause suffering and sorrow, as to bring peace and joy.

And so today, as I make my last landing in a "heavy jet," I unabashedly, gratefully and humbly acknowledge the quiet, incredible heroism of the woman who made it all possible. She is the Wind beneath my wings, my Rose, the purpose for my life, the reason God put me in the world.

I love you, Christine. Because of you, I am the luckiest man on Earth. I fly today for you, and with you, and at last, to you.

Your loving husband,

Bob

THE POSTS

. . . . . .

February 20, 2017
*"The earth is the Lord's and the fullness
thereof, the world and those who dwell therein;
for he has founded it upon the seas, and
established it upon the rivers." (Psalm 24)*

Chris rested well yesterday. Good numbers, and she appears stable after her surgery last Thursday. We are quite certain that she can hear, so we play music, we talk with her, and we pray with her. She will soon be ready for transport to the next "stepdown" facility, an LTAC somewhere in the Boston area. Please keep praying for a bed to open up at Spaulding in Cambridge. They have accepted her clinically; all we need is a bed.

While Chrissy is physiologically stable, her condition is fragile, and the danger of infection and illness are the most serious threats, given the delicate condition of her immune system. We have to keep her healthy while her brain continues to heal. Time is both a friend and an enemy.

Yesterday, I "reached out my hand and touched the face of God" for the last time from the cockpit of a commercial airliner. It was a beautiful day to fly - clear skies, unlimited visibility, warm temperatures, and a wonderful crew. It was a memorable "last hurrah" in a very complex and dynamic environment, where every single flight brought another glimpse of the beauty of God's creation. It was an honor and a privilege to lead the many good people who enabled me to enjoy a 30+ year career doing something I truly loved to do.

Effective leadership, whether on a battlefield, in a cockpit, or on a factory floor, requires two key attributes: competence and humility. Both are necessary to earn the trust and respect of those who look to us for guidance, or who trust us to make decisions that can profoundly affect our lives.

Competence is the result of hard work, learning all that we can about a particular subject or process.

Humility, though not in vogue in today's "me" society, is the result of understanding that every single person ever created is an integral part of God's plan for mankind; that we all have "a piece of the puzzle." That understanding comes from only one source: respect for Almighty God as the author of all life

As a society, we value competency in secular matters. Companies require varying combinations of technical training, college degrees, advanced degrees, and certifications as a condition of employment. They do this to ensure the quality of their work product.

But how about the "work product" of our relationships? How many of us seek "advanced degrees" about how to strengthen our relationships and deepen our love for others?

To respect Almighty God as the author of all life, we must be able to SEE the face of God in every person we ever encounter along our life's journey. Jesus Christ showed and taught us everything we need to know.

From his humble birth in a manger in Bethlehem, to His ignominious death on a Cross at Golgotha, he taught haughty and humble alike how to lead others in the thing that really matters most: the salvation of our souls.

His competence in understanding God's workings "amazed" those in the temple. And His humility confounded the ungodly, and set us free from sin.

To truly follow Him, we have to see God's face in every person we encounter. We also have to make sure that it is God's face we show to those we meet along the way.

Enjoy the journey!
Bob

. . . . . .

February 21, 2017

> *"I will bless the Lord at all times; His praise shall continually be in my mouth. My soul makes its boast in the Lord; let the afflicted hear and be glad. O magnify the Lord with me, and let us exalt His name together." (Psalm 34)*

Chris continued to rest quietly for much of the day yesterday. Good numbers though her heart was beating faster than we like for a period of time yesterday. Such variances remind us that her "central command" - her brain - has experienced a devastating injury which manifests itself in occasional fluctuations of her "numbers."

Administrative work related to her transfer from DHMC to a Long Term Acute Care (LTAC) facility is in process. Please keep praying for Spaulding in Cambridge, as they have accepted her clinical records, and are working with the insurance company to gain authorization for admission there. We still do not know whether a bed is available. I offer that uncertainty up to God this morning in my prayers. Please pray with me.

An incredible friend whose love and counsel have brought me through some of my darkest days once shared a seemingly obvious thought: "No matter where I go, there I am." It seems obvious, but it speaks to taking responsibility for where we are in life, and understanding that it's the choices we make that put us where we are; that each day brings a new set of opportunities to make choices that can make a difference in our own lives and in the lives of others.

Putting faith into practice is an acquired skill. Just like a muscle, if we exercise our faith, it grows stronger. If we don't, it atrophies, and, either deliberately or out of neglect, we put our lamp under a wicker basket. We relegate our Godliness to obscurity.

During those times in my life when I've felt that God is farthest from me, it is I who have chosen to be farthest from Him. God does not abandon us; we abandon Him, either by making conscious choices to do the wrong thing, or by failing to nourish our souls.

One day, when seeking counsel from a Priest, he asked me, "How's your prayer life?" And it came to me (it's not rocket science) that at those times when I've been farthest from God, my prayer life has been weakest. In fact, it was sometimes nonexistent.

I believe that prayer holds the secret to living a good life. When we pray, we invite God to fill our hearts and shape our minds. It is through prayer that we gain God's grace - modern-day manna from heaven that nourishes our souls as we sojourn through life. It is through prayer that we can discern the will of God, as we open ourselves to His guidance.

Today, may you feel the hand of God on your shoulder, no matter where you may be, or what you may be doing. And if you're not sure He's listening, say a prayer. Because He is waiting to be asked.

No matter where I go, there He is. :-)

Bob

. . . . . .

February 22, 2017

> *"...Yea, though I walk through the valley of the shadow of death, I will fear no evil, for Thou art with me..." (Psalm 23)*

Today, Chrissy begins the next phase of her recovery - at Spaulding Rehabilitation Hospital in Cambridge, MA. :-)

Shortly after arriving at DHMC yesterday, I was advised that Chris was ready for discharge, that Spaulding had accepted her for rehab, and that a bed had opened. Two hours later, we were on our way.

We arrived at Spaulding at about 2:30PM. An hour later, she was in her bed amid a flurry of activity. This is a "no-nonsense" hospital, among the best in the world, whose purpose is to do everything humanly and medically possible to return those suffering brain and spinal injuries to a normal life. If it can't be done here, it can't be done. Make no mistake - Chrissy's condition is still very serious, and she is very fragile. But DHMC has done all it can do, and now it's up to the Spaulding rehab team to pick up where DHMC left off.

Her rehab team will be led by a team of 7 doctors in various specialties, who will assess her condition and develop a rigorous rehab program that fits her specific type and level of brain injury. As has always been the case, it is up to Chrissy's will to live, the hand of God, and medical science... and our faith in God and the power of prayer.

From morning to night this day, I will pray in thanksgiving to Almighty God, whose power and mercy have saved Christine and placed her in the best place in the world to effectuate her recovery. What we have asked for in faith, He has delivered in fact.

THE POSTS

Further, God is using her adversity to strengthen His presence on Earth. There is a divine paradox in the fact that though Chris is unable to speak, she is reaching people all over the world. At the end of this post, I'm sharing (with her permission) a message I received from a woman of faith in Arusha, Tanzania, East Africa. What better proof of the power of prayer?

Sing praise to the glory of God, who has truly done wondrous deeds.

Bob

· · · · · · · · ·

Hallow Bob, Congratulation for ur retirement, I think this will be nice time to ur wife ever as you will be together on her hand side.

Me, my family and praying team are praying together for you again today around 6:00 pm our time.

I just see my self In ur family situation by now, God is going to do more job for Chriss health. She is going to rise and shine again. I pray all the positive sign to her body and very fast recovering.

Bob one of my friend I know in Tanzania was about to buried but he wake up from dead body. He was in the mortuary already (I can say it might be doctors and nurses mistake but I believe that God did something to him that is beyond the human power and ability). It was shocked but her wife were having lots of faith even when his husband told to be dead. She said loudly I Refuse, My husband is alive, she prayed and prayed while calling her husband asking him to wake up. God is there with ur family and for the faith you have, something good is going to happen to ur wife again. Be blessed and your always in my prayer Bob. As we are friends I know that I need to play part as a friend to your family especially in this hard time.

Also one of my friend here in Arusha is travelling tomorow to USA (Seattle) I don't know how far is your place from Seattle, I will like to send a letter prayer. Would you like to receive my prayer gift? If Yes, please help me your contact and my friend hosting family Mr Rick and Sharon Reuter of whom I know will help the letter to reach you.

I will be happy for your positive response right now as I'm meeting the friend who is travelling around 4: 00 pm my time.

Be blessed Bob.

. . . . . .

February 23, 2017
"...Make me to know thy ways, O Lord; teach me thy paths. Lead me in thy truth, and teach me, for thou art the God of my salvation; for thee I wait all the day long..."

Yesterday, Day 1 at Spaulding, began a series of physical, medical and neurological tests that will establish the baseline from which Chrissy's rehab program will be built, and from which her progress will be measured. Doctors, nurses, therapists and specialists are evaluating everything - and I do mean everything - to determine her state of consciousness, her physical state, and her neurological ability to function. Once they know where she is, they will determine where she can go and how to get there. In many ways it is an inexact science, but these men and women are the best in the world at rebuilding the lives of those who have suffered brain and spinal injuries.

This change in facilities has brought a very definite change in mission. And that change in mission is redefining the "terrain" for our walk of faith.

The first phase of the journey took place at DHMC. They dealt with the issues that presented imminent threats to Chrissy's life. There was a sense of urgency, as her "numbers" were constantly monitored, and any significant change brought a rapid medical response. Things changed every day, as the medical procedures to keep her alive, and then to stabilize her, were performed and her convalescence constantly monitored. That phase of the journey is over. It was your prayers - working in a realm that produces miraculous outcomes beyond the ken of science - that enabled her to defy the overwhelming odds against her survival. There was imminent danger, and we drew the energy for our prayer efforts from the very real threat of imminent death.

But the game has changed. As we transition from "staying alive" to "learning to live," we pivot to a new set of conditions, in which things will change very slowly, and the riveting attention of her trauma is replaced by the long, slow struggle of rehabilitation. Chris faces a completely new set of challenges, in a completely different environment, with a totally new regimen to overcome them. But even amid these less-urgent challenges, we must maintain the intensity and volume of our prayers.

I love studying physics, and have come to characterize my journey of faith as a vector: a quantity having both magnitude and direction.

We all experience forces that change the direction of our lives. Some are constructive, and some are not. Either way, these changes can affect the magnitude of our faith as well as its direction.

I've learned that the only way to maintain or increase the magnitude of my faith is by praying, every single day, and often throughout the day, to bring God's grace to my soul as I weather the storms — and the joys — of life. It is God's grace that provides the energy to keep my faith vector headed in the right direction without sacrificing magnitude.

Physics isn't only about matter and energy. It's also about God. If it was good enough for Albert Einstein, it's good enough for me. :-)

Magnitude and direction.
Bob

. . . . . .

February 24, 2017
To thee, O Lord, I call; my rock, be not deaf to me, lest, if thou be silent to me, I become like those who go down to the Pit. Hear the voice of my supplication, as I cry to thee for help, as I lift up my hands towards thy most holy sanctuary." (Psalm 28)

The testing and assessment period continues at Spaulding, with "good numbers" except for an elevated white blood cell count which the team is watching very carefully. Chris has no fever, so there's no sign of infection or illness — the two major threats to her life due to the severity of her brain injury. And her coma is proving to be a significant obstacle to her progress. The team has started her on a medication recently discovered to bring people out of coma.

So today, and going forward, I have a special prayer request. Starting today, please include the following 3 things in your prayers: (1) please pray that Chris remains free from illness and infection; (2) please pray that she awakens from her coma; and (3) please pray for our family as we begin this next phase of our journey.

I was thinking about "prayer" yesterday, and about the incredible gift of being able to speak directly to God. It took a few minutes for that to sink in. When we pray, we are speaking directly to the Creator of the Universe. When we pray, we are communicating directly with the Savior of Mankind. When we pray, we are personally petitioning the Author of All Life, the Alpha and the Omega.

If we had a personal audience with the President of the United States, wouldn't we wear our "Sunday best?" Doesn't it make sense, then, that when we visit with Almighty God, we should be in our spiritual "Sunday best?"

When we pray, we are approaching Yahweh in his sanctuary. We are approaching Absolute Truth and Infinite Power. We are approaching the Source of All Life. We are approaching the Alpha and the Omega.

Can we even comprehend the enormous power of God, and the incredible, sacred gift of prayer that enables us to approach Him?

Jesus fasted and prayed, and humbled himself to die on a Cross. When He prayed at Gethsemane, he was so fervent in His prayer that He sweated blood. Before we pray, it might better prepare us if we spend a few minutes truly understanding what is about to happen.

Because humility in the presence of Almighty God is always appropriate.

"O God, be merciful to me, a sinner."

Bob

February 25, 2017

*"I will sing of thy steadfast love, O Lord, for ever;
with my mouth I will proclaim they faithfulness
to all generations. For they steadfast love
was established for ever, they faithfulness
is firm as the heavens." (Psalm 89)*

Chrissy's white cell count remains more than double what is normal, so lab tests and cultures are ongoing as her team tries to identify the cause. She has no fever, and a chest x-ray ruled out pneumonia, so they've put her on a broad-spectrum antibiotic to combat as many possible causes as possible "in general" before the lab tests identify the specific cause. She is in a near-constant state of neurological sleep, and the team's lead doctor indicated that they'll start to increase the dosage of the "wake-up drug" as they gain more insight into her baseline neurological, physiological and medical conditions.

The tumultuous emotions we experience along the way continue to challenge us. We work hard to corral and dispel them, but we're not always successful. Within the context of my failures, I'm reminded that others, too, are having to deal with sorrow, anger, fear and uncertainty.

My humanity chastens me, as we walk "in the valley of the shadow of death." When I walk in faith, I step outside of myself, and notice that everyone in this valley is carrying a similar cross.

Failures represent deviations from Christ's pronouncement that "Thou shalt love the Lord they God with thy whole heart, and thy whole soul, and thy whole mind, and thy whole strength; and thy neighbor as thyself." He sets the standard of perfection that we as Christians are called to attain. None of us do, because none of us can. The problem started a long time ago, when we traded away spiritual perfection for a bite of an apple.

The entire history of mankind is a story of spiritual wandering; it is a story where time after time, man abandons God, falls into sin, wanders in the desert, and returns to God. It is the story of mankind as a whole, and it is the story of each of us as individuals.

Except for Jesus Christ, "who was conceived like us in all things but sin."

When our humanity gains the upper hand and we transgress God's laws, conscience leads us to repentance and atonement. Many, however, give up on actively living their faith because we can never attain what God expects of us. This is an immense tragedy. A person that feels this way can't possibly understand the incredible act of salvation consummated at Calvary. It's up to us to share it with them.

Jesus Christ died on the Cross for us. His blood paid the price for our sins, and reopened to us the gates of Heaven. Instead of despair, we transcend our sins by understanding that Calvary bridged the gap between Perfection and our failure to attain it. Christ's death on the cross means that each new day is another opportunity to live as He would have us live: free from the bondage of sin, and bringing His message to those suffering spiritual separation from God.

Enjoy this day. Rejoice in the steadfast love of God.

Bob

. . . . . .

February 26, 2017

> *"The Lord answer you in the day of trouble! The name of the God of Jacob protect you! May he send you help from the sanctuary, and give you support from Zion! May he remember all your offerings, and regard with favor your burnt sacrifices." (Psalm 20)*

Yesterday, two things happened that serve as "the substance of things hoped for, the evidence of things unseen."

First, Chrissy's white cell count dropped from 24,000 to 12,000. Normal is 4,000-10,000. We're headed in the right ...direction. :-)

Second, not every time, but twice while standing next to her, when I said loudly, "Chris, this is Bob. If you can hear me, blink your eyes," she did. These were not the fluttering eyelids of reflex or subconscious response. She clearly, deliberately blinked her eyes. :-)

I believe that God's hand is present in these small signs of improvement, and I am grateful beyond words for your continuing prayers. I also believe that acts of God and the workings of science are not mutually exclusive. :-)

Today is Sunday. It is a day of worship, prayer and renewal. it is a benchmark for our lives, a recurring and regular source of new beginnings along our pathway to eternity. Setting Sunday aside for worship gives structure to our lives, and spending dedicated time with God gives us the grace we need to sustain our faith in a decidedly secular world.

Sunday is that special day ordained for us to "give God His due," to make modern day "offerings" and "burnt sacrifices." It is a day of thanksgiving for the good in our lives, of evaluating where we can do better, and committing to do so. Each Sunday provides both an end and a new beginning, for which we should be thankful.

Dedicating Sundays to renewing our faith and refreshing our souls with God's grace is what God intended. It reminds us that He alone is the author of our lives and the keeper of the clock.

God gives us our Sundays, and asks us to join Him. He provides us with the opportunity to bind up our spiritual wounds and recharge our souls with grace for the coming days. He provides us a chance to be healed, and the means to do so, if we seek Him.

When Jesus cured the ten lepers, he gave them new life. On Sundays, He does the same for us. Our faith is the key to eternal life, a precious gift from God that helps us transcend our trials in this world. Sunday worship is our way of returning to God to thank Him.

"Were not ten cured? Then where are the other nine?"

Have a truly blessed day. Spend it with the Lord.

Bob

. . . . . .

February 28, 2017

"Praise the Lord! Praise the Lord, O my soul! I will praise the Lord as long as I live; I will sing praises to my God while I have being. Put not your trust in princes, in a son of man, in whom there is no help. When his breath departs he returns to his earth; on that very day his plans perish." (Psalm 146)

Good numbers yesterday, and the team today (Tuesday) is increasing the dosage of the "wake-up drug." Chrissy was out of her bed in a special wheelchair for about an hour and a half, in addition to her morning therapy session. I did "range of motion" exercises with her, moving and flexing her fingers, wrists, forearms, upper arms, toes, feet, ankles, and legs. It is joyful work, enlightened by faith, delivered in hope, and driven by my love for her.

Yesterday was my fifth consecutive day staying in Cambridge and attending Chris at Spaulding. The psychological and emotional demands of the long journey ahead are becoming more noticeable, as I learn to "invest," and not merely "spend," my time with her. Lauren, Stephanie and Hunter are coming to Cambridge today for several days, so I can take a "mental health break" while we maintain our family presence with her. Having family speaking to her, and holding her hands, and praying, and playing music and reading books with her is of significant benefit to brain injury recovery.

Since "A-day" - the day Chris was stricken with her aneurysm - I have learned the meaning of what I call "relational deprivation" - the complete absence of meaningful communication with the most important person in my life. My conversations with my life partner, which she can hear at least some of the time, are totally one way. Chris neither initiates nor responds to conversation. But it is not because she won't; it is because she can't.

In our daily lives, how many times do we inflict "relational deprivation" on others? How many times do we disrespect others by not giving them our undivided attention when they are trying to engage us? How many times are we distracted (texting, internet, TV, etc.) during the course of conversation? How many times to we listen, and not hear?

A recent article quoted a study, conducted among thousands of couples, which proved that it took at least three attempts for the woman in a relationship to convey a message to her male counterpart - the most important person in her life.

It is tragic when relational deprivation is caused because a loved one can't communicate. It's sadder still if it happens when they can.

Are we so used to being with someone that we subconsciously "tune them out?" Do we inflict "relational deprivation" on the most important people in our lives? Do we inflict it on God when He speaks to us during the day?

It's been said that Wisdom is best learned from the experiences of others. So men, please respect the lady you asked to share her life with you, by giving her your complete, undivided attention when she speaks.

Because one day, she may not be able to.

"Go placidly amid the noise and haste, and remember what peace there may be in silence..."

Bob

. . . . . .

March 1, 2017

"Blessed be the Lord, my rock, who trains my hands for war, and my fingers for battle; my rock and my fortress; my stronghold and my deliverer, my shield and He in whom I take refuge..." (Psalm 144)

Chrissy had a mixed day yesterday. Good numbers, but the nurses had to suction her more often than "normal," because her mouth secretions kept interfering with the trake and causing her to cough and her breathing to be labored. We also found a small "raw spot" on the right side of her head, where the shunt (under the skin) rubbed against the pillow and caused a small abrasion. Though small, this type of break in Chrissy's skin can cause an infection. And an infection could kill her.

Deep down inside, I feel it. Dread. Like a spiritual rodent, it gnaws away at my faith. I dread what I know, and what I don't. I dread the certainty of today, and the uncertainty of tomorrow. I dread that she may die, and I dread what life might be like if she lives.

Dread. It is real, a corrosive acid that eats away at the underpinnings of our faith, challenging our belief and jeopardizing our souls. Dread. All day. All night. Every day. Every night.

There are times when I sense the hounds of hell lurking in the shadows of the night, looking to devour my faith, to destroy my family, to tear us to pieces and thus mock what we claim to believe, what God has ordained.

Chrissy lies in a strange bed in a strange place, with strange people coming and going, turning her and cleaning her every two hours, brushing her teeth, clipping her nails, moving her limbs, suctioning her mouth, cleaning her trake, bathing her body, lifting her out of and back into bed, positioning her head, and doing for her everything you and I do without so much as a second thought. She cannot move, except for the occasional fluttering of her eyelids, the opening and closing of her mouth, the slight movement of her toes every once in a while. If she has an itch, she cannot scratch it. If she feels afraid, she cannot say it. If she is in pain, she can't convey it. She is absolutely, totally, completely helpless.

Her condition can evoke horror and dread, shoals lying in wait for the unwary, ready to shred their faith and add them to the graveyard of souls who foundered in the storm-tossed waters of life.

We tame the horror and quell the dread by standing strong in our faith. We believe in an all-powerful, all-knowing God that so loved the world that He gave his only Son to die for us. Chrissy's tenuous situation only underscores the reality we Christians acknowledge today, Ash Wednesday: "Remember, man, that thou art dust, and unto dust thou shalt return."

We transform the acid of dread into the mortar of faith through prayer. Praying alone and with others, praying all day, every day, we repel the forces of evil that seek to drag us down. We reject the notion that evil will win. We declare that God is our champion. We proclaim that Jesus is Lord.

We repudiate Satan, and all his works, and all his wiles; all his tricks that tempt us to doubt and lead us into despair.

We repel the horror, and reject the dread. We embrace our faith. We sail on through the storms of life, guided by the light of Christ, strengthened by the power of prayer, humbled by the grace of God, and convicted by His promise of eternal life.

Believe, surrender, see, grow, and witness: Jesus Christ is the Way, the Truth and the Life.

Be SPECTACULAR today. :-).

Bob

. . . . . .

March 2, 2017

> *"Unless the Lord builds the house, those who build it labor in vain. Unless the Lord watches over the city, the watchman stays awake in vain." (Psalm 127)*

Yesterday the doctors changed the type of trake Chrissy uses, and her breathing has become easier, as the new one enables her to better deal with her oral secretions. Also, Lauren, Stephanie and Hunter got to watch her physical therapy session, as the therapists strapped her to a specially constructed metal table and rotated it so she was "standing up", even though she is unable to do so on her own. They did this to evaluate how her pulse and blood pressure react after lying horizontal for a full 6 weeks. We have some renewed concern about possible infection, as her white blood count has started climbing again. The doctors are doing lab tests and cultures on everything, to try to identify the cause and head it off as soon as possible. Infection and illness remain the greatest threats to Chrissy's survival.

As I watched her yesterday, it dawned on me that we and the Spaulding staff provide 100% of the inputs to her senses, however acute they may be. Everything she is experiencing is the direct result of what we say and do. We work diligently to provide a completely positive environment, because that environment directly influences her outcomes.

There's a saying (or at least, there used to be a saying) in the computer world, "Garbage in, garbage out." It means that the results a computer delivers are totally dependent on the quality of data input by its operator. It's one of the reasons pilots triple-check our navigation waypoints before pushing back from the gate. Inputting an incorrect latitude or longitude can produce catastrophic consequences.

Our lives are no different. If we put garbage in, we're going to get garbage out. The quality of our lives and the content of our character (MLK) reflect the nature of the "data" (nourishment) we provide for our souls, minds, and bodies.

In the 6 weeks since Chris was stricken, I have essentially stopped watching TV. I spend much more time praying, reading the Bible, doing recreational reading, and looking around me at the stunning beauty of God's creation and the incredible way He engineered it. I am much more aware of the things I can influence, and much less concerned about those that I can't.

For Lent, one of the things I'm giving up is "worry."

We don't know whether Chris will be alive tomorrow, much less what her life will be like if God allows her journey to continue. But then, we don't know whether WE will be alive tomorrow, or what OUR lives will be like if God allows OUR journey to continue.

Are we meaningfully enriching our lives by seeking out "good" data in a secular world that bombards us with garbage? What kind of music do we listen to? What kind of movies do we watch? What kind of books do we read? What kind of food do we eat? Do we smoke, chew, do drugs, drink to excess? What kind of role models do we seek out?

Our minds, souls and bodies need "good data" to deliver the results God wants us to achieve with our lives. It is completely our choice, an exercise of our free will, as to whether the things with which we nourish ourselves are Godly, healthy and wholesome.

Garbage in, garbage out. The choice is ours.

Bob

. . . . . .

March 3, 2017

> "For I know that the Lord is great, and that our Lord is above all gods. Whatever the Lord pleases he does, in heaven and on earth, in the seas and all deeps. He it is who makes the clouds rise at the end of the earth, who makes lightnings for the rain and brings forth the wind from his storehouses." (Psalm 135)

THE POSTS

Yesterday was a day of progress as well as uncertainty. Physical therapy is rigorous, and Chrissy rested for much of the day after her session. The new trake has made a big difference in her ability to cough up secretions, and has significantly improved her breathing. During the afternoon, I called and spoke to her over the phone. When she heard my voice, her head turned left, then back to the right. It was just a slight movement, only an inch or so each way, but it was movement. 😊 :-) And her heartbeat, which had been somewhat fast, immediately slowed. Her left foot was moving quite a bit earlier in the day, and pretty much stopped by evening. This is consistent with the schedule of her "wake-up drug." When her eyes open, they seem to be focusing more. And twice, when she opened her eyes, Lauren told her, "Mom, look at me." And she did. 😊 :-)

Good numbers, except that her white cell count is climbing again - 16,000 - and no clear indication of why. A chest x-ray ruled out pneumonia. There is some concern that the shunt may be a problem. An infection specialist is now on the team, and may have Chris transported to Mass General for a CT scan to check the shunt and its components for possible infection

We continue to wait, watch and pray.

I spent most of yesterday at home, recharging after my 6-day stint in Cambridge, and catching up on the bills and the paperwork that make the world go round. As I worked, my subconscious continued to wander, and it landed on the concept of "belief," and specifically what I believe with regard to Chrissy's situation.

For 6 weeks, faith has guided my footsteps. "Believe. Surrender. See. Grow. Witness." Each of these words is a journey in itself. Together, they could be considered "words to live by."

Since Chris was stricken, I have continuously said that I "believe" in God, in the power of prayer, in the guidance of the Holy Spirit. But those are "general" beliefs. They served to propel me into the "arena of faith." Now, as a gladiator in that arena, I am surrounded by opponents. I believe that I will vanquish them. However, what I believe, and what actually happens, may be very different. Regardless of this, I BELIEVE I am going to achieve victory.

Believing is not based on knowing. It is based on NOT knowing. (Back to Hebrews 11:1: "Now faith is the substance of things hoped for, the evidence of things not seen.")

Believing is the act of committing to an outcome that is impossible to explain or achieve using our human faculties.

People have recovered from Chrissy's condition. This is fact.

Chris is going to recover completely from her condition. This is faith.

Today, and every day, BELIEVE!

And pray that God will reward the constancy of our faith, and the strength of our belief.

"Through Him, all things are possible..."

Bob

. . . . . .

March 4, 2017

> *"Praise the Lord. I will give thanks to the Lord with my whole heart, in the company of the upright, in the congregation. Great are the works of the Lord, studied by all who have pleasure in them. Full of honor and majesty is his work, and his righteousness endures forever. (Psalm 111)*

THE POSTS

Yesterday was a quiet day for Chris. Her white cell count dropped a little (16,400 to 15,500), and in the absence of any fever or other indication of infection, the team decided to hold off on ... transporting her to Mass General for a CT scan of her brain. Good numbers continue, and after having been away for 2 days, it seems that she is gradually becoming more active, with her eyes opening, and her feet and mouth moving more than I've noticed before. I decided that Friday night was movie night, so we watched "Secrets of the Ya Ya Sisterhood" - one of her favorites - before I turned in for the evening.

A little over 6 weeks ago, the journey Chris and I had planned experienced an abrupt change of direction. The source of that change was catastrophic, and its consequences were immediate and drastic. But while our temporal lives have greatly changed. our journey of faith remains the same. A change in direction in this life can not affect our primary goal of attaining Heaven in the next.

The conversion of the apostle Paul began with a bolt of lightning. Several days later, he regained his sight and realized that God had another plan for him. He accepted that change of plans, and spent the rest of his life as one of God's most outspoken and effective disciples.

But conversion doesn't always require a lightning bolt. More often than not, it comes as the result of small things that momentarily catch a person's attention, providing an opportunity for us, with a word or a gesture, to allow the Holy Spirit to enter that person's life and begin the process of conversion.

Some say that "luck" happens when opportunity and preparedness meet. I believe life's collisions represent opportunities, and our faith represents preparedness. Our every encounter with people or circumstances presents an opportunity to bring someone closer to Christ because of that "collision." And living our faith requires that we do just that.

Here's wishing you a lucky day. 😊

Bob

. . . . . .

March 5, 2017

"My heart is steadfast, O God, my heart is steadfast! I will sing, and make melody! Awake, my soul! Awake, O harp and lyre! I will awake the dawn! I will give thanks to thee, O Lord, among the peoples. I will sing praises to thee among the nations. For they steadfast love is great above the heavens, thy faithfulness reaches to the clouds..." (Psalm 108)

Good numbers yesterday, including white cell count, which dropped about 30% to just above normal - 10,500. I actually took her for our first "walk" - a brief journey around the floor in her wheelchair. (I really wanted to organize a wheelchair race, but discretion got the better part of valor. LoL) Chrissy's eyes opened for part of our walk, and I'm sure she knew she was moving. Such exertions wear her out, and so she rested much of the rest of the afternoon. We can tell when she is "sleeping" and when she's "awake" - though awake has a somewhat different connotation right now. She is very gradually showing signs of increased awareness.

In aviation, we have some basic rules for dealing with emergencies. "Aviate, Navigate, Communicate" is probably the best known among them. It simply means that we must maintain our priorities during an emergency, or the outcome may be a smoking hole in the ground. "Aviate" - keep the aircraft flying. "Navigate" - know where you are and where you're going. "Communicate" - declare the emergency, inform stakeholders of the situation, and request assistance if necessary.

When we face a crisis in life, "Aviate, Navigate, Communicate" can save us from the potential "smoking holes" of physical, emotional, psychological and spiritual disaster.

It is faith that enables us to follow this rule during life's emergencies, and thus manage the crisis at hand. First, we keep the aircraft flying; survive. Next we devise a plan to arrive safely at destination. And finally, we communicate - with friends and relatives, and most importantly, with God.

By the way, "Aviate. Navigate. Communicate" doesn't only apply to emergencies. It also applies — perhaps even more — to life under normal circumstances.

We live our lives under an incredible array of assumptions. We assume we're going to awaken in the morning. We assume the sun is going to provide a morning. We assume we'll remain in good health. We assume that our job will be there when we get to the office. We assume the car will start when we turn the key in the ignition. We assume our flight will depart, and on time. We assume that when we see our loved ones, they will be the same as when we left them.

We assume so much because we have built our world into a place where these assumptions work almost all the time. Almost. But there are exceptions, and sometimes they're catastrophic.

So when we open our eyes in the morning, when we see sunshine coming in our window, when the car starts, when the flight leaves on time - in fact when ANYTHING happens as we planned and assumed it would or should, we should THANK

GOD that the billions of assumptions and conditions under which we continue to live our lives remain intact.
  Because it doesn't have to happen that way.
  Today is Sunday.
  Aviate. Navigate. Communicate.
  And keep holy the Lord's day. ☺ :-)
  Bob

· · · · · ·

March 6, 2017
  "O give thanks to the Lord, call on His name, make known His deeds among the peoples! Sing to Him, sing praises to Him, tell of all His wonderful works! Glory in His holy name, let the hearts of those who seek the Lord rejoice! Seek the Lord and His strength, seek His presence continually! (Psalm 105)

Chris had a rough time dealing with her oral secretions for much of the day yesterday. It is really hard watching her cough, as her entire torso heaves from the effort. But it does clear her throat, and I believe it ultimately it paved the way for what happened later in the day. Good numbers, and her white cell count is down to 10,500.
  I try to watch a movie with her every afternoon - our matinee date, if you will. We were watching "The Bucket List" (with Jack Nicholson and Morgan Freeman), and paused the movie so her nurses could do her scheduled turn. (She has to be turned every 2 hours to prevent skin breakdown.) Turning her, like coughing, seems to stimulate her, and her eyes will open and sometimes her mouth will move. After the nurses were finished and had left,

we resumed watching the move. As I pushed the "Play" button, I gazed at her and said, as I do often throughout the day, "I love you, Mrs. G."

And her eyes opened - right eye completely, left eye about half.

And her lips mouthed the words, "I love you." 😊 :-)

I looked at Joe and Naomi, who visited Chrissy both Saturday and Sunday, and I said, incredulous, "Mom just said, "I love you!"

No words can express what my heart felt at that moment. So I did what anyone would do: I wept. I wept tears of joy, tears of hope, tears of determination, tears of thanksgiving.

Chrissy stayed "with us" for about 10 more minutes before slowly lapsing back into unconsciousness. Her periods of "wakening" seem to be lasting longer, but she still spends most of her time "asleep."

I thank God for this small sign, for this small miracle from a woman who was not even supposed to survive, but whose life continues on as an example of God's power and compassion. If we have faith, God can accomplish the impossible through us. Your prayers for the past 47 days have raised our cry to the Almighty. They have lifted Christine up to Him and He has shown, again, that through Him all things ARE possible.

And so, in a world in which God's work is so often dismissed by cynicism or smothered by pragmatism, we dare to be different. Of our own free will, we choose to REJOICE in the presence of God and His promise of salvation.

Chris and I and our family love every one of you, and we need you with us as we continue to wait, watch and pray for her complete recovery.

By the way, I carry a package of mustard seeds in my pocket. I don't even know it's there. 😊

THE POSTS

BELIEVE!
SURRENDER!
SEE!
GROW!
WITNESS!
REJOICE!
"Today is the first day of the rest of your life."
Bob

· · · · · ·

March 7, 2017

> "O Lord, my heart is not lifted up, my eyes are
> not raised too high; I do not occupy myself with
> things too great and too marvelous for me. But
> I have calmed and quieted my soul, like a child
> quieted at its mother's breast; like a child
> that is quieted is my soul." (Psalm 131)

I left Chrissy yesterday after spending four days with her, and headed for Concord for the afternoon, then home. Good numbers, but she had a really bad morning coughing and gagging, and the respiratory therapist and RN worked patiently and diligently to perform "mouth care" and "trake care" and remove the very thick mucous secretions that her mouth and throat continue to produce. The pulmonologist (lung and breathing doctor) checked her lungs to ensure they were clear. They are. Shortly thereafter, a CNA gave Chris her morning bath, and she was resting quietly when I left.

When I left, my mind was I a state of near-riot, as I had to deal with the million "what-ifs" that raced through my head as

I, her staunchest advocate, was leaving her? After all, she is unable to communicate in any way, and her total dependency is a terrifying reality, fraught with all manner of imagined dangers.

A few years ago, in a completely different set of circumstances, I memorized Psalm 23. It popped into my head as I was leaving Spaulding Hospital, and it took me to a quiet place that enabled me to quell the fear and guilt of leaving Chris alone.

How do we tune out the countless distractions that constantly assail us, and take a spiritual "cleansing breath" to quiet our bodies and minds, and refresh our souls?

Doing so enables us to restore order amid chaos and tranquility amid turmoil. It provides the "green pastures" and "still waters" where we can restore our souls, even amid the storms of life.

It enables us to do as Jesus did when confronted with challenges, especially in the form of "people in high places," some of whom doubted Him, and others of whom sought to entrap and ultimately kill Him.

With one exception, and that was His anger at the shameful disrespect shown by the moneychangers in the temple, Jesus never "lost His cool." He paused, collected His thoughts, and carefully chose the words He used to respond rather than react. His use of parables, and the way He asked questions, showed His Way to those who were truly seeking peace.

Learning how to find that quiet place, even in the midst of a hectic day, can save your life, and

restore your soul... And someone else's.

Have a quiet day. ☺ :-)

Bob

March 8, 2017
"...But I will hope continually, and will praise Thee yet more and more. My mouth will tell of Thy righteous acts, of thy deeds of salvation all the day..." (Psalm 71)

Yesterday was a day of mixed results. Good numbers, white cell count still a bit elevated, but not much. Chrissy was transported to Massachusetts General Hospital (MGH) for a routine follow up CT scan of the shunt, and to compare the condition of her brain with the very first CT scan she had on the day the aneurysm burst (Jan. 18th). Upon returning to Spaulding, the doctors immediately called her back to MGH for another CT scan, this one from the top of her head to the bottom end of the shunt in her abdomen. The team of doctors reviewing the first CT scan had discovered several things.

Good: the ventricles of her brain have returned to normal size, and the CSF within them is clear. indicating that the blood that had been contaminating it is gone.

Not so good: the shunt is doing what is called "over-sumping" - draining too much CSF. This may require another surgery to replace the current non-adjustable shunt valve with one that can be adjusted so that over-sumping does not occur

Second not so good: they discovered a subdural hygroma. This is an enlarged area of CSF between the dura - the protective membrane between the brain - and the brain. It is not uncommon in cases of hydrocephalic brain injury caused by aneurysms. An analogy would be as follows: in a tire with a tube (remember those?) if the tube represents the brain, the tire represents the dura (membrane around the brain), and air represents CSF, a subdural hygroma would be a bubble of air between the tube and the tire. I'll find out more today about the specifics and implications of this condition, and our path forward.

As a young Midshipman at the Naval Academy, I took up skydiving. The first few jumps were on a static line - a line attached to the plane which automatically pulled the ripcord on the parachute in case the new jumper froze up and forgot to do it. After that, I was introduced to the world of free fall - jumping from the plane and falling through thousands of feet of sky until a preset altitude (we wore an altimeter on our wrist), at which time you pulled the ripcord, the chute presumably opened, and you landed safely in the drop zone.

One jump technique we used to enjoy was called a "hop and pop." The plane would take us up to 12,500 feet, and we'd jump, free fall for five or ten seconds, pull the ripcord, and then float for ten minutes or so to a controlled landing, hopefully in the drop zone, but not necessarily. Winds aloft affected the direction of our "flight," and sometimes blew us significantly away from our intended point of landing.

Thinking about the past 7+ weeks, I realize that this is so much like a "hop and pop." After the initial "emotional free fall," I pulled the ripcord of belief to open the parachute of faith. I am now drifting in prayer — yours, mostly — towards a landing somewhere in the drop zone of life. I don't know where it is, and winds aloft taking me in directions I can't control, but I've gone from "free fall" to "free flight," and I'm ok with it. Chrissy and I are together in our parachute, and we're going to be just fine, no matter the winds, so long as we steer our chute towards green pastures and beside still waters.

God really is in charge. The winds of life will take us many places we never thought we'd go. But at the end of the "jump," God is there, always and forever, waiting for our landing.

But don't take my word for it. Take His. 😊 :-)
Bob

. . . . . .

March 9, 2017

> *"O Israel, hope in the Lord! For with the Lord there is steadfast love, and with him is plenteous redemption." (Psalm 130)*

Good numbers yesterday, and Chrissy was very restful. Our faith continues to lead us as we wait, watch and pray.

I was awakened last night, very late, by the soft light of the moon shining in the window nearest my bed. It bathed all of creation in its quiet glow, dispelling the darkness and exposing every natural and manmade hazard as far as the eye could... see.

In the darkest nights of our lives, our knowledge of God's law is just like moonlight. There is no hazard — physical, mental or moral — which is not readily apparent under that light. If we choose to travel life's roads without the benefit of that light, we will stumble over every hazard we encounter in the darkness.

We are called to walk in the Light. In fact, we are called to be a light to others. Even when we choose darkness, even when we trip and fall, God loves us enough that He offered up His Son to die for us, a Light for all ages. But unlike the moon, which clouds of sin and doubt can obscure, Jesus is the Light of the World, a Light that cannot be extinguished, a Light that will show us the way to Heaven. All we have to do is embrace the Light, to accept Him as our Way, our Truth and our Life.

When we embrace the Light that is Christ, we become light for others who may be walking in darkness. They cannot make a choice to embrace the light if they don't know they have one. Their salvation depends on coming to Christ, coming out of darkness and into the Light. In a sense, their salvation depends on us, because every single one of us is called to show forth that Light.

When we accept our universal Christian mission to share the light of God's love with everyone we meet, we begin to change the world, one person at a time.

Be a superstar. Be brilliant today. ☺
Bob

. . . . . .

March 11, 2017

> *"O Lord, thou hast searched me and known me! Thou knowest when I sit down and when I rise up; thou discernest my thoughts from afar. Thou searchest out my path and my lying down, and art acquainted with all my ways."* (Psalm 139)

Chris remains in good hands at Spaulding. Good numbers again yesterday, and it seems her eyes are opening more than they have been, and staying open longer than in past weeks. She actually tracked Joseph with her eyes at one point yesterday. We won't know until Tuesday, after another CT scan, whether she'll need additional surgery to replace the shunt valve that's causing the hygroma. We know she is getting the best possible care, and we are doing our part by praying and being with her every day.

Though her body is broken, Chris continues to inspire. The heart that loved us every day of our lives still loves us without limit or reservation. The hands that cared for us every day of our lives now touch us with their stillness. The smile that brightened every day of our lives now warms us from within. And even in the silent stillness of her affliction, she continues to teach us more about life and faith and love every day of this journey. We continue to take each day as it comes, guided by faith, lifted by hope, and strengthened by God's love for us.

Today is Saturday, and that brings to mind... housekeeping! It's a healthy, normal part of a purposeful life. It's how we keep we our physical homes clean and tidy. And It's a good day to do some spiritual housekeeping as well, to sweep out the dirt, dust and cobwebs of laziness and sin, and make our spiritual homes - our souls - clean and tidy. We do it by setting aside ample time to sit down and perform an "examination of conscience" - examining our lives in the light of God's commandments. And in those instances where we have fallen short, we can rid ourselves of the stain of sin by truly repenting of our transgressions, making restitution where appropriate, and accepting the gift of God's forgiveness.

Only then; only if we are truly sorry for our sins, repair the damage we have done by committing them, and truly do our best to avoid sinning again, can we attain the salvation God intends for us. It's there waiting, but we have to do our part. We'll all fail again, because we're human. But God's not rescinding His promise.

Oh, I almost forgot - there is one more thing. There is the matter of believing that Jesus Christ died a horrible, agonizing death, nailed to a Cross to forgive our sins. Every one of them. For every one of us. Forever.

So today, do some housekeeping. Challenge yourself. Think about your life.

Then think about eternity. :-)

Bob

THE POSTS

. . . . . .

March 12, 2017

> *"...Bless our God, O peoples, let the sound of His praise be heard, who has kept us among the living, and has not let our feet slip. For Thou, O God, hast tested us." (Psalm 66)*

Chrissy had good numbers again yesterday, and she is definitely beginning to "awaken." I'm back at her bedside, seeing it firsthand. Her eyes are opening much more often, wider, and for longer periods of time. Another small triumph: Because I can't kiss her lips (infection risk) I kissed her on the right side of her nose, while I was holding her hand, and her hand actually moved. Ever so slightly, but it moved. Three different times. And Joe and Naomi said she moved one of her legs several times yesterday before I got to the hospital.

I'm asking all to pray specifically that the subdural hygroma which showed up last week on her CT scan be healed. If healed, it will mean Chris doesn't need another operation. Every time she has surgery, it really sets her back for at least a week, as the anesthesia severely affects her central nervous system, which is very, very fragile as a result of the hemorrhage.

It's Sunday morning, and we know where we should be. :-)

When I'm away from Chris, I sometimes grow weary from "The Struggle." It is something much deeper than merely being tired. It drives down to my core, and causes distractions which would ordinarily not even slow me down, to bring me almost to a complete stop.

At various times in our lives, we all face "The Struggle." It can be physical, emotional, psychological, or financial. But ultimately, it always winds up being spiritual. Circumstances wear us down and set us adrift. And drifting souls are Satan's playground. He and his minions thrive on spiritual weariness, for that is when we are most vulnerable to sin.

The world around us provides ample evidence of the constant battle between good and evil. Scripture tells us of the war between "powers and principalities." Every minute of every day, we have to be on guard against spiritual weariness that can allow evil to gain traction in our lives.

What is The Struggle that stands between who we are, and who God wants us to be? Once we know what it is, we can deal with it. Sometimes it's very subtle, sometimes it hits us like a tsunami. But whatever it is, reading God's word and praying to Him for wisdom and guidance will ALWAYS enable us to find it, see it for what it really is, and defeat it.

Jesus told paralytics, "Rise, take up your pallet and walk." And "Go your way, your faith has saved you."

So don't just stand there. Start walking. :-)

Bob

. . . . . .

March 13, 2017

> "...O God, from my youth thou hast taught me, and I will proclaim thy wondrous deeds. So even to old age and gray hairs, O God, do not forsake me, till I proclaim thy might to all the generations to come. Thy power and thy righteousness, O God, reach the high heavens..." (Psalm 71)

THE POSTS

Another steady day for Chris, good numbers, and though she rested most of the day, she opened her eyes and seemed to follow along as we watched "Return to Me" on the DVD player (our Sunday matinee movie.) She was almost cough-free for the entire day, but at the one point when she did cough, it was so strong that she blew the valve off the end of the trake! And then, something you have to see to believe, she actually sneezed 4 times. These are all signs pointing to a direction we want to go, but the future remains completely unpredictable. Compared to where she was 7 weeks ago, though, we are making definite progress. Please keep up your prayers.

I am neither a priest, nor a pastor, nor a minister, so what I write isn't "ordained." But I do ask God's guidance each day as to what I should share with you, as I awaken and pray in the silent stillness of morning. I'm getting messages of appreciation for my daily posts from all over the world. This has become a new ministry in my life.

I believe each of us has a specific role to play in God's plan of salvation, a ministry that we were created to perform. And though all of us, at one point or another in our lives, stray from the road to Heaven, God's promise is that salvation awaits those who accept Jesus Christ, repent, and follow Him. But we can't do this if we don't know "the rules of the game."

Over the past few days, I've been getting a consistent message that I should write about the Ten Commandments. So tomorrow, I will begin to do just that. It is Lent, a time of repentance and preparation for the events that reopened Heaven to us: the crucifixion, death, and Resurrection of Jesus Christ.

Long ago, God gave us the rules. Then He gave His Son to die for us because we continue to break them. Why on Earth would we not want to keep those rules in mind as we walk our daily journey?

Heaven only knows. :-)

Bob

. . . . . .

March 14, 2017

> *"...Blessed is the man who makes the Lord his trust, who does not turn to the proud, to those who go astray after false gods!..." (Psalm 40)*

The unpredictability of brain injury recovery struck again yesterday, as Chrissy's white cell count jumped to 16,000. The team ordered a chest x-ray, blood work, and precautionary antibiotics against possible infection. She had a low grade fever early, but that subsided by around 11 AM.

From what I have seen and learned, I know that prayer is going to be the foundation of her recovery. We are not daunted by facts, as faith is not ruled by facts. Faith is larger than life, and delivers results that defy explanation. Either we believe in God and His infinite power, or we do not. There is no middle ground. So we remain resolute today, as every day, as we pray for God to purge all infection from Chris, to heal the subdural hygroma, and to return her to full health.

"I am the Lord thy God. Thou shalt not have strange gods before me."

This First Commandment frames our relationship with Almighty God. It stands in direct contradiction to our human nature, which Satan used in the Garden, tempting Adam and Eve to believe that they could become like God through an act of willful disobedience.

"Strange gods" come in all sizes and shapes. They entrap our minds and bodies, altering our relationship with God by enticing us to place greater importance on the things of this world than on whatever mission God may have in mind for us. The First Commandment is first because it establishes the natural order of the universe, and our position within it. When we set God aside in pursuit of other priorities, we undermine the foundation of God's eternal promise.

As we pursue any of the entire spectrum of worldly "treasures," we are lured away from our primary purpose in life: to seek God in everything we do, every day of our lives.

Jesus warned us that we cannot serve two masters, that we must choose between His way and the way of the world. Seeking God is our primary mission on Earth. It doesn't mean we can't seek success in the world. It means we're called to use the things of this world in pursuit of God's kingdom.

What are the "strange gods" that tempt or enslave us? Are there things in our lives that we love more than God?

If we truly respect God as the Master of the Universe, then we respect His creation. We respect ourselves, and every other human being, for we are all created in His image and likeness. We respect the glory of His creation.

If we respect God as the Author of All Life, we don't stick needles in our arms, or powder up our nose. We don't abuse the incredible gift of procreation, and then compound that mistake by ending the life of an unborn child. we don't savage the planet or the flora and fauna over which He gave us dominion.

We respect God. We humble ourselves before Him, and we understand that any thought, word or deed that takes us in any direction other than towards Him, places something other than God at the center of our lives.

"I am the Lord they God. Thou shalt not have strange gods before me."

It's the single most important priority in our lives.

Bob

. . . . . .

March 15, 2017

"O Lord, our Lord, how majestic is thy name to all the earth! Thou whose glory above the heavens is chanted by the mouth of babes and infants..." (Psalm 8)

Yesterday was another restful day for Chris. Good numbers except for the elevated white cell count, as we await the results of various lab tests to try to identify the cause, aware of the serious threat posed by infection. Physical therapy continues as well. We couldn't visit because of the snowstorm, but our prayers are with her, as are God's angels.

In reflecting on the Second Commandment, there are differing opinions on exactly what it is. So I'm going to go with what I was raised with, and leave it to God to decide whose version is right. The language in the Bible is the same either way; it's men who interpreted the Bible hundreds of years ago who disagreed on God's priorities. That's way above my pay grade. I'll just move forward knowing that my heart's in the right place. :-)

"Thou shalt not take the name of the Lord thy God in vain."

Mankind is not capable of defining or comprehending "infinity." Yet God created infinity and everything finite as well. He has created things we can't even begin to comprehend. He created each of us as well, miracles in our own right, in His image and likeness.

Do we speak the name of God with the awe and reverence it deserves? Do we understand Who and What we are speaking of when we use His holy name? Some even refuse to say "God," but instead refer to "Him whose name we dare not speak."

Have you noticed that our movies and television shows are increasingly integrating profanity into all forms of entertainment? It's becoming a "normal" part of the lexicon of mass media. Our society is normalizing the debasement of the holy name of God. Our children are being taught that irreverence and profanity are ok.

Using profanity disrespects the name of God, when instead, everything we do should be focused on reverencing Him. When we speak, our mouths should proclaim the glory of God. And our every word should reflect the fact that we're made in His image and likeness.

God bless you.

Even if you didn't sneeze. :-)

Have a spectacular day.

Bob

. . . . . .

March 16, 2017

"...How precious is thy steadfast love, O God! The children of men take refuge in the shadow of thy wings. They feast on the abundance of thy house, and thou givest them drink from the river of thy delights. For with thee is the fountain of life; in thy light do we see light." (Psalm 36)

Good numbers yesterday, and Chrissy's white cell count is coming back down. It's still out of bounds, but is headed in the right direction. Lauren, Derry, Stephanie and Hunter are with her (yesterday and today), and I'm quite sure she is happy they are there. A follow-up CT scan is scheduled for next week, to assess the physical condition of her brain and determine whether the subdural hygroma has improved, worsened, or stayed the same. Please focus on praying that the hygroma goes away, and that Chris returns to consciousness.

"Remember thou keep holy the Lord's day."

When God created the world, He worked for 6 days, and rested on the 7th. Scripture tells us, " So God blessed the seventh day and hallowed it, because on it God rested from all the work that he had done in creation."

What does it mean to "hallow?" It means "to make holy." It means not only that we are blessing the day to glorify God, it means we are using the day to see the glory of God in all that exists around us.

It means that we try to comprehend the incredible engineering and artistry of creation. it means we stop to consider the amazing gift of human life, the intermingling of chemistry, matter, consciousness, intellect and soul that defines each and every human being ever created. All of us. From Adam and Eve to the end of time. Uniquely made in the image and likeness of God.

Out of true reverence for Almighty God, and dedicated reflection on the enormity and intricacy of His works, comes what I believe is the single most important and least evident component of human character: humility.

God himself "hallowed" the seventh day. He rested, and looked out over the work He had completed. Shouldn't we do the same? Is it too much to ask to dedicate one day each week to studying God's word, seeking God's grace, and finding our place in God's kingdom?

Every Sabbath, God invites us to His banquet. Every one of us has a seat reserved at His table.

All we have to do is accept. Humbly.

Only then can we "go in peace, to love and serve the Lord and one another."

Have a blessed day. :-)
Bob

. . . . . .

March 17, 2017

"...When the righteous cry for help, the Lord hears, and delivers them out of all their troubles. The Lord is near to the brokenhearted, and saves the crushed in spirit..." (Psalm 34)

Chris rested quietly yesterday, as her white cell count continued dropping towards normal. Her medical team has isolated the infection, and the antibiotics are working. I thank God for this. Giving thanks is so important - it isn't enough to just recognize the manifestations of God's power and love. God wants us to communicate our joyful thanks as well as our times of distress. Remember the ten lepers?

I'm postponing the "Ten Commandment Series" for a day to share what's in my heart with you. I believe it's during times of silence that God speaks to us most clearly. This morning was one of those times. So here goes...

The person I love most in this world lies motionless in a bed in a faraway place. Unable to see, speak, or move, she is completely dependent on others for every aspect of her existence. We see so much good being done, yet there is little measurable progress. My heart leaps with joy when she opens her eyes, but that joy is beset by uncertainty because we don't know whether the Chrissy we know and love still exists; we don't know whether her personality is still alive within her broken body; we don't know whether what we see is cognitive act or brain stem reflex. And there's no way to find out.

The question of whether or not Chris is "here" constantly wears on me, hour after hour, day after day, week after week, month after month, working to undermine my belief that she is going to recover. This whole situation is really a war between faith and doubt, hope and despair, love and death.

This war takes its pound of flesh one day at a time. It torments, consumes, and exhausts. It tempts me to pull back from life, to become absorbed in the wait and immersed in the uncertainty; to disengage from everything because I do not want to live life without her. I don't want her not to be standing in the kitchen smiling when I get home. I don't want to accept that I'm getting used to her not being here. But I am. And I hate it.

From time to time, I've felt spiritual weariness and despondency, as anyone might in similar circumstances. And these only go away when I let go of my anguish and place it in God's hands. Just as Jesus prayed during His anguish in Gethsemane, so we should pray when we're beset by sadness.

Through prayer we transcend doubt and despair.
Through prayer, we replenish our reservoir of faith.
Through prayer, we choose to Believe.
We opt to Surrender.
We start to See.
We begin to Grow.

We learn to Witness.

And then we Rejoice.

We Rejoice because we experience the healing power and the loving mercy of God. I cannot conceive of a world without it. Maybe that's what Hell is all about.

So whether you're soaking up sunshine or beset by a tempest, my fervent prayer is that you will find God's loving arms around you this day.

Peace be with you.

Bob

. . . . . .

March 18, 2017

> *"Sing to God, sing praises to his name; lift up a song to him who rides upon the clouds; his name is the Lord, exult before him! Father of the fatherless and protector of widows is God in his holy habitation. God gives the desolate a home to dwell in; he leads out the prisoners to prosperity; but the rebellious dwell in a parched land." (Psalm 68)*

Yesterday, the medical team lead (MD) contacted me to share both good news and bad, as is often the case with brain injuries. Good... news: the infection has been defeated, and Chrissy's white cell count is down to 6,000. (Normal range is 4,000-10,000). Bad news: her liver enzymes spiked way above normal, possibly a result of the antibiotics and other medications she's been receiving for the past week or so. So - off the meds, no dosage increase of Amantadine (the "wake up" drug), and... wait. If the problem persists, she'll be transferred to Mass. General Hospital (MGH).

Bad news notwithstanding, we know there will be many more ups and downs along the long, slow road to recovery. Our faith levels the mountains and fills in the valleys along the way. And prayer sustains that faith, and helps us keep our eye on the prize.

"Honor thy father and thy mother."

The first three Commandments deal with our relationship with God.

The rest govern our relationships with one other.

The Fourth Commandment actually lays the entire foundation for lawful authority. It ratifies the primacy of the traditional family unit, one man and one woman, as God's intended "building block" of civilization. It establishes the obligation of children towards their parents, and by inference the obligations of parents to act honorably for the good of their children. It also speaks to how government should treat its citizens, and how citizens should act towards government.

"Honor thy father and thy mother" cuts both ways. A supportable corollary for parents and those in authority is "Honor they sons and thy daughters."

If we do the job God wants us to do as parents, we lay the necessary foundation for preserving our way of life. We protect and nurture God's preference for the traditional family unit. We instill values and discipline in our children to empower them to learn, grow, and succeed. We teach them how to bring responsible change to our society and its institutions. And our institutions and leaders treat those in their charge with respect and dignity. Riots in our streets, disobedience of the law, and disrespect towards those in authority are direct consequences of disregard for the Fourth Commandment.

But so are police brutality, judicial misconduct and government corruption.

Someone once propounded that "The hand that rocks the cradle rules the world." We do well to rock that cradle with care and with wisdom.

Thank you, God, for another sunny day. Help me be light to all whose lives I touch on my journey.

And now...

Rock on! :-)

Bob

. . . . . .

March 19, 2017

> *"...Oh, send out thy light and thy truth; let them lead me, let them bring me to thy holy hill and to thy dwelling! Then I will go to the altar of God, to God my exceeding joy; and I will praise thee with the lyre, O God, my God..." (Psalm 43)*

Good numbers yesterday, though we wait for Chrissy's liver enzyme levels to come back from the lab. They were off the charts yesterday (bad), and we pray that the measures taken by her team will return them to normal. Her breathing is improving, and the RT (Respiratory Therapist) last night shared that starting today (Sunday), they're going to try to keep the one-way valve on her trake both day and night. It's been on only during the day, so this decision is a cautious measure of confidence in Chrissy's ability to manage her oral secretions and breathe normally. We are slowly but surely making progress towards removing the tracheostomy.

As I learn more and more about the human body, I'm driven to question how anyone cannot believe in God. Our bodies are incredible marvels of science and engineering, with organs, senses, and systems working every second of every day, month after month, year after year, to produce the amazing gift we call "life." How casually we treat (and mistreat) something which is truly incredible. How arrogant and disrespectful that we act so nonchalant about the amazing miracle of life.

"Thou shalt not kill."

Some interpret the original language to say "Thou shalt not murder." Using the word "murder" allows for the possibility of taking human life in defense of oneself or another. It also allows for waging just wars to confront and defeat regimes that are inflicting evil. The Holocaust and "ethnic cleansing" come to mind.

No discussion of the Fifth Commandment is complete without considering abortion. The fundamental premise of abortion is that a "fetus" is not a "child." But the science is categorically non-debatable: a new human life is created, evidenced by its unique genetic code, at the moment of conception.

Consider the sin of a nation whose judges declare that the mother of a newly conceived child is entitled to kill it. Consider the seismic shift away from respecting God as the author of all life when a nation establishes in law the right to destroy it.

Then consider the catastrophic impact of legalized abortion on every single one of the Ten Commandments, as the moral underpinnings of our civilization.

At its core, abortion is a matter of personal convenience. And while bearing a child is most certainly not "convenient," that child is a unique creation of Almighty God, made in His image and likeness. And we are morally bound to respect it.

In today's world, we have wonderful alternatives to abortion - alternatives that save mothers from living the rest of their natural lives under the horrific moral torment of knowing they destroyed that for which God uniquely ordained them.

But then, I could argue that we do have precedent. After all, we did kill Jesus Christ for being politically and morally "inconvenient."

"Thou shalt not kill."

So don't.

You'll be glad you didn't.

Bob

. . . . . .

March 20, 2017

> "...Thus they became unclean by their acts, and played the harlot in their doings. Then the anger of the Lord was kindled against His people, and he abhorred His heritage; he gave them into the hand of the nations, so that those who hated them ruled over them." (Psalm 106)

Chris rested most of the day yesterday, after being "awake" (eyes open, but not responsive) for a brief period in the early morning. Numbers are good, liver enzymes down some, but nowhere near where they should be. So we're watching and praying that they return to normal. She's scheduled for another CT scan at MGH on Tuesday to check the status of the subdural hygroma. We're praying that it is subsiding/improving; if not, it will likely require surgery to install an adjustable valve in the CSF shunt. This is concerning because the impact of anesthesia on her already-fragile central nervous system has severely impacts her progress.

"Thou shalt not commit adultery."

This commandment is self-evident in its own right. It is fundamental to social order, and speaks to the importance of the family unit as God's ordained "building block" of civilization. It charges us to honor our promise of fidelity, made to our spouse and sworn to Almighty God in the presence of witnesses (who are thereby charged to do everything within their power to keep the marriage intact.)

The Sixth Commandment also speaks to the issue of modesty, and (here's that term again...) respecting God as the author of all life. We are commanded to see every man and woman as uniquely created in His image and likeness. Jesus himself said that anyone who so much as looked at another person with a sexual connotation is guilty of the sin of lust. By the way, how we dress, and how we allow our children to dress, are both considerations within the context of this Commandment. Presenting ourselves in such a way as to invite inappropriate thoughts is also disrespectful of God's intended use of our bodies.

Prostitution, pornography, and related "industries" pander to the deadly sin of lust. They are morally destructive, as they exploit the beautiful gift of human sexuality, repudiate the virtues of modesty and chastity, and debase God's sacred gift of procreation. They do it for the money. Billions of dollars flow to these purveyors of filth and evil every year, as they grow rich at the expense of the moral fiber of our nation and the innocence of our children. Let's not forget that the scrapheap of history is piled high with civilizations whose downfall was preceded by moral decay.

When we subvert God's moral design, we wreak havoc on our families, and sow the seeds of immorality in the hearts and minds of our children. Those seeds are regularly exploited by the entertainment and fashion industries, which use our natural inclinations as tools for profit, drawing young people towards immodesty and promiscuity in thought, word and deed.

Temptations challenging our obedience to the Sixth Commandment are everywhere. We're bombarded with sex and the lure of evil on TV, in the movies, and on our streets. But there is no temptation that can stand against the name of Jesus. He is our weapon - the only weapon - against the ever-present challenges to virtue and fidelity.

So when you see something, say something.

"Jesus." :-)

Thanks for your prayers. I love you.

Bob

. . . . . .

March 22, 2017

"...The Lord loves those who hate evil; he preserves the lives of his saints; he delivers them from the hand of the wicked. Light dawns for the righteous, and joy for the upright in heart. Rejoice in the Lord, O you righteous, and give thanks to His holy name!" (Psalm 97)

Good numbers yesterday, though Chrissy's liver enzymes are still way too high. She'll be going over to MGH for a follow-up CT scan to compare with last week's scan. The team needs to determine if there's any change to the subdural hygroma. We pray it is improving, because if not, another surgery is likely. Also, they capped her trake yesterday morning, but she didn't do well with it, so it was removed and the one-way valve reinstalled. They are pushing her, and that's good. It's what rehab is all about. But she just wasn't ready for the cap.

"Thou shalt not steal."

Most of us take the Seventh Commandment at face value. We define theft in terms of stealing a candy bar, robbing a bank or cheating on taxes. But there's a lot more to it than just theft of tangible assets.

If stealing things for which restitution can be made is a sin, how much greater is our sin when we rob people of things for which restitution cannot be made? How grave is our sin when we rob others of the dignity of their person, their peace of mind, or the joy in their hearts? If stealing the fruits of a man's labor breaks God's law, how much greater is our sin when we steal the fruits God's labor?

Then there's the issue of time. Time is capital that God has given each one of us to invest in His plan of salvation. And although our allotment is finite, we really don't know how much we have. But what we do know is that regardless of how much we're given, God expects a good return on His investment. We might want to be asking ourselves, "Are my priorities robbing the time God's wants me to invest in His plan of salvation?"

But don't worry about it too much.

We'll have all eternity to reflect on the answer.

Take time to do some of God's work today. The hourly wage isn't much. But the benefits are spectacular. ☺

Bob

. . . . . .

March 23, 2017

"O God, thou art my God, I seek thee, my soul thirsts for thee; my flesh faints for thee, as in a dry and weary land where no water is. I have looked upon thee in the

sanctuary, beholding thy power and glory. Because they steadfast love is better than life, my lips will praise thee. So I will bless thee as long as I live; I will lift up my hands and call on thy name." (Psalm 63)

Yesterday's news was not what we had hoped for, as the radiology team at MGH reported the results of Tuesday's CT scan. The subdural hygroma has gotten slightly larger, and the ventricles in her brain are enlarged and showing some blood mixed in with the CSF. Chrissy is scheduled for surgery on Monday, April 3rd, unless the situation becomes more unstable, in which case they will admit her through the Emergency Room and take her right into surgery. The reason for the delay is to purge the aspirin (blood thinner) from her system to minimize the possibility of continued bleeding before, and uncontrollable bleeding during the operation. Her liver enzymes continue to move towards normal, significantly better than the past 4 or 5 days. We continue the emotional roller coaster ride that time after time lifts us up with positives, then knocks us down with disappointments. I call it the "up-downs," and they're just a part of the journey. So we steady our emotions with prayer, staying grounded in our faith as we frame this mortal journey within the context of eternity.

I have asked several men and women of deep faith to join me in laying on hands and praying over Christine on Sunday afternoon. I don't yet know the exact time, but I'll share it with you as soon as arrangements are finalized. I'm asking each of you, across the world, to join us in prayer from your homes, churches or wherever you may be during the time we are praying over her.

Some will wonder if I've taken leave of my senses. The answer is "Yes!" and here's why:

Our senses feed our intellect, which requires physical evidence to validate concepts and ideas, or confirm the existence of material objects. Our senses and our intellect thus become limiting. They hinder, and sometimes prevent embracing our faith and the empowerment it can bring to our lives. They introduce doubt as to our ability to engage God's power to accomplish the mission He has given each of us in this life.

I've never found a better definition of "faith" than that found in Hebrews 11:1. Walk with me as I examine its words:

"Now faith is the substance of things asked for, the evidence of things unseen."

"Now" means exactly what it says: right here, at this time, and in this place.

"...the substance of things asked for" defines something which has not happened, something which does not yet exist, something which we have defined, but is not yet real.

"...the evidence of things unseen" defines the physical manifestation of events which our senses cannot detect, confirm or validate, and our minds cannot explain.

So yes, I am taking leave of my senses.

Jesus spent His life healing the sick and curing the infirm in body and spirit. He told us that if we had faith the size of a mustard seed, we could move mountains. This wasn't a metaphor, something intended to convey an idea. It was a challenge to us to grow in faith to the point that we could enable God to work through us to accomplish things that most consider impossible.

There is nothing lukewarm or ambiguous in God's promise to "be with us, even unto the end of time.". And we cannot be lukewarm when we accept that Promise. It's all or nothing. We're either "in" or we're "out." We can't "sort of" have faith.

The idea behind Jesus' exhortation to greater faith was to attain a level of belief by which we could invoke the power of God to accomplish things beyond what our limited human abilities and faculties could deliver or comprehend.

I believe.

Do you?

See you on Sunday. :-)

Bob

. . . . . .

March 24, 2017

> *"...What shall I render to the Lord for all His bounty to me? I will lift up the cup of salvation, and call on the name of the Lord. I will pay my vows to the Lord in the presence of all His people..." (Psalm 116)*

Yesterday was a "so-so" day for Chris, as some periods of coughing interrupted her restful times. She was in her wheelchair upright for about 2 hours, with a neck brace in place because her neck muscles aren't able to hold her head upright. We continue to wait, watch, and pray, as we count down the days until her surgery on April 3rd. We pray that any bleeding in her brain has stopped. Please pray with us.

Important Note: Our Healing Service for Christine will take place at 2:00PM EDT, Sunday, March 26, 2017. Some of us will be at the hospital; most will not. I humbly ask that you join us at that time to pray for her full recovery. I know God will hear you.

"Thou shalt not bear false witness against thy neighbor."

This Eighth Commandment is fairly self-explanatory, but has very broad implications in our lives. Think about how much of today's "news" is unsubstantiated rumor, hype or innuendo. Whereas news media used to seek truth to inform us, it now bears false witness to deceive us.

Deceit and misrepresentation are evident today more than ever before. Because of social media and the internet, a falsehood or partial truth can travel around the entire world in less than a second. A person's entire life can be destroyed with the push of a button, without ever firing a shot.

There's another aspect of "bearing false witness" that I'm learning about. Since beginning to write my morning posts on Facebook, I've been "friending" everyone without hesitation. Today, I learned that there are people on Facebook promoting and practicing immorality. They are using Facebook to serve Satan, even as we use it to serve God.

One of my daughters warned me about this today, as I have "friended" many without hesitation. That some have strayed from God's path is not "on me;" it is "on them." It is not my choice that they choose evil; it is theirs.

But what IS "on me" is letting them know of God's plan of salvation, of the incredible act of redemption consummated at Calvary on Good Friday 2000+ years ago.

So rather than "unfriending" those who are living in sin, I'm going to do as Jesus did. He didn't run from sinners. He befriended them, and gave them a chance to redeem themselves and gain eternal life.

We are charged by Christ's apostolic exhortation to share the Good News of salvation with all people. I don't care if Christ is not in your life right now. My goal is for this ministry to introduce you to Him, so you, too, can learn of His promise, to stand with us in the warmth of God's infinite love, and to turn your life around.

Christ never "unfriended" any member of the human race. He chastised, advised, admonished, taught, and exhorted, but He never said, "I reject you." Instead, He gave His life for us - each and every one of us - so we could reject sin, repent of our transgressions, atone for our misdeeds, and achieve eternal life.

God's invitation to Heaven is eternal and unconditional. Except for one thing. We have to answer His call. We have to "take up our cross and follow Him." We have to say "Yes!" to His RSVP.

I truly hope, no matter how grievous your sins, that you will reach out to the promise of eternal life that was paid for by the blood of Jesus Christ on the Cross. His outstretched arms invite all into God's loving embrace.

And last time I checked, everyone loves a hug. :-)

God bless you.

Bob

. . . . . .

March 25, 2017

> *"...Open to me the gates of righteousness, that I may enter through them and give thanks to the Lord. This is the gate of the Lord; the righteous shall enter through it. I thank thee that thou hast answered me and has become my salvation..." (Psalm 118)*

Yesterday was a better day for Chris, much less coughing, and Joe and Naomi reported that her eyes were open occasionally throughout the day. Her white cell count is elevated slightly again (11,000), but not a cause for concern at this point. Thrush is a constant problem, and may be the reason for the increased white cell count. The PT people are keeping her as limber as possible. We have a Family Conference scheduled for next Friday (3/31) and then surgery the following Monday (4/3), if all goes according to plan.

Because so many ask me how I deal with what happened, I decided that today, I'm going to let you in on my secret.

Have you ever been physically tired to the point of exhaustion? You stop your work, eat supper, get a good night's sleep, and awaken the next morning ready for the new day. You might have some aches and pains, but nothing too serious.

But a different kind of exhaustion, a "multi-dimensional" weariness attacks us when we deal with the many aspects (physical, intellectual, financial, mental, spiritual) of a personal catastrophe. And a hearty meal, a good night's sleep and some Ben-Gay aren't going to provide the kind of recovery we need. Things come at you from all directions, a literal avalanche of legal, medical and financial issues, faith questions, relationship challenges, and many more. It keeps on coming, and coming, and coming, until you're ready to throw up your hands and yell, "Uncle!"

I yelled "Uncle!" the day of Chrissy's hemorrhage. I saw right away the oncoming avalanche and threw my hands up to Almighty God because I knew I was going to need Him in a big way to handle the ensuing train wreck in our lives. I asked Him to save Chrissy, and to give her and me and the kids the grace and strength we were going to need to play the cards in the hand we were dealt.

And He has.

There will be times when we're embattled on all fronts. Just like parachuting from a stricken airplane, I let go of everything, and "through it all, I take the fall, and do it [His] way." It's simple, but it's never easy.

God's love is infinite, and He gives us every opportunity to accept Jesus Christ as our Savior, pick up our crosses, and follow Him. All you have to do is ask. :-)

God bless you this day, and every day of your life.

Bob

PS - Please don't forget to pray with us tomorrow at 2PM EDT. We are praying over Chris and asking God to restore her to complete health.

. . . . . .

March 26, 2017

> "He who dwells in the shelter of the Most High, who abides in the shadow of the Almighty, will say to the Lord, "My refuge and my fortress; my God in whom I trust." For He will deliver you from the snare of the fowler and from the deadly pestilence; He will cover you with his pinions, and under his wings you shall find refuge; His faithfulness is a shield and buckler. You will not fear the terror of the night, nor the arrow that flies by day, nor the pestilence that strikes in darkness, nor the destruction that wastes at noonday. A thousand may fall at your side, ten thousand at your right hand; but it will not come near you. You will only look with your eyes and see the recompense of the wicked. Because you have made the Lord your refuge, the Most High your habitation, no evil shall befall you, no scourge come near your tent. For He will give His angels charge of you, to guard you in all your ways. On their hands

they will bear you up, lest you dash your foot against a stone. You will tread on the lion and the adder, the young lion and the serpent you will trample under foot.

Because he cleaves to me in love, I will deliver him; I will protect him because he knows My name. When he calls to Me I will answer him; I will be with him in trouble. I will rescue him and honor him. With long life I will satisfy him, and show him My salvation." (Psalm 91)

Chris had a good day yesterday, good numbers, white cell count back to normal, and her eyes are opening more and more. Her right leg is definitely moving some without external stimulation. No way of knowing if it's a reflex, but it's moving. Not often, but noticeably when I'm holding her right hand, her fingers make an almost-imperceptible grasping motion. Her eyelids are definitely opening more, and her eyes occasionally track from side to side. Interestingly, as Naomi found out, Chrissy will stay "awake" for long periods of time (half an hour or more) when we show her "Stampin' Up" videos on YouTube. :-)

Today is Sunday. But it will not be an "ordinary" Sunday, if there is such a thing. Because today at 2PM, we will pray with one voice across the entire world, laying on hands and bringing God's healing touch to His faithful daughter, Christine. We lift her up with complete confidence in the words of Jesus Christ, the Son of God, our Way, our Truth, and our Life:

"And Jesus answered them, "Have faith in God. Truly, I say to you, whoever says to this mountain, 'Be taken up and cast into the sea,' and does not doubt in his heart, but believes that what he says will come to pass, it will be done for him. Therefore I tell you, whatever you ask in prayer, believe that you have received it, and it will be yours." (Mark 11:22-24)

...for thine is the Kingdom, and the Power, and the Glory, forever. Amen.
BELIEVE!
Bob

. . . . . .

March 27, 2017

"...For God alone my soul waits in silence, for my hope is from Him. He only is my rock and my salvation, my fortress; I shall not be shaken. On God rests my deliverance and my honor; my mighty rock, my refuge is God. Trust in Him at all times, O people; pour out your heart before Him; God is a refuge for us..." (Psalm 62)

Good numbers yesterday, some coughing, but overall a quiet day for Christine. It provided a welcome backdrop for our Prayer Service. Thank you to our daughters who downloaded music onto my computer, and prepared song sheets and Scripture readings. Thank you to the five who prayed with me over Chrissy in her hospital room. And thank you, more than words can ever convey, to every one of you around the world who prayed with us for our beloved wife, mother and friend.

As we gathered in the hospital room, there was an aura of quiet confidence, a gentle but unwavering certainty about the intercessory power of prayer and the healing power of God. We began by singing some of Chrissy's favorite hymns, and then reading from Scripture. And then we prayed, long periods of silence followed by softly whispered prayers from the heart, punctuated by more readings from scripture and a few more hymns.

God was in that room yesterday. I could feel it. With our eyes closed and our hands on Christine's broken body, an intense peace came over us as we prayed for God to heal His daughter. We were totally immersed in bringing God's healing grace to Christine.

And then after about an hour, it was gone. No one said "Stop," it just faded away. We conversed quietly for a few more minutes, bade one another farewell, and went on about our lives as if stopping in to ask God to heal a friend was as ordinary as going to the store for a loaf of bread.

When we truly believe, we don't need explanations or physics or chemistry. We are immersed in the "incomprehensibleness" of God. We cannot truly understand any of it — the infinity of His power, the vastness of His love, or the universality of His mercy. But we know God is there, just like the force of lift on an airplane wing. We can't see it and we can't touch it, but we can see certainly see the consequences of its absence.

"Now faith is the substance of things hoped for, the evidence of things unseen."

One of the people praying in the room with us was a doctor. So was St. Luke, who authored one of the four Gospels.

I wonder if these men of science are on to something. Just sayin'... ☺

Bob

. . . . . .

March 28, 2017

"Blessed are those whose way is blameless, who walk in the law of the Lord! Blessed are those who keep His

testimonies, who seek Him with their whole heart, who also do no wrong, but walk in His ways..." (Psalm 119)

Another good day yesterday, good numbers, as Chrissy continues the long journey towards recovery. Every day I see very subtle but definite signs that something is going on. We have no way of knowing what is happening, only that it's happening. When I went into her room yesterday, I took hold of her right hand and said, as I always do, "Good morning Mrs. G!" And her entire body "stretched," and she turned her head towards me. Yet later, during her half-hour of physical therapy, she was totally unresponsive to loud noises and visual stimulation. She seems to respond to us, but is unresponsive to her medical team. The uncertainty of what's happening tortures logic, plays on emotions, and consumes us if we try to make sense of it. So we don't. We leave Chrissy's course and destination in God's hands. We do it through prayer, because there is no other way to reconcile the inconsistencies (and there are many) we see and feel every day.

For over two months now, we've led much-altered lives. The stress is enormous as we deal with the utter uncertainty of Chrissy's condition, the logistics of keeping one of us with her every day, attending to household tasks and duties, and the deafening silence of her absence from our home. The incongruity of her being here, and at the same time not being "here," is psychologically and emotionally draining, no matter how hard we try to wrestle this reality to ground.

Our family dynamics have changed, forced changes which were neither welcome nor healthy. We've all been running full speed ahead, and the "noise level of life" has become a cacophony. Circumstances are pummeling us individually and as a family, and I felt that even though we're together and talking to each other constantly, we're losing touch with each other as we cope individually with what happened to the heart and soul of our home.

Have you ever noticed that the more you say, the less you communicate? The louder you talk, the less people hear? Last night, I asked Lauren, Stephanie and Hunter (our grandson, age 7) if we could just sit together in silence for half an hour in the living room, forcing a temporary stop to the frenetic physical and mental activity which has overtaken our inner peace. I wanted to just "be," together.

I've said many times that God whispers to us in the silent aftermath of tragedy. But we have not had that silent aftermath, because Chris is still alive, so instead of silence, we've had more "noise" to deal with. So last night, we created silence through an act of will. And God filled that silence that just moments before was overrun by anxiety, anger, confusion, and uncertainty.

No matter our path in life, we will experience collisions which dramatically affect where we're going and when we get there. But God has given us the ability to stop everything and push the "RESET" button. We can walk over to those green pastures and lie down beside those still waters.

When we choose silence over the din of the world, we enable God to refresh our souls.

So be quiet. Today. ☺

Bob

. . . . . .

March 29, 2017

"Out of the depths I cry to thee, O Lord! Lord, hear my voice! Let thy ears be attentive to the voice of my

> supplications! If thou, O Lord, shouldst mark iniquities, Lord, who could stand? But there is forgiveness with thee, that thou mayest be feared." (Psalm 130)

Really no change yesterday, as we move one day closer to surgery. We continue to wait, watch, and pray.

A couple of interesting things happened yesterday, things for which there isn't really an explanation...

Yesterday afternoon, one of her team members wheeled Chris to a music therapy session given by a guitarist, after which the nurse returned her to her room. A few minutes later, the guitarist came in, guitar in hand, and played some songs for her. His last song was the Neil Diamond best-seller, "Cracklin' Rosy." At the end of the song, Lauren and Stephanie noticed a single tear rolling down Chrissy's cheek. A single tear, for no physical reason...

Then last night, I was home alone in our bedroom shortly before midnight, catching up on the endless stream of paperwork that continues to arrive every day, when a small camera case which had been sitting on a windowsill since just before Chrissy's incident, fell off the window sill and rolled a couple of feet across the floor. There was no wind, no earthquake, to thunderclap, no cat playing nearby, no nothing. So I picked it up, put it back on the window sill, and went back to my paperwork. And ten seconds later, it happened again...

There is no physical explanation for these two incidents. But they happened. One manifested itself on Chrissy's person, the other happened 110 miles away, at home.

Did you ever wonder what happens to our souls when we're near death? There are myriad accounts of "NDE" — Near Death Experiences" — in which the spirit of an afflicted person actually leaves the body, and returns to it some time later. These are the accounts of doctors, clergy, and people like you and me.

During the entirety of His life, Jesus used signs, as God has used supernatural signs to "wake us up" since the beginning of time. He continues to do so today. I know — not believe, but KNOW — of the presence of souls in this world. I can say with certainty that they're here at certain times, and for specific reasons.

When there is no physical explanation for something that happens, do we dismiss it as some sort of trick? Do we scoff at the possibility that the soul of a loved one is trying to communicate with us?

Don't.

Do you remember Jesus' last words as He was dying on the Cross? He was a man like us in all things but sin. And as He approached death's door, His exact words were, "Father, into thy hands, I commend my spirit." He was asking God to accept His soul into Heaven. He had accomplished His mission on Earth, and his soul was leaving for Heaven. Literally.

Did I mention to you that Neil Diamond was Chrissy's favorite pop singer? Or that the camera case that flew off the window sill was sitting on top of a small carrier we use to bring Communion to the sick and dying?

"Now faith is the substance of things hoped for, the evidence of things unseen."

How about the evidence of things that ARE seen?

BELIEVE.

And keep your eyes and ears open.

Bob

· · · · · ·

March 30, 2017

> "O Lord, my heart is not lifted up, my eyes are not raised too high; I do not occupy myself with things too great and too marvelous for me. But I have calmed and quieted my sol, like a child quieted at its mother's breast; like a child that is quieted is my soul." (Psalm 131)

Interesting day yesterday, as the Physical Therapists really worked Chrissy hard on a bicycle in the rehab gym. Good numbers, but with the combination of sitting up in the wheelchair for several hours and the "workout," her heart started acting up, so it was back to bed for the day.

It's not surprising that her heart isn't able to sustain much stress. She has been lying down, without conscious muscle movement to create the need for her heart to work harder, since January 18th.

Physical fitness is the result of proper nourishment, adequate rest, and regular exercise. Spiritual fitness is no different.

We get "proper nourishment" for our souls by reading and listening to the Word of God, at home and in church. Building virtuous communities depends on building bonds of faith when we gather together in worship, so that our relationships outside of church are framed within the context of Christian fellowship. When we do this, we build the groundwork for "practicing what we preach" in our everyday lives.

Spiritual rest is found in prayer and meditation, when we allow our souls to escape the din of everyday life to a "place" of stillness and quietude. This refreshes us. It sharpens our senses and replenishes grace, strengthening our ability to resist temptations that would lure us from godliness into sin.

Finally, "spiritual exercise" is the integration of conscience into our thoughts, words and deeds. It is the active practice of our Christian faith, the promotion of virtue and the rejection of evil, by example, in our interaction with those we meet in the normal course of our lives.

Question: "How do you eat a thousand-pound hamburger?"
Answer: "One bite at a time."
Question: "How do we change the world?"
Answer: "One person at a time."

Eat right, get enough rest, and exercise. Physically and spiritually. Be ready to resist and strong in your rejection when temptation strikes.

Because as much as God wants you in Heaven, Satan wants you in Hell. And he's working out all day long, every single day until the end of the world.

So for God's sake, be strong.

Bob

. . . . . .

April 1, 2017

> *"Lord, thou hast been our dwelling place for all generations. Before the mountains were brought forth, or ever thou hadst formed the earth and the world, from everlasting to everlasting thou art God. Thou turnest man back to the dust, and sayeth, "Turn back, O children of men!" For a thousand years in thy sight are but as yesterday when it is past, as a watch in the night." (Psalm 90)*

THE POSTS

Yesterday, Friday, we had our first Family Conference at Spaulding. Every member of Chrissy's team was there: Physical Therapy, Respiratory Therapy, Speech and Language Therapy, two doctors, the social worker, and all our immediate family, either in person or on a conference call. The consensus seems to be that parts of Chrissy's brain were badly damaged by the severe hydrocephalus (overpressure) caused by the hemorrhage. While all her organs are working, the center(s) of the brain responsible for receiving and processing the signals sent by her sensory organs (eyes, ears, nose, tongue, fingers) are badly damaged. It's too soon to establish any permanent prognosis, though she has shown slight improvement since arriving at Spaulding. Monday's surgery will address the cause of the subdural hygroma, and should facilitate the brain's healing. Time will tell. We've known since Day 1 that we are in for a very long journey.

After the conference, which lasted over an hour, we went to Chrissy's room to visit with her. And it's very clear that something is changing. Her right arm, right leg, right foot and toes, and her left foot and toes were moving intermittently, sometimes in a reflexive spasm, sometimes more deliberately. Her right hand and arm pulled my hand towards her; her eyes were sometimes wide open, sometimes just barely, sometimes closed. It is the most active I've seen her since I kissed her good-bye on January 18th.

Life is short. We spend much of it engaged in worldly pursuits, rushing to make deadlines, meet obligations and pursue "success." In our hectic world, it's very easy to lose sight of the incredible architecture of creation. Stop and think about the Hand that designed everything from the subatomic structure of the atom to the planetary balance in our solar system;

from the invisible Nanoarchaeum equitans to the magnificent Balaenoptera musculus. (Google them. ☺)

Consider the intricacies of the human mind, body and soul, the incredible marvel that is a "person." Then consider that there are 7.4 BILLION such persons on planet Earth, each made in the image and likeness of Almighty God. And then try to grasp the fact that there are an infinite number of solar systems and galaxies, stretching on and on and on without end.

At the end of the day, we have two choices. We can acknowledge (but not comprehend) the awesome power of God as the architect of creation, or we can write off the incredible world we live in, the organisms that populate it, and the forces that keep it all in balance as products of some cosmic happenstance.

"From everlasting to everlasting, thou art God."

Wrap your head around that. "FROM everlasting..." — a quantity we are unable to comprehend; "TO everlasting..." — yet another quantity we can't comprehend; "thou art God."

Since before time began, and beyond its end, God simply "is." Timeless. Alpha and Omega, yet without beginning or end. From the most minute subatomic particle to the unquantifiable vastness of space without end, God is.

We is too.

So be. ☺

Bob

. . . . . .

April 3, 2017

"The law of the Lord is perfect, reviving the soul; the testimony of the Lord is sure, making wise the simple; the precepts of the Lord are right, rejoicing the heart;

THE POSTS

> *the commandment of the Lord is pure, enlightening the eyes; the fear of the Lord is clean, enduring forever; the ordinances of the Lord are true, and righteous altogether. More to be desired are they than gold, even much fine gold; sweeter also than honey and drippings of the honeycomb." (Psalm 19)*

Restful day yesterday (Sunday), good numbers, legs and feet moving sporadically, right arm moved twice, right hand squeezing mine when she coughs, eyes open from time to time, sometimes tracking, sometimes unseeing, head turning from side to side when I wash her face... That's what's we can see happening on the outside. Which means something's happening on the inside.

Today, Chris undergoes the surgery to replace the shunt that's "over-sumping" the CSF from her brain. I've worried about both the condition and the operation for three weeks, and I've felt very tired lately.

A lifelong friend who I hadn't seen in months "dropped in" unannounced for the weekend. He is a man of great faith, and we spent a few hours discussing what has happened, the relevance of faith, our need for reliance upon God, and then we prayed over Chris together.

It's interesting how God just sort of brings what we need when we need it, letting us know in His own special way that we're not alone, and that He is listening. Last night, for the first time since January 18th, I slept through the night.

"Worry" kills. It triggers harmful physiological reactions (cortisol, sleeplessness, high blood pressure, etc.). It also endangers our souls by leading us away from God, who wants us to have "faith as of a little child." Time spent worrying is time spent headed in a direction that is contrary to God's plan for us. Jesus told us not to worry, when He spoke about the birds of the air being fed every day without building storehouses full of grain; and flowers in the fields, who don't buy clothes but whose beauty surpasses even Solomon in all his splendor.

Message? "God will provide."

Satan loves worry. It lets him sow seeds of doubt and despair that challenge our faith. He preys on our human nature, trying to lure us away from the certainty of prayer which reinforces our relationship with God. Satan wants us to worry, to be afraid, to doubt the power of God, to surrender to our humanity rather than reaffirm our divinity.

"Doubt" is as dangerous as an open flame near a can of gasoline. It is dangerous to the body, and hazardous to the soul. Just as we douse the open flame, we "extinguish" the doubt. We do so by focusing on the suffering of Jesus Christ on the Cross, and understanding that His crucifixion and death already triumphed over the burden of doubt which assails us. In prayer, we lift up our uncertainty to The One who through His suffering, death and resurrection, already took care of it. We walk away from Satan's ruse because it's already been defeated.

When in doubt, pray. No matter what is tempting you away from God's love, pray.

Jesus did.

Bob

. . . . . .

April 5, 2017

Very quick update: If all goes as planned, Chrissy will receive a CT scan this morning (Wednesday),

> then be transported back from Mass. General to
> Spaulding Rehab. The CT scan will establish the
> baseline from which we will measure the regression
> of the subdural hygroma and the return to normalcy
> of her brain ventricles. These in turn should facilitate
> her recovery. Nothing is for certain, except that
> your prayers have helped her, strengthened us, and
> continue to glorify God as the author of all life.

I'll be continuing my "regular" morning posts as the logistics and travel demands settle down again post surgery. I apologize if I in any way disrupt or interrupt your faith journey with the inconsistency of my posts. It is not because I'm not inspired. But as Jesus said when He saw His disciples asleep at Gethsemane, "The spirit is willing, but the flesh is weak." Please forgive me for letting you down. Please know that I will continue our journey with you.

God bless you, as we approach both the solemnity and the joy of the single most important event in human history: the fulfillment of God's promise to redeem all mankind by sending His Son to suffer a horrific death on a Tree. Remember the words of John the Baptist: "Make straight the way of the Lord..."

Lift high the Cross.

I love you.

Bob

・・・・・・

April 6, 2017

> "...For ever, O Lord, thy word is firmly fixed in the
> heavens. Thy faithfulness endures to all generations;
> thou hast established the earth, and it stands

THE POSTS

fast. By thy appointment, they stand this day; for all things are thy servants..." (Psalm 119)

Chris is back at Spaulding Rehab Hospital, and resting quietly after her 3-day trip to Mass. General for surgery. We believe we've addressed the physiological impediments to her neurological recovery, and I look at today as the starting point for moving ahead. Yesterday's CT scan established the new baseline for evaluating her neurological progress. And so, our journey continues...

Modern aircraft are engineering marvels, the product of over 100 years of technological invention and innovation. Pneumatic, environmental, electrical, hydraulic, fuel, and other systems are designed with built-in redundancies which give us a very high reliability factor. We protect critical systems, because a critical system failure could force us to crash land far short of our intended destination.

But aircraft components do fail from time to time. In the electrical system, for example, when we lose a generator, either the crew (manually) or the system (automatically) performs what is called "load shedding." This eliminates unnecessary electrical demand to ensure that we have power for systems critical for safety of flight. Lights, galley power, and entertainment systems — things that are not directly related to safety of flight — drop off line, reducing electrical demand and preserving power for core functions. The aircraft is designed to get rid of things that are nice to have, to protect power for the things we have to have.

I've learned a lot about "load shedding" since January 18th. We suffered catastrophic damage to the heart of our family. We dropped every activity not directly required to save her life. We "load shed" our activities down to the bare minimum needed to survive.

As we transition from "emergency" to "recovery," just like a Boeing 777, we're beginning to reverse the "load shedding" we performed to deal with the crisis. And I'm suddenly becoming aware of how much I don't need, nonessentials that clutter the roadway to Heaven, that distract us from our core mission in life: to love the Lord with our whole heart, our whole soul, our whole mind and our whole strength; and our neighbors as ourselves.

"Load shedding" doesn't require a catastrophe. Our Lenten journey is intended to make us evaluate our lives in light of that core mission. We have a perfect opportunity to discern whether we're too attached to the things of this world, and to consider where the temptations and distractions of this world might be taking us.

Some prudent load shedding might just ensure that we make it to our intended destination.

Godspeed.

Bob

. . . . . .

April 8, 2017

"Thy testimonies are wonderful; therefor my soul keeps them. The unfolding of thy words gives light; it imparts understanding to the simple. With open mouth I pant, because I long for thy commandments. Turn to me and be gracious to me, as is thy wont toward those who love thy name. Keep steady my steps according to thy promise, and let no iniquity get dominion over me." (Psalm 119)

Quiet day again yesterday, as the nurses reported that Chris is resting comfortably. The Physical Therapy team reported that the tone of her leg muscles is improving. I know what this means physically; I need to know what it means neurologically. We continue to wait, watch, and pray.

So do Christians everywhere.

Evil exists. It comes in the form of thoughts, words and deeds. It is scalar: individuals can be evil; groups can be evil; organizations can be evil; and nations can be evil. Evil can result from what we do, and from what we fail to do.

Political philosopher Edmond Burke wrote, "All that is necessary for the triumph of evil is that good men do nothing."

To challenge evil, we first must recognize it. We need a conscience well-developed enough to discern the presence of evil. Though we're born with a soul, we're not born with a conscience. Conscience is forged during our formative years, and is reinforced by the practice of virtue within the framework of values held by those entrusted with our care. More than anything else, conscience is shaped by "the hand that rocks the cradle."

Developing conscience depends not only on our example in actively living by and attesting to the laws of God; it also requires teaching the importance of living a virtuous life so we can perpetuate our civilization. If we remove ourselves from being active participants in the war between good and evil, are we not then the "good men" of Burke's quotation?

When confronted by evil, our social inclination is to avoid conflict. But what is our moral obligation? We are called on to act. To understand this, we must differentiate between "tolerance" and "accommodation."

Jesus tolerated evil, but he never accommodated it. He admonished sinners, and told us of a different Law than "the law of the jungle." He let us know we have an option to accept God's love, repair our moral shortcomings, and change our lives forever. He single-handedly changed the world. So can we.

Jesus calls upon us to live our faith. While we may tolerate evil, we do not have the moral option to accommodate it. It is not within our purview to cede the moral authority or eternal validity of God's laws. There are no innocent bystanders in the battle between good and evil, only victors and vanquished. Living not for the glory of this world, but for the glory of God's eternal kingdom, carries a price. We can pay it now, or we can pay it later.

Please stay out of debt.

In faith,

Bob

. . . . . .

April 10, 2017

"Happy are those whose help is the God of Jacob, whose hope is in the Lord their God, who made heaven and earth, the sea, and all that is in them; who keeps faith forever; who executes justice for the oppressed; who gives food to the hungry." (Psalm 146)

Chris continues to recuperate from last Monday's surgery, with little change to her physical condition. We're now learning in real terms the glacially slow pace of recovery from brain injuries, as her brain seeks new ways to control neurological processes and transmit neurological impulses to trigger conscious muscle movement. It will be another 2-3 weeks before even the effects of the surgery are measurable with a CT scan. And then, all we'll have done is establish a baseline for measuring future neurological progress.

Dealing with the day-after-day "sameness" of Chrissy's condition is difficult. We want to see measurable progress, but we don't see it happening. Frustration mounts: "Lord, we're doing our part. We BELIEVE. We've been praying for almost three months now; please give us a sign that our prayers are working."

Fact is, we want a Lazarus, and while that's not happening, our prayers ARE working. Chris was not supposed to survive, but she is still here almost 3 months down the road. She is physiologically sound, despite the neurological devastation caused by the hemorrhage. She has weathered the initial trauma, 6 surgeries, 10 ambulance rides, pneumonia, infections, and reactions to medication. Her extremities are beginning to move, her eyes are opening, her head turns occasionally, she clearly expresses pain, discomfort, and displeasure with her facial expressions, and she sometimes responds to the presence of loved ones. That IS measurable progress, if we remember the situation at the "starting line."

If we're "complete" in our prayers, we're being transformed in body and spirit. We're transcending the understandable human desire to validate our efforts with visible results. We're placing every bit of the outcome completely in God's hands. We're experiencing SURRENDER.

Surrender brings transformation, and with it, we get a very small sense of the vastness of eternity. Consider that we're praying to the God who shaped and ordered everything from the atom to infinity. "Awesome" is what this is all about.

We facilitate emotional, psychological, physical and spiritual harm when we persist in our human inclinations and rebel against things we can't control. Rather than fighting these things, we're much better served to embrace them, to transcend the adversity, accept its consequences, and place the angst, anguish, and anger in the God's hands. Because we are simply not equipped to deal with them.

This week, we commemorate the crucifixion and death of the Son of God for our sins. Jesus Christ's last words were, "Father, into Thy hands I commend my spirit." He surrendered himself to the Father with His last conscious act.

Surrendering our humanity to God's will is a tall order. But it's no taller than the Tree of Salvation upon which hung the Savior of the world. We can do it. We must do it.

Believe me.

Bob

. . . . . .

April 12, 2017

> *"Thy word is a lamp to my feet and a light to my path. I have sworn an oath and confirmed it, to observe thy righteous ordinances. I am sorely afflicted; give me life, O Lord, according to thy word! Accept my offerings of praise, O Lord, and teach me thy ordinances. I hold my life in my hand continually, but I do not forget thy law." (Psalm 119)*

On Monday morning, the same doctor who examined Chrissy on admission to Spaulding, examined her again. He hasn't seen her in the intervening 7 weeks. She remains in a vegetative state, but is beginning to show signs of progress, as I shared in my last post. His description of Chris's condition sent an electric jolt through me: "Compared to when she arrived, her condition today is remarkable."

To God be the glory. Our prayers are being heard, and Chris is gaining ground against all odds. We have a very long way to go, but we are moving forward, even if slowly. Please keep praying.

"Life is what happens to our plans," my dad once told me, with a knowing smile on his face. He wasn't wrong. Plans speak to a vision for the future; they engender a sense of purpose. We don't plan for ambivalence, and we don't strategize for ambiguity. Our dreams are little more than flights of fancy absent plans to achieve them. We have financial plans, career plans, family plans, and house plans.

God also has a plan, His plan of salvation, and He gave each of us a role in that plan. He also gave us free will to choose whether to accept that role. Unenlightened by God's laws and unrestrained by obedience to His will, our free will can lead us straight to Hell.

Faith is the lighthouse that warns us of spiritual shoals in our voyage of life. It is the beacon that keeps us clear of the rocks of sin and death. Faith reframes our every experience into an opportunity to better understand God's plan and to refine our sense of purpose in life. It transforms tragedy into triumph, sadness into serenity, doubt into discernment.

But plans don't bring success. Execution brings success. It's not what we say we're going to do that matters; it's getting it done that counts. A plan establishes a trajectory, with benchmarks and milestones to measure progress. It's up to us to invest the "sweat equity" to make it happen.

In aviation, we live by maxims, one of which is, "Plan your flight, and fly your plan."

Salvation is no accident. See you in the friendly skies. ☺

Bob

April 14, 2017

> *"Trust in the Lord, and do good; so you will dwell in the land, and enjoy security. Take delight in the lord, and He will give you the desires of your heart. Commit your way to the Lord; trust in Him, and He will act. He will bring forth your vindication as the light, and your right as the noonday." (Psalm 37)*

Chris continues to make progress even though she remains in a vegetative state. Her tracheostomy is now capped during the day, and she is managing it well. Next step - cap it both day and night, for a week or so to ensure that she can breathe without it. And then, they will remove it — a major step forward in her recovery. Though we do not know what tomorrow may bring, we do know that God hears us if we remain steadfast in prayer.

Today is Good Friday. It is a day of contradictions, symbolized by the perpendicular arms of the Cross. It is a day of brutality and Mercy. It is a day of envy and Generosity. It is a day of cruelty and Compassion. It is the end of the Old Law, and the beginning of the New. It is a day of defeat, and a day of Transcendence. It is the day in which Jesus Christ suffers temporal judgment and death in this life, so we can escape eternal Judgment and Death in the next.

The best sermon I ever heard was preached by a Naval Academy Chaplain, Commander Bob Ecker, while I was a Midshipman. It's power lay in both the message and how he delivered it. Father Eckert climbed up into the pulpit, and began speaking. He captivated us as he took on the role of Pontius

Pilate. And in the course of that sermon, he rationalized away his surrender of the innocence of Jesus Christ to the trappings of this world: wealth, power, status, and popularity.

On this day, we commemorate the Price paid for our salvation. We witness in horrifying detail the triumph of evil over innocence, of deceit over honesty, of sin over virtue, of death over life. The message of Christ was killed this day, for all the world to see.

We cannot allow the horror of "Good" Friday to be lost on us. We must contemplate, in minute detail, the agony and torture Jesus Christ suffered to free us from sin and death. He took on Himself the weight of every sin ever committed in the history of the world. Every single transgression of God's law was hung on Him, just one week after we took to the streets to honor Him on Palm Sunday.

As disciples, we must grasp the sense of desolation that gripped His followers as they watched the Son of God fall prey to the bloodlust of the mob, the political ambitions of the powerful, and the envy of the clergy. We are the rabble that called out "Give us Barabbas!" We are Pontius Pilate, who washed his hands of the murder of an innocent man. We are the guards who whipped Christ and tore open His flesh at the pillar. We are the jailers who fashioned the crown of thorns and gleefully jammed in onto His head. We are the crowds who jeered and spat at Him as He walked silently to His death. We are the soldiers who tore off His garments and sold them in pieces. We wielded the hammers that drove the nails, we stood and taunted Him as He suffered, and we laughed at Him until He died.

Whatever the weather today, we as Christians must be very aware of the spiritual storm around us as the battle of Powers and Principalities rages on. For this day, we must understand what we face in the spiritual wasteland of a world in which innocence was murdered, compassion was killed, and evil has prevailed.

Today, we are called to understand the desolation of a world in which sin has conquered mankind. Even as we killed Him, Jesus loved us: "Father, forgive them for they know not what they do." Jesus Christ forgave us, even as we drove nails into His hands and feet, and a spear into His side.

When we choose evil, do we really NOT KNOW what we are doing? Really?

At 3pm today, stop for a minute and consider that the Son of God just finished paying the price for our eternal salvation. Then say "Thank You" with the rest of your life.

Bob

. . . . . .

April 16, 2017

> *"But an angel said to the women, "Do not be afraid; for I know that you seek Jesus who was crucified. He is not here; for He has risen as He said. Come, see the place where he lay." (Matthew 28:5-6)*

Christine's tracheostomy is now capped 24/7, and she is managing it without any issues. This means she is breathing on her own, normally, and that the end of the trake is in sight! Once it's gone, I can take her outside (in her wheelchair) into the fresh air of newly arrived Spring, and share with her the beauty of God's renewal. We do not know what is to be, but we are thankful to God for His healing touch.

First light. The Sabbath has passed, and I'm taking some flowers to the tomb of the man I thought was the Messiah. Just a week ago, everything was so beautiful, as the people honored and praised Him. And then, just like that, out of envy, I suppose, the rabbis finally managed to have Him killed — by the Romans, no less. I can't stop hearing the hammers as the soldiers drove spikes through His hands and feet. I can't forget His voice, forgiving them even as they inflicted unspeakable agony on Him. I don't know what to think or believe any more. I want to believe He was the Son of God, but I watched Him die, saw Him taken down off the Cross and laid in this tomb. And then they rolled that huge stone — the one right there — across the door. They even left two soldiers as guards. And now they are gone, the rock has been moved, and His body isn't here, even though I saw it wrapped in burial cloths, lying right there. The cloths are laying on the ground, and I'm being told He has risen from the dead. I don't know what to believe.

Imagine trying to sort out the conflicted "facts" assailing mind and body, standing at the door of the tomb 2000 years ago. Back then, it wasn't a story read from a Book, it was reality. Family and friends were stunned and horrified. They had scattered after the Crucifixion, gone to who-knows-where after their Friend died on a Cross. Look, you can't kill God; He just "is." But I know what I saw, and I know about death, and that man was DEAD. Now I'm told He's not, that He's alive, and He's gone on ahead. I don't know what to believe...

First light. Not only the first light of day, but the First Light of salvation, the lifting of the veil of darkness that has hung over mankind since The Fall, the inevitable descent into sin and death that results when mankind seeks its own will rather than seeking the Amazing Grace we need for salvation.

The Son of God humbled Himself to die on a Cross for us, and reopened the gates of Heaven.

As we celebrate the Resurrection of Jesus Christ from the dead; as we sing and rejoice in the fulfillment of God's Promise to send a Savior; as we commemorate the sealing of the New Covenant with the Blood of the Lamb; as we try to comprehend the Infinity of God's love for us, understand that at the end of the day, our only fitting response is to reaffirm Almighty God as the Author of all life, God of Judgment and God of Mercy, upon whom our salvation rests.

Awe is defined as an emotion variously combining dread, veneration, and wonder that is inspired by authority or by the sacred or sublime. Our God IS an awesome God, and if we do our part, He will raise us up on eagle's wings, bear us on the breath of dawn, make us to shine like the sun, and hold us in the palm of His hand.

BELIEVE.
SURRENDER.
SEE.
GROW.
WITNESS.
REJOICE.

Humility... It does a body good.

God bless you in the glory of His risen Son, and grant you peace and joy on this Resurrection Day.

Bob

· · · · · ·

April 18, 2017

"So they drew near to the village to which they were going. He appeared to be going further, but they constrained him, saying, "Stay with us, for it is toward evening and the day is now far spent." So he went in to stay with them. When He was at table

THE POSTS

with them, He took the bread and blessed, and broke it, and gave it to them. And their eyes were opened and they recognized him; and he vanished out of their sight. They said to each other, "Did not our hearts burn within us while he talked to us on the road, while he opened to us the scriptures?" (Luke 24: 28-32)

Yesterday, we rode the ambulance over to MGH for a post-op exam of Chrissy's last operation. The PA who examined her indicated that this was the last surgery needed to address the physiology of her brain. I asked about any sense of direction, and she stated clearly that it's far too soon to make any pronouncements or predictions. After we returned to Spaulding, the team's backup MD examined her and told us that Chris has now arrived at the physical "starting line" for her neurological recovery. In their words, it's now all about time and therapy.

Three months ago today, our family's earthly life changed forever, the result of an event totally unforeseen, incredibly tragic, and breathtakingly transformative. In the ensuing journey, we've traversed deserts of despair and crested mountains of doubt; we've withstood tsunamis of fear and scaled cliffs of anguish; we've choked on the bitter bile of regret, and tasted the cool sweet water of God's forgiveness.

Spaulding Rehab Hospital's motto is: "Find Your Strength." It's a marvelous credo that captures the essence of who they are and what they do. They help, they coach, they love, they push, and they teach.

God also uses adversity to teach, and through Chrissy's affliction, we've learned. We've learned about the wonderful if unheralded compassion of friends and strangers. We've learned about the indispensable need for faith to guide us on our journey. We've learned to recognize what's important in life, and what isn't. And we've found our strength:

"He is risen as He said."

Find your strength. Follow Him.

Bob

. . . . . .

April 20, 2017

"And these three men, Shadrach, Meshach, and Abednego, fell bound into the burning fiery furnace. Then King Nebuchadnezzar was astonished and rose up in haste. He said to his counselors, "Did we not cast three men bound into the fire?" They answered the king, "True, O king." He answered, "But I see four men loose, walking in the midst of the fire, and they are not hurt, and the appearance of the fourth is like a son of the gods." (Daniel 3:23-25)

Yesterday was another of the many days in which we will see little change externally, as Chrissy's brain works to continue to heal, seeking to organize and find new pathways for the neural impulses that are starting to make their way to her limbs and extremities. This will be a long, slow process, but our faith remains strong and our hearts resolute that God's amazing work will continue. It took three months to get to the starting line. It will take many more months to run the race. Your prayers are so important, and I constantly visualize the day she will see, hear and speak to us. The absence of her voice in our lives is physical. The sight, sound and smell of a person are real. So is their absence. I wait in faith for the day she will say, "I love you."

Have you ever taken stock of how much time we spend working to appear "normal" (whatever that is.) We buy clothes; we put on makeup; we "stay between the lines." We wouldn't wear pajamas to work, or bathing suits to church, because these would violate "normal." We seek to represent ourselves as carefree, healthy, rational, and therefore approachable.

But what's also "normal" is the fact that every one of us, without exception, either is or will one day be tossed into a "fiery furnace" that rocks our world and challenges our faith. We'll mask the fact that we're in that furnace, and we'll work to hide its smoke and flames, and the burns those flames inflict. It could be a catastrophe, or winning the lottery. It could be the death of a loved one or an adulterous affair. It could be substance abuse, or spousal abuse. It could be financial trouble or loneliness. But there will be a furnace, and we will be tossed into it, bound hand and foot by our own weaknesses, and sometimes we'll actually jump into it because we yielded to temptation.

Whatever the issue in our lives that binds us and hurls us into the furnace; whether it's sorrow, doubt, despair, exhilaration, success, health, wealth or failure; whether it's one of the cardinal sins of wrath, greed, sloth, pride, envy, lust, or gluttony; whatever the "king" that rules you and seeks your spiritual or physical death, never, ever, forget that there's always a Fourth Person who will appear with you in that furnace if you seek Him. And if you listen to Him, He will save you from that fire.

We are all willful creations of Almighty God. When we live as He wants us to live, we receive the grace — the "manna" — that nourishes our souls on the journey through this life. Grace flows from knowing and loving God. And knowing and loving God come from praying, and listening, and being as much a friend to Him as He is to us. Do we really, truly, know God as a friend, and Jesus as a companion?

What is your fiery furnace? And with whom are you walking through those flames?

Loving Him, and loving you,
Bob

. . . . . .

April 22, 2017

"Let the words of my mouth and the meditation of my heart be acceptable in Thy sight, O Lord, my rock and my Redeemer." (Psalm 19)

Chrissy's numbers remain good, and her feet and limbs continue twitching, not in response to any conscious thought that we're aware of, but they're moving nonetheless. Her brain continues to seek new pathways to communicate with her muscles. Her case manager hinted that they're considering "decannulating" her next week — removing the tracheostomy. This is a significant step forward, but it's one which requires caution, hence the decision to wait a few more days. We're ok with it.

While I was praying for Chrissy on the drive home from the State House yesterday, I decided to pray specifically for her to regain consciousness. That is the true "game-changer" that will showcase the miracle of her recovery. I have believed from the outset that she will return to us. When doubt has reared its head,

I've prayed harder, and I've asked you to pray harder, and God has heard our prayers every single time. Now, I'm asking all of you who pray for Chris to use the following prayer: "Jesus, Lord, please wake her up." Over and over, from around the world, let this be our prayer. "Jesus, Lord, please wake her up." God will hear and answer us.

As I'm writing this, I'm listening to the singing of Andrea Bocelli, Sara Brightman, and Luciano Pavarotti. The stunning purity and incredible range of their voices are a magnificent tribute to the power and glory of God. They are gifts, intended to bring beauty and joy to our world, and to glorify God every day of our lives. They bring us joy. They inspire us - IF we use them as God intends.

Inspiration can come in many forms, and from many places. It can come from within or without. It is at times born of tragedy, and at times born of joy. It can transform the anguish of sin into the peace of forgiveness. It can lead us and others closer to God and salvation.

Today, I'd like to share some thoughts with the men who might read this post.

In the 3 months since Chris was stricken, I've begun to understand just how much she sacrificed during our life together. She was always there for me and for the kids. She forgave my transgressions, and her love of God and family never wavered. If not for her, we wouldn't have the beautiful children and grandchildren God has given us. Because of her, each of us is leading the life we have chosen. She always gave of herself, but never asked for herself.

Do you love your wife? I love mine. But I missed the boat many times and in many ways, because I failed to truly understand the incredible sacrifices she made for me, for our family, and for my successes. She always put us first. Always.

It's not enough to merely "love" our wives. As "husbands" and the heads of our families, we are called to inspire our wives and children with our faith, honor them with our fidelity, lead them with our virtue, respect them with our speech, and enlighten them with our love of God. Much too often, I let other things come before Chris, and inadvertently sent a message that I had chosen not to be her inspiration, that being her hero wasn't my priority, that I had made a conscious choice that neither honored, respected or inspired her. That's not something I'm proud of. And though she forgave me, the point is that it should never have happened.

Spare yourself the heartache of looking back with regret because you made the wrong choice. Instead, do something today, and every day of your life, to not only love, but to inspire the woman God put into your life, and into your hands. Be SPECTACULAR for her, and to her, and because of her.

You'll never regret it.

Bob

. . . . . .

April 24, 2017
> *"...The pastures of the wilderness overflow, the hills gird themselves with joy, the meadows clothe themselves with flocks, the valleys deck themselves with grain, they shout and sing together for joy." (Psalm 65)*

Christ's Resurrection consummated His triumph over evil and His victory over death.

Understanding the truth of the Resurrection will give purpose to our lives and meaning to our existence. There is no "sort of" to believing. Either we do, or we don't; and if we do, then our faith must be transformational.

Have you ever noticed that artists evidence a certain radiance in their portrayals of Jesus after the Resurrection? I believe we can manifest this same radiance in our lives, radiance born of our absolute faith in the certainty of Christ's triumph over sin and death.

Radiance isn't intrusive or loud. It's not a "clanging bell" or "clashing cymbal." In fact, radiance makes no sound at all. Yet in its silence, in the mystery of its origins, it can captivate and inspire. It is born of our acceptance of the Absolute Truth that Jesus Christ, the Son of God, died for us and reopened the gates of Heaven. When we really, truly comprehend the incredible Truth of salvation, we will radiate that Truth.

As we read God's word, as we pray, as we worship, as we sing, as we grow in faith, we will undergo a transformation, and we will begin to show forth the radiance born of knowing the Truth. We have new life in Christ — the Way, the Truth, and the Life — as we walk with quiet certainty towards Heaven.

Be radiant in your faith, and dispel the darkness.

Bob

. . . . . .

April 26, 2017

"...How precious is thy steadfast love, O God! The children of men take refuge in the shadow of thy wings. They feast on the abundance of thy house, and thou givest them drink from the river

> *of thy delights. For with thee is the fountain of life; in thy light do we see light..." (Psalm 36)*

On Monday, after posting my update but before leaving the hospital to return to NH, the pulmonologist approached me as I was sitting with Chris after her physical therapy session. He shared that today, Wednesday, the team will be discussing whether to remove her tracheostomy, and if all members of the team agree, they will remove it this afternoon. ☺ Then he motioned me out of earshot of Chris, and let me know that complications could arise that might require re-intubating her with a ventilator, or installing another tracheostomy. And then he gently asked The Question: If a problem did arise, what did I want them to do? I knew what he was asking, and I knew he had to ask it. It's the same Question we were asked 3 months ago when Chrissy was in extremely critical condition at DHMC: Do I want the person I love most in this world to live or to die if things take a turn for the worse?"

After a few moments of reflection, I gave him the same answer I gave DHMC: I wanted all possible measures taken to keep her alive. Though her progress has been extremely slow, we are light-years ahead of where we were at the start of this journey. We don't yet know the full effects of the new shunt valve that was installed 3 weeks ago, but we do know that it has brought her to the point of being able to breathe on her own, and thus remove the trake: evidence of meaningful progress.

At this point, my job — and I ask you to pray with me — is to keep my eye on the ball: "Jesus, Lord, please wake her up."

Way down deep, I deal with another question: am I making decisions because they are what Chris would want, or because they are what I want? It is a constant, relentless companion, 24/7, day after day, week after week, month after month. Seeking the answer to such questions sometimes takes us places we don't like to go, to discover things we don't like to know.

But I'm quietly confident in my decision for two reasons: First, it's what Chris would do if it was me lying in that bed. Second, I know that years ago, without any hesitation whatsoever, she put her life completely in my hands when she signed her living will, with absolute trust and confidence that I would do what is best for her when the chips were down. I did the same with her. And that's powerful medicine.

Now for the rest of the story...

Just a few minutes before I was asked The Question, I watched as the woman I love was hoisted off the physical therapy platform with a hydraulic lift, completely limp, unable to sit up, see, speak or move. I watched the therapists wipe the drool off her chin. And for just a split second, during my "moment of reflection" when the pulmonologist asked me The Question, I wondered which way to go.

When life brings fear, doubt and uncertainty, we only need to go back to the basics. So I did. Hebrews 11:1. It never gets old, because God never gets old. You know the real rest of the story:

BELIEVE.
SURRENDER.
SEE.
GROW.
WITNESS.
REJOICE.
Have a happy day. ☺
Bob

THE POSTS

. . . . . .

April 28, 2017

> "...Thou visitest the earth and waterest it, thou greatly enrichest it; the river of God is full of water; thou providest their grain, for so thou hast prepared it. Thou waterest its furrows abundantly, settling its ridges, softening it with showers, and blessing its growth. Thou crownest the year with thy bounty; the tracks of thy chariot drip with fatness. The pastures of the wilderness drip, the hills gird themselves with joy, the meadows clothe themselves with flocks, the valleys deck themselves with grain, they shout and sing together for joy." (Psalm 65)

Good news! Wednesday morning, the team made the decision to remove the trake, and that afternoon, they took it out. So far, Chrissy is handling it well, though they're keeping her under close watch to make sure she manages the transition without any complications. She got a shampoo and styling Monday, something long overdue since her hair was pretty chopped up from her surgeries. So now it's all the same length, short the way she likes it, and I'm sure that's making her happy. ☺

Yesterday morning, I awakened, did chores, and for the first time this year, went out into our garden. Chris and I loved working together in that garden; it brought us a lot of laughter over the years, and I'm looking forward to the day we can laugh together again. Jesus, Lord, please wake her up.

I took stock of the garden and the raised beds in which we grow most of our vegetables. I went to work, cleaning out debris from this past fall and winter, and pulling up the weeds that have already begun to grow in the fertile soil. Those weeds just sort of creep in, but can quickly take over the soil that's waiting to receive the starts and seeds that will deliver our harvest. I cleaned up three of the raised beds, and will soon get to the rest of them. It takes time and constant attention to keep weeds from winning...

Life is the garden in which we grow the crops we'll bring to God's table when He calls us home. With our free will, we can fertilize and cultivate that garden, or we can let weeds and debris overtake it and choke out our harvest.

Scripture is God's handbook on how to plant and fertilize our gardens. Prayer and grace provide the nourishment to enable our crops to grow. And God's love — evidenced through the sacrifice of His Son on the Cross at Calvary — is the sunlight that makes it all possible.

It's up to us to do our part. It begins with accepting Christ as our Savior, and by choosing to cultivate crops that will be pleasing to God when we're called to our final harvest. Never forget that there is one who comes in the night, sowing weeds and seeking to ruin our harvest. Those weeds start as small seeds — temptations — and without consciously attending to them, they will grow and overtake our lives. They come in many shapes and sizes, and they will clutter our lives and choke our harvest unless we tear them out by the roots — all of them, every time they sprout.

It's that time of year again — time for spring cleanup — in the garden outside, and in the garden of our lives. Prepare your soil, and choose your seeds carefully. Keep watch every day for the weeds that will try to overtake your life. And tear them out by the roots.

Happy gardening.
Bob

. . . . . .

April 30, 2017

> "...My soul is feasted as with marrow and fat, and my mouth praises thee with joyful lips, when I think of thee upon my bed and meditate on thee in the watches of the night; for thou hast been my help, and in the shadow of thy wings I sing for joy. My soul clings to thee; thy right hand upholds me..." *(Psalm 63)*

The trake incision is healing quickly, and Chrissy's journey continues in a positive direction. We continue to wait, watch and pray: "Jesus, Lord, please wake her up." Today, after Mass, I'll be making my usual Sunday morning drive south to Spaulding to be with her today, tonight and part of tomorrow. This afternoon, I'll be wheeling her down to the auditorium for her own private piano recital. It's been said that "Music is the language of the soul." I agree, and today, for the first time since Jan. 18th, I will play for her. :-)

Yesterday we hand-washed Chrissy's car, and while doing so, we left the keys in the ignition. When we opened the driver-side door, the car's warning and caution system lit up like a Christmas tree, and we were serenaded by its assorted bells and chimes, installed to alert us to systems problems in the car.

In modern jet aircraft, we have very complex caution and warning systems to monitor everything on the aircraft — flaps, landing gear, engine operating parameters, airspeed, altitude, door position, pressurization, smoke, fire, hydraulics, fuel systems, oxygen levels — the list is exhaustive. It's exhaustive because the consequences of a system failure at Mach .86 and 40,000 feet can be catastrophic. Careful attention is given to engineering these caution and warning systems so that pilots are made aware of problems before they become catastrophic. Then, millions of dollars are spent training to recognize, respond, and deliver safe outcomes for any problem that may arise.

As we reflect this day, Sunday, it might be a good idea to check our own spiritual "Master Caution and Warning System." If it's not in good repair, it can't alert us to the spiritual and moral dangers which abound in the hazard-riddled environment of today's secular world. If we're unable to discern the presence of evil, it's much more likely that we'll fall victim to it. Reading and meditating on the Word of God, and sharing it with those we meet, develop, maintain and strengthen our ability to discern and reject evil on life's journey.

If airlines spend millions to protect our lives in getting us safely from New York to Shanghai, how much more is it worth for us to install and maintain our spiritual Warning and Caution Systems to protect our souls on the trip from here to eternity?

Happy Sunday!
Bob

. . . . . .

May 2, 2017

> "...Oh send out thy light and thy truth; let them lead me, let them bring me to thy holy hill and to thy dwelling! Then I will go to the altar of God, to God my exceeding joy; and I will praise thee with the lyre, O God my God..." (Psalm 43)

THE POSTS

Yesterday, the rehab doctor advised that the neurologist reduced Chrissy's dosage of the "wake-up drug," amantadine, because of its side effects. She was having almost-continuous muscle spasms in her arms, legs and feet. And because her overall progress isn't what it should be at this point in her rehab, she'll be visiting MGH this week for an MRI to help the neurosurgeons determine whether her brain stem was affected by the aneurysm. They'll also check whether the current setting on the adjustable shunt valve has reduced the subdural hygromas caused by over-sumping of the original shunt. We continue to wait, watch and pray.

Ups and downs are part of any recovery process, but knowing this doesn't make the "downs" any easier to deal with. I spent much of yesterday subconsciously rejecting the facts that I have, in search of "facts" that I want. The battle went on into the night, and finally, at 2:15AM this morning, unable to sleep, I picked up my Bible and read of the miracles Jesus performed while He was here on Earth — beautiful accounts of His compassion for the suffering. I also thought about the many miracles that have been performed in His name in the centuries following His Resurrection. Jesus showed us that our faith can unleash the healing power of His love.

God's love for us is the most powerful painkiller ever put at our disposal. It was purchased on Good Friday, and it's free for the taking. It calms our troubled souls, quiets our restless minds, and heals our broken hearts. And you'll never die of an overdose.

As I pondered the doctor's comments at Chrissy's bedside yesterday morning, I kept coming back to the amazing power of faith. If we truly believe, we can transform horror into beauty, fear into courage, anguish into joy, and death into life. We can transcend the worries of this world because we know what awaits us in the next.

After reading the Bible for about 15 minutes, I turned off the light and began silently reciting the 23rd Psalm in my mind. I never finished. Interestingly, the last thing I remember is "He restoreth my soul."

Next time a troubled heart or restless mind is keeping you awake, try this: take two Gospels and call me in the morning. And please remember that someone you meet today is needing this prescription.

So go forth and be God's pharmacist. ☺

Bob

. . . . . .

May 4, 2017

> "...Why are you cast down, O my soul, and why are you disquieted within me? Hope in God; for I shall again praise him, my help and my God." (Psalm 43)

Waiting for the MRI, and then waiting for its results. Waiting for her to awaken, and waiting to go on with life. Waiting, and watching, and praying. "Jesus, Lord, please wake her up."

Some days it stays dark even after the sun is up. It's about the questions, the ones we ask inside, the ones that can rip and rend and shred our souls.

It's about why I don't choke on the irony of it all, as the heart of our family can't move, but we can't stop. It's about the duality of time as the days drag on, one interminable second after another, but weeks and months fly by in a blur. It's about why I wait, but God doesn't wait, and the world doesn't wait, and do I wake up hating that we go forward but she does not? hating that every day, I open my eyes to the beauty of God's creation, and she opens her eyes to God only knows what?

Ask me how every single day I push aside a goblet of guilt to drink the water of life, while she eats and drinks through a tube. Ask me how I deal with the gut-wrenching unfairness of it all - to her, to the family, to what we hoped and dreamed our retirement would be, to what she deserved after almost 40 years of sacrifice.

Ask me, and I will tell you: I pray. Constantly.

We don't get to choose what life brings our way, but we do get to choose how we deal with it. I freely admit there are times when I'm alone that I have to consciously, and sometimes even verbally repel horror, doubt and despair. So I reach for God in the darkness, and He's always there.

Faith enables us to gain the upper hand in battle. "There are no atheists in foxholes," and that includes the spiritual war for our souls. Prayer strengthens our faith, and our faith enables us to conquer adversity and become who God wants us to be. Yes, it's sometimes really hard to see God's will amid this firestorm. But He is here walking with me as if in a modern-day version of Daniel in the furnace. I invited Him into the fire, and He is here.

"Come to Me, all ye who labor and are heavy burdened, and I will give you rest."

As Spring slowly frees us from the last desperate clutches of winter, life begins anew as all creation awakens to the wondrous choreography of God's incredible ballet.

I think I'll join the celebration. Music, Maestro!

I am truly the luckiest man alive. ☺

With you in faith,

Bob

May 6, 2017

> *"...In your majesty ride forth victoriously for the cause of truth and to defend the right; let your right hand teach you dread deeds! Your arrows are sharp in the heart of the king's enemies; the peoples fall under you..." (Psalm 45)*

We should learn today if Chrissy can undergo an MRI so the team can get a better look at her brain stem. The doctors need very specific information about the size, shape and mass of the platinum coil used to block the aneurysm, because MRIs use a very strong magnetic field to map the affected area. Also, the opening in her throat where the trake had been is just about completely healed, with only a very small Band-aid over it now.

"Find your strength." That's Spaulding's motto, and it fits. It's incredible to watch them work, bringing people back to leading functional lives after devastating brain and spinal injuries. They are pushing patients to reach deep down inside and work harder than they probably ever have before.

Reaching deep is something most people never have to do. As a midshipman at the Naval Academy, and as a Marine, I learned how our military "helps" recruits learn just what they're capable of accomplishing by driving them to the limits of their strength and endurance. We make those who want to be Marines learn how much heart, grit, and determination they really have within. This is how we prepare to defeat the enemy.

As recruits go through the exhausting rigors of Basic Training, a new ethos develops, a fierce sense of loyalty to each other, much stronger than any other bond most of us ever experience. This ethos is the foundation of our warfighting capability. In the heat of battle, warriors aren't fighting for a nation. They are fighting for each other. Imagine a world where people fight for each other rather than for themselves; where helping the others in our "unit" survive and succeed becomes our driving raison d'etre.

In the spiritual battles of life, our training will ultimately determine whether we defeat the enemy. We owe it to ourselves, our families, and the world to keep our swords sharp, our shields strong and our faith resilient as we pursue victory. Whether physically, intellectually, financially, professionally, or spiritually, it's imperative that we constantly train to win — in this life and the next.

Semper Fidelis.

See you in the gym.

Bob

. . . . . .

May 8, 2017

> "...Gracious is the Lord, and righteous; our God is merciful. The Lord protects the simple; when I was brought low, he saved me. Return, O my soul, to your rest, for the Lord has dealt bountifully with you..." (Psalm 116)

The MRI has been scheduled for May 9, and we hope to learn more about the road ahead from the results. We're not sure what the news will be, but we'll accept it and move on in faith. The scab from the trake is about the size of a pencil eraser, and should be completely healed in a few more days. She's having muscle spasms from her neck to her toes, mostly on her right side — a side effect of Amantadine (wake-up drug), so the dosage has been reduced. Her eyes are open much more, and we're now waiting for her to start making conscious responses to requests and commands

Yesterday (Sunday), I sat with Chris and talked with her. We went to a Sunday-afternoon music hour in the auditorium, and afterwards, I played the piano for her. I rode her around in her wheelchair, and I read to her, (Hope Heals, by Katherine and Jay Wolf). And we looked outside at the incredible beauty of Nature, as the Earth dons the trappings of Spring, and life begins anew.

I prayed for her (Jesus, Lord, please wake her up.).

And I prayed with her.

Our Father, Who art in Heaven, — You are my God, and you've created for me a place of indescribable beauty, peace and perfection, which can be my eternal home if I follow your Law.

Hallowed be Thy name. — Even though I'm far from perfect, I still pray to you and speak your holy name. May I always use it with awe and reverence, for you are the Author of All Life.

Thy kingdom come. — I look forward to the day when the trials of this life are replaced by the perfect peace of Heaven.

Thy will be done on Earth, as it is in Heaven. — I'll try to act as You would have me act, in everything I say and do, towards all whose lives I touch today. I'll seek your will today, and every day.

Give us this day our daily bread, — Help me take care of those in my charge, at home and at work. Please provide us with food to nourish our bodies and grace to nourish our souls.

And forgive us our trespasses, as we forgive those who trespass against us. — Help me bear witness to your New Covenant, knowing that forgiveness, not retribution, is the road I must travel to get to Heaven. Help me be deserving of salvation, which was only made possible by the death and Resurrection of your Son, Jesus.

And lead us not into temptation, but deliver us from evil. — Help me to recognize and avoid the dangers of sin, that I may avoid spiritual death, and gain eternal life with you in Heaven.

Amen.
So be it.

For thine is the Kingdom, the Power, and the Glory, now and forever...

Bob

· · · · · ·

May 11, 2017

"I waited patiently for the Lord; he inclined to me and heard my cry. He drew me up from the desolate pit, out of the miry bog, and set my feet upon a rock, making my steps secure. He put a new song in my mouth, a song of praise to our God. Many will see and fear, and put their trust in the Lord..." (Psalm 40)

It is with a joyful heart that I share with you that the results of the MRI were precisely what we were praying for. Chrissy's brain stem is totally intact, the new shunt valve is working exactly as planned, and the subdural hygromas are shrinking. Her dosage of Amantadine has been reduced again, and though she is still vegetative, she is much more "awake" — her eyes open for longer periods, and her muscle tone is improving slowly as the drug-caused spasms are diminishing.

Waiting for the MRI results wasn't easy. The constant uncertainty wore on us, and when it began to color my world, I looked up and handed my fear up to Him, and reaffirmed that He's got this.

We push back against fear and dread with faith. Whenever confronting our uncertainty, we only need to look at where we started, and where Chris is today, and we can only smile. We put our trust in Almighty God, because He's the only One who can deliver the outcome for which we continue to pray: "Jesus, Lord, please wake her up."

The tug-of-war between hope and fear is something we all face at some point in our lives. Whether we win that contest reflects our faith; it reflects the degree to which we can supplant our human inclinations with the grace that comes from the Holy Spirit. As Pentecost nears, recall that the disciples were in hiding after the death and Resurrection of Our Lord, gathered in a room, confused, concerned and afraid. When the Holy Spirit descended (tongues of fire on their heads), they immediately began to preach, each in his own native tongue, and the people understood what they were saying, and began to convert to the New Law: "Thou shalt love the Lord thy God with thy whole heart, and thy whole mind, and thy whole soul, and thy whole strength; and thy neighbor as thyself."

I feel renewed and refreshed this morning, as the love of God for Christine vanquishes our fear and our doubt. When God said, "I will be your God, and you will be my people," He offered us the best deal in the world.

BELIEVE.
SURRENDER.
SEE.

GROW.
WITNESS.
REJOICE.

How incredibly lucky we are to have the framework of our faith as the context for what we see! Almost 4 months ago, our wife, mother, and friend was supposed to die. Today, she continues to gain ground as we pray for her to return to fullness of life, and she fights to return to fullness of life, and God brings her closer to fullness of life.

So today, please pray with me in thanksgiving. We dialed 9-1-1, and God responded to our call. I got on my knees this morning, and looked at the Crucifix on our wall, remembered where we were on January 18th and where we are today, and just nodded my head in affirmation, because no words can express the gratitude in my heart. Who can doubt God's power, majesty and love: for Christine, for our family, and for each of us who continue to believe in miracles? Because we are watching one happen right in front of our eyes, one day at a time. That miracle may bring Chris back to us, or it may bring her home to Heaven. But for right now, I know what my eyes see, and my ears hear, and what it means: "Now faith is the substance of things hoped for, the evidence of things unseen."

I love God. I know He has a plan, and it's not mine to know, but I trust Him.

Some would call it a leap of faith.

And I'd reply, "You bet your life it is!"

Have a SPECTACULAR day. ☺

Bob

· · · · · ·

May 14, 2017
"...We have thought on they steadfast love, O God, in the midst of thy temple. As thy name, O God, so thy praise reaches to the ends of the earth..." (Psalm 48)

The MDs have reduced the Amantadine dose to the minimum, as Chris seems more awake, though still not conscious or aware of her surroundings. Her eyes are open more, but she can't yet see. We remain resolute in our belief that God is working a miracle when we compare where we were Jan. 18th and where we are now. We reinforce that belief with prayer.

Praying is the easy part. What's much harder is accepting and living the paradox that although we continue to live, our lives have no direction, because we wait and watch. Life revolves around trying to make sure one of us visits with her every day — a major factor in recovery, as the sound and presence of loved ones is cited as essential by every survivor of this type of brain injury.

No matter what I do, what I say, or where I go, Chris is the priority in my life. The paradox is that she is not here, but the circumstances of her absence color everything. I am trying to get to a place that allows me to accept that it's ok to do things, to enjoy recreation, to continue to live life without her, even though she's not here. Except that she is here. So how do I wait, while continuing to live? I am able to wait because I believe she will be back, and I will wrestle this dichotomy of living-while-waiting until God completes His miracle. 😊

Today is the one day each year we set aside to honor our Moms. It's a day that means the world to Christine, because she loved our kids without reservation or condition, and gave everything she could to nurture them and raise them up to be loving, caring, responsible participants in life. She sacrificed, as all good mothers do, without complaint, because she understood that children are a gift from God, and we as parents are the stewards of those gifts. Nothing — and I do mean nothing — came between her and her sense of obligation as a mother. Thank you, Chrissy, for being the mother you were and the mother you are. Thanks also to my Mom, for the love and the lessons you shared which put me on track to achieve my successes in life. Thanks especially for the single most important gift of all — my faith.

How much our mothers have done for us! How they loved us, and cared for us, and feared for us, and taught us, and hoped for us, and worried about us, and encouraged us, and coached us, and disciplined us, and sacrificed for us. We should be celebrating the vocation of motherhood every day!

After the shepherds had visited the stable and shared what the angel had told them, and everyone was trying to figure out what was going on with this Child in a manger, Luke wrote, "And Mary kept all these things, pondering them in her heart."

Today is the day we get to reflect on the wonderful role God gave the mothers in our lives.

Today, we get to keep these things, and ponder them in OUR hearts.

Honor (thy father and) thy mother. You'll be glad you did.
Bob

. . . . . .

May 17, 2017

"...Have you not known? Have you not heard? The Lord is the everlasting God, the Creator of the ends of the earth. He does not faint or grow weary, his

> *understanding is unsearchable. He gives power to the faint, and to him who has no might he increases strength. Even youths shall faint and be weary, and young men shall fall exhausted; but they who wait for the Lord shall renew their strength, they shall mount up with wings like eagles, they shall run and not be weary, they shall walk and not faint..." (Isaiah 40:28-31)*

Yesterday, one of the RNs told Lauren that when entering the room, she called out to Chris, and Chris turned her head and looked at her. Chris is still not conscious, but she is increasingly more "awake." They're using a cool mist vaporizer to prevent her mouth from getting coated by oral secretions because she's a "mouth breather." And they're aggressively treating a very small sore which we're watching very closely to make sure it's healing. She had a light physical therapy session, and is still non-responsive. Her eyes are open for longer periods of time, though she's not seeing anything as far as we can tell. Jesus, Lord, please wake her up.

Four months ago, on January 18th, our lives changed forever in a way we never imagined. Since then, we've been together, and through faith and prayer — yours and ours — we've made it to this day. Chris wasn't supposed to survive. The doctors and nurses and aides worked hard, Chrissy fought hard, and we prayed hard, all day, every day. God heard and answered. It was our faith that got us to where we are today, and it is our faith that will guide the remainder of this this journey, no matter where it takes us.

This day, our daughter Lauren, who flew in with her husband, Derry, from Seattle on the night of Chrissy's hemorrhage, will be flying back home. Both she and Derry have been heroic in their commitment to caring for Chris, as she took humanitarian drops from her college courses and used all her FMLA leave and personal vacation days so she could be here, caring and advocating for Chris and helping us at home with all the tasks involved in everyday life. Derry returned to Seattle after about a week and has been working overtime to cover their bills. He has managed to fly back to NH twice to visit and help as he is able. "Thank you" doesn't even come close.

There is a great deal of sorrow in Lauren's heart as she returns to Seattle after being close to her Mom and to us for the past 4 months, even as there is joy because she is returning to her home, to her pets, and to the person she loves most in the world. Derry, thank you for being the quiet hero, doing what needed to be done so Lauren could be here to help. To Lauren, thank you for your unhesitating advocacy for Mom, whose condition and recovery have benefited greatly because you were here paying close attention to every detail of her care. I know your heart aches because you won't be here, close to Mom, close to us, and keeping close watch over things. Mom knows you were here, and that you continue to pray with us, even as the business of life calls you away. You helped keep things going in our home, and stood ever vigilant at Mom's bedside. Please remember that there is always sunshine above the clouds, that I (and all of us) love you both beyond what words can convey. I could not be more grateful for your presence during this tempest.

To Stephanie and Hunter, you have stayed the course and risen to the daunting challenges Mom's situation has presented, even as you deal with the challenges in your life and the questions about what our tomorrows will bring. I have been amazed at the patience of a 7-year-old who has spent many days in a hospital room with his Yaya, never complaining, but always watching and trying to understand what has happened, asking questions and sharing thoughts and feelings that at times amaze us. Do not fear, there is nothing we cannot overcome so long as we keep sight of God's presence and seek to do His will every day. He has always provided, sometimes in ways that took us by surprise. But He always does, and always will. You have traveled faithfully, every day at first, and then every week as Mom's situation changed, to help make sure that one of us was with her every single day, with very few exceptions.

Joseph and Naomi, you gave up a very large part of your military leave, and you continue to give two days of your lives every week to keep Mom company at Spaulding — no trifling sacrifice as you continue your naval career. You put your Masters Degree on hold so you could help carry the burden. I know it, and I'm sure Mom knows it too. Your steadiness under pressure has bolstered me more times than you know as we navigate our way towards Mom's recovery. Naomi — your insights into what Chris likes and needs to speed her recovery are both wonderful and deeply appreciated.

To each of you, I offer the following. When we first arrived in NH 21 years ago, we sat down as a family, designed a family crest, and decided on a family credo. With few exceptions, you have each shown forth the values that Mom worked so hard to teach you. I know that you have made her heart glad, as you have made mine glad, in the way you came together to face the fear and uncertainty this situation brought upon us, and that come with each new day. It is our faith that enables us to deal with the ups and downs in this life, and my prayer for each of you as we continue forward in our individual and collective journeys, is that you will always know that God is with you, that as much as Mom and I love you, He loves you more, and that He is always here with us as we wait, watch and pray.

With all the love a dad could possibly muster, I thank each of you for the Compassion, Commitment and Courage you have shown to Mom, to me, and to one another. You will face other tragedies and storms in your lives. But none of them can withstand the power of prayer and the strength of God's infinite love for us. Remember — there's always sunshine above the clouds. ☺

I am truly the luckiest man alive.

dad

. . . . . .

May 27, 2017

> "...I am the Lord, that is my name; my glory I give to no other, nor my praise to graven images. Behold, the former things have come to pass, and new things I now declare; before they spring forth I tell you of them..." (Isaiah 42:8-9)

Our Family Conference at Spaulding took place Thursday, May 25th, at 1pm. It was everything we hoped it wouldn't be. To sum it up, the medical/physiological assessment is that Chris has pretty much reached the highest level she is going to attain, and that further treatment will not produce any better outcome. She is, and will remain, in a vegetative state, and will require 24-hour complete care for the rest of her life. We left the conference room, and spent the next 9 hours with Chris, talking to her, playing her favorite music, praying, and just being with her.

I'd be less than honest if I didn't say that the initial impact of the team's assessment was crushing. It colored everything in my world for the next two days. Yesterday (Friday), after some committee work at the State House, I visited a residential assisted living facility especially founded for brain and spinal injury patients. The difference between it and Spaulding is that Spaulding maintains doctors on staff; this facility does not (but they're not far away.) They will develop a comprehensive PT, OT and ST regimen for Chris, and will actually engage her in more physical activity than Spaulding to stimulate her cognitive functions. It is a beautiful place, and we are readying ourselves to adapt to this new paradigm.

Dread, anger, sorrow and emptiness assail us at these times. We're human. But when viewed in the context of our faith, and by reflecting on the totality of this experience from its onset, a different outlook emerges. It is not imagined, and just as evolution and creationism can rationally coexist, so we remain resolute in our belief that Christine will recover.

We rejected the finality of the clinical assessment at DHMC, and we do so here. Chris IS opening her eyes more; she is occasionally turning her head in response to our voices and our touch; she is beginning to make sounds as though trying to speak — all this after we were told very early on that she would likely not survive.

DHMC was wrong, and Spaulding is wrong. In both cases, their assessments were based purely on physiological tests and conclusions. But we are so much more than physiological beings. We have hearts, and we have souls. And Chrissy has an amazing amount of both. God will be the One who makes the final call. Until that time, I am trusting in Him, and praying to Him, and allowing Him to continue to work His miracle.

"Now faith is the substance of things hoped for, the evidence of things unseen."

I remain resolute in my faith, and I ask you to remain resolute in your prayers. Chris needs them, and we need them.

Because "our God is an awesome God." And we're not done until He says we're done. ☺

Have a SPECTACULAR day.

Bob

. . . . . .

June 1, 2017

> "Love is patient, love is kind. It does not envy, it does not boast, it is not proud. It does not dishonor others, it is not self-seeking, it is not easily angered, it keeps no record of wrongs. Love does not delight in evil but rejoices with the truth. It always protects, always trusts, always hopes, always perseveres." (1 Corinthians 13:4-7)

Chris remains comfortable and resting. I left her Sunday evening, and though we haven't been able to visit her this week, I'm smiling. Because tomorrow, June 2, we'll be with her to celebrate her birthday. ☺

As I think about what she means to me, what she has done for me, what she has given up for me for 35+ years, I think of the times when I "coulda/shoulda/woulda" and remember things that diverted my time and attention away from the most important person in my life. So men, as you balance the business of life with the business of eternity, here's something to think about.

Do you know what you have? Do you KNOW what you have? Do you know how much God loves you? Do you not see it in the one He created to be with you, to share your hopes and dreams, to laugh with you, and to cry with you? To trudge with you across life's deserts and to dance with you at life's banquets?

Do you see her dreams when you look into her eyes? Do you understand that those eyes look up to you to be her hero? Do you understand how sacred the trust she has placed in you, the gentle, special, beautiful tabernacle of her heart which she has asked you to love, honor and cherish? Do you understand the sacred, precious, created-by-God-for-you-alone gift of her life which she has put in your hands, to deliver to the end of your shared time on Earth intact, complete, and heaven-bound?

Do you KNOW what you HAVE? Because if you don't see God's love in giving her to you, and if you don't treat her as the most precious gift you will ever receive, you are missing the mark, and may one day know sorrow and regret beyond the reach of words.

Love her. LOVE HER. Make her the most important thing in your life. Because if she isn't, then you're failing in the most important job you will ever have. No matter wealth or power or prestige, if you lose her heart, you lose your soul.

Love her.

Because GOD made HER for YOU. And your job is to make sure she knows it - every single day of your life.

Bob

. . . . . .

June 2, 2017

"But Ruth said, 'Entreat me not to leave you or to return from following you; for where you go, I

THE POSTS

> *will go, and where you lodge, I will lodge; your people shall be my people, and your God my God; where you die I will die, and there will I be buried. May the Lord do so to me and more also if even death parts me from you.'" (Ruth 1:16-17)*

(This Bible verse really isn't about husband and wife, but it is all about love and loyalty. So I took some "poetic license" and used it as the prelude to this post, because it embodies the love and loyalty of the most beautiful girl I ever met. ☺)

Friday afternoon, September 14, 1979, we met at the Back East Deli in Oak Harbor, WA, through the unlikely combination of music, friends, laughter and a meatball sub. We talked, danced, laughed, and at the end of the evening, drove over to your apartment. We spent the night together, but not the way some might think during those wild and crazy days. No, instead, we sat on the floor of your apartment, at opposite ends of the coffee table, cross-legged, and talked and laughed until 7 the next morning. We were young, and in the prime of our lives, and the world was our oyster. And there was something about you...

I remember being with you when the US beat the USSR in the 1980 Olympics. We were at the Officer's Club at NAS Whidbey Island, and the CO had ordered all hands to the bar to watch the game. I remember you walking a very inebriated Marine instructor pilot back to his BOQ room, and taking off my shoes after I crashed and burned on my bed. What a day that was! The world couldn't believe that Mike Eruzione and the amateur US Olympic hockey team had beaten the much-favored Russian professionals. And there was something about you...

THE POSTS

    I remember flying you out to Roche Harbor and Friday Harbor for lunch while we were courting; kicking back at the San Juan Jazz Festival; watching them filming "An Officer and A Gentleman" at Whidbey Island, with my Marine Corps flight students as extras. Then there was the drive from Whidbey Island to Eugene to meet your Mom and Dad, and asking him - a truly wonderful loving father and husband — if I could marry you, and him giving me his blessing. I remember changing the air filter every 40 miles or so as we drove your baby-blue Mustang up and down I-5 through the volcanic ash from Mt. Saint Helens. And there was something about you...

    I remember you and Jo, and Tom Mushyn and I, spending the weekend at your place on Queen Anne Hill in Seattle, a weekend of nothing but lasagna, manicotti, and Italian bread. I remember driving back to Whidbey Island at 4am that Monday morning with a pan of each in the back seat of my Datsun, and having it for dinner for the next 3 days. I remember flying the rented airplane from Oak Harbor to Eugene to be married, standing near the altar, best man at my side, and wondering who was that dazzlingly beautiful, petite, dark haired, blue-eyed girl dressed in white and walking down the aisle with your Dad, until I realized it was you, and we became husband and wife, and our journey began.

    I remember the Sunday morning a couple of months after we were married, and you were on Reserve weekend at the Naval Hospital at Whidbey Island, and I got the call from brother Bob that your Dad had died unexpectedly, and I drove to the hospital and told the doctor on duty, and took your hand and led you to an empty room and told you that he was gone to heaven. I remember holding you while you cried and wishing more than anything else in the world that I could bring him back to you and take the hurt away, and knowing that I couldn't. And there was something about you...

I remember the camping trip, and the day you told me we were pregnant with Joseph, and the awe and amazement when he was born; getting the news that I had been accepted into the FBI as a Special Agent, and the 16-week separation while I was at Quantico going through New Agents training, and getting our orders and moving to Denver.

I remember the day I came home to 4555 South Delaware in Englewood, and you were sitting on the couch with tears running down your beautiful face, and I asked why, and you said it was twins. I remember the burly OR nurse who invited me out of the delivery room when the girls were imminent and Stephanie's heartbeat was way down because the nurse wouldn't let you lay on your side even though you told her that's what you needed to do, and they were born, and our world was about double-feedings and diaper service because we couldn't afford all the Pampers they needed.

I remember leaving the FBI and flying the Jetstar 731 all over the world, and you at home with newborn twins and a 3-year-old son, and your Mom and Mary Pat coming to Broomfield to help while I was gone. And there was something about you...

I remember the day my Dad died, July 16th, 1986, and I was at the hospital with him, and you called me and told me that in the midst of sadness, you wanted me to know that United Airlines had just called and I had a class date of August 4th, and God gave me the incredible privilege of sharing the skies with angels and eagles for the next 31 years. And there was something about you...

THE POSTS

I could go on and on about the incredible journey you made possible, the joy you brought to my life and to our children, the things we did, the places we went, the sacrifices you made, Christmas presents, Stampin' Up, coloring Easter eggs, homeschooling, First Communions, Confirmations, the surprise Valentine's day trip to Paris, our walks on the beach in Kauai, Maui, Washington, Oregon, Newport, Puerto Rico, the trips to Disney with the kids, Eagle Crest, our sailboat excursions in the Pacific Northwest, skiing, snowboarding, moving from Whidbey Island to Eugene to Denver to Tacoma to Warren, a frozen Niagara Falls, steaming with Joseph on CG-52 from Pearl Harbor to San Diego, and so, so much more. The tapestry of life we wove together is a story of life rich beyond measure, because you made it all possible.

Christine Michele, through it all, every single minute of every single day, through thick and thin, ups and downs, sadness and joy, darkness and light, there was always something about you.

And there always will be. Always and forever.

I love you, Mrs. G.

Happy birthday. ☺

Bob

. . . . . .

June 5, 2017

> *"...And now my soul is poured out within me; days of affliction have taken hold of me. The night racks my bones, and the pain that gnaws me takes no rest..." (Job 30:16-17)*

The last two times I've gone to visit Chris at Spaulding, when I walked into her room, her eyes have been wide open — as wide as is possible. I am positive that, although still blind, she's trying to see. One by one, small indications of new brain activity seem to be manifesting themselves. Today, people from the assisted living facility are coming to Cambridge to evaluate Chris as a potential resident. I am irreversibly committed to continuing her PT, OT and ST so long as any signs of improvement, however small or seemingly inconsequential, continue.

Sleep has been difficult lately. The swirling undercurrent of questions I don't want to ask and answers I don't want to entertain keeps my mind in high gear as I wrestle with them. Sheer exhaustion usually wins out; but the result isn't generally the kind of good rest I need.

I shared my battle against fatigue with one of the CNAs taking care of Chris. She is a very compassionate lady, an immigrant from a place where not too long ago, men armed with machetes and driven by hatred almost wiped out an entire civilization while the world stood idly by. This woman knows God. And she knows, too, the swirling undercurrents that drown you with wakefulness and rob you of rest.

She knows.

She knows the darkness, but she is at peace, because through it, she found The Light. It emanates from her like a lighthouse beacon for beleaguered ships in a pitch-black night on a storm-tossed sea. Her bright, beautiful, quiet smile lights up the room as she cares for Chris with love like a mother for a child.

She knows.

As I told her of my weariness, she gazed at me, touched my arm and said softly, "You must give your struggle to God so you can rest. You see, you have a watch. But God has the time."

Peace be with you. Sleep tight. Tonight, and every night for the rest of your life.

And don't worry about the time. 🙂

Bob

. . . . . .

June 10, 2017

"...Fear not, for I have redeemed you; I have called your name, you are mine. When you pass through the waters I will be with you; and through the rivers, they shall not overwhelm you; when you walk through fire you shall not be burned, and the flame shall not consume you. For I am the Lord your God, the Holy One of Israel, your Savior..." (Isaiah 43: 1-3)

Twice over the past week or so, Chris has vomited from the presence of secretions in her throat. Both times, she managed to clear her airway without aspirating anything. (Aspiration brings with it the threat of pneumonia.) Other than that, there's been no significant change in her condition, as we wait for a bed to open at the assisted living facility we have chosen. Sadly, this will happen when one of their current residents dies. This is a real person with a real family in the last stages of hospice care. Please pray for this person, for the family, and for the hospice team which is with them in the final days of life's journey. May God's peace descend upon them and remain with them forever.

For the past month, I have been fighting: fighting Chrissy's condition, fighting our situation, fighting myself, and fighting the inexorable process that is leading us towards a possibility I do not want to admit, and a decision I don't want to have to make.

Christine's life, while God's to give and to receive, is now in my hands. She entrusted to me the right to decide, in the event she was not conscious, when the quality of her life has reached the point that it's time to allow her to die with dignity, with certain faith-based conditions.

My incredible life partner trusted me to care for her "for better or for worse, for richer or for poorer, in sickness and in health, until death do us part." I never once thought it might entail having to decide for her when her life should end. But that thought is my constant companion now; it never goes away. I thank God every day for her faith and mine, for Scripture, and for the privilege of approaching Him in prayer for wisdom, strength and guidance as our journey continues.

If we one day have to make that decision, we'll frame it in our faith and make it as a family, because Chris always put our family first, often without notice or thanks. Possible future decisions notwithstanding, we remain resolute in our prayer, "Jesus, Lord, please wake her up." And we continue to see signs, however tiny, that her brain is working to find its way back to consciousness.

Life's distractions can obscure God's intended purpose for us. Husbands and wives, please dedicate time, every single day, to reverence the level of trust you place in one other. Do it together. Reaffirm the love you professed at the altar and the faith with which you professed it. Understand that your marriage is a sacrament, sworn before God, friends and family; a pledge to live a virtuous life and to sustain the God-given model for human happiness. Introduce the element of "awe" into your relationship. Because our God is an awesome God, and your marriage is an awesome sacrament.

In everything that happens to us or because of us, we're called to manifest our trust in Almighty God. What better way to do so than to humbly acknowledge and prayerfully reaffirm, together, reverence and gratitude for entrusting your lives to one another?

Do it! Don't let distractions steal time, energy, life, or joy from your sacrament.

Believe.

Surrender.

See.

Grow.

Witness.

Rejoice.

"For I am with you, even unto the end of time."

Bob

. . . . . .

June 16, 2017

> "...Trust in the Lord with all your heart, and do not rely on your own insight. In all your ways acknowledge Him, and He will make straight your paths. Be not wise in your own eyes; fear the Lord, and turn away from evil. It will be healing to your flesh and refreshment to your bones..." (Psalm 3)

Chris remains physically stable, with little change to her neurological condition. We continue to stand beside her, strong in our faith, but also mindful that we are entering month 6 as we continue to pray for more significant neurological improvement. She remains at Spaulding for now, due to an acute shortage of facilities and beds for severely brain-injured patients. Our efforts are being assisted by an independent case manager who knows the "ins and outs" of state and federal regulations (there are many) and the options available to us. We are deeply grateful for her help and her friendship.

"Life is what happens to your plans." My Dad shared these words with me many years ago before his passing, and as I look back at what has happened to Chris and at the many detours and changes that brought us to where we are, those words certainly ring as true as ever.

Chrissy's affliction is the most difficult challenge our family has ever faced. It has tried our patience, tested our stamina, and measured our faith. And it will continue to do so with each passing day, as we pray for God's hand to bring her back to life, but begin to acknowledge that God's way of "waking her up" might not be temporal but eternal.

Our acceptance of life's challenges is put to the test by their severity. It's easy to sing with a joyful heart when things are running smoothly; it becomes more difficult as the severity of the trial increases. Sometimes, it's hard to "sing a joyful song unto the Lord," but that's what we're called to do.

Does God "will" misfortune to enter our lives? I don't think so. What happened to Chris, and what happens to each of us, is known to God before it ever occurs. But God doesn't cause it to happen. It happens as a natural consequence of our physical existence. Whether it's a brain hemorrhage, or an auto accident, or a fall in a bathtub, it is a natural consequence of life on Earth and the temporal nature of our physical bodies. It is our love of God, and His love for us, that enable us to transcend grief, misfortune and catastrophe as we continue our journey towards eternity.

How did Jesus maintain His love of the Father throughout His ordeal at Calvary? (1) Knowledge of Scripture, (2) intense prayer, and (3) understanding His role in God's plan for the salvation of mankind. He knew what had been prophesied, and that He is the Lamb of God, chosen to suffer and die as the necessary precursor to the Resurrection that's the foundation of Christian belief.

These same three elements that empowered Jesus Christ to willingly accept death on the Cross show us how we, too, can walk peacefully "through the valley of the shadow of death."

When fear and doubt begin to weigh me down, I read the Bible, immerse myself in prayer, and search for a way to use what has befallen us to advance God's kingdom. I know that God didn't "will" this to happen to Chris or to us. But I do know that He expects me to use it to bring us all closer to Him. And therein lies the road to "the peace that surpasses all human understanding."

So... Take spiritual nourishment from Scripture. Pray fervently to the Father to find our way forward. And learn to love God in everything we do, no matter what.

Or, said another way, "Eat. Pray. Love." ☺

God bless you today and every day of your life.

Bob

. . . . . .

June 18, 2017

> *"...Your wife will be like a fruitful vine within your house; your children will be like olive shoots around your table. Lo, thus shall the man be blessed who fears the Lord..." (Psalm 128)*

No report on Chris today, as I haven't yet left to visit her. But Joseph and Naomi were with her yesterday, and report that she is resting quietly, with no notable change to her condition. We continue to pray...

Wide awake at 3:20AM, thinking about the gift of fatherhood, and praying in the quiet predawn darkness. Prayers of thanksgiving. Prayers for Christine. Prayers for our children. Father's Day. Sunday, appropriately. Today is, first, the day we set aside to worship God. And then, this Sunday, it's the day we choose to remember and honor our dads.

Thank you, God for giving us three unique, beautiful, amazing, purposely-created-by-You-to-fulfill-Your-purpose-on-Earth children; children we coached and guided and taught and disciplined and loved without condition or measure; three gifts from Heaven, placed into our lives and entrusted to us to prepare for this life, and for eternity. We are rich beyond measure...

Chrissy... sitting next to your hospital bed, grateful that you made me a dad. Knowing that you made it all possible, and needing you to know that I know. Gazing at you, silent and still, the heart of our family. Knowing the amazing, multi-tasking, patient, tolerant, caring, selfless, protective, loving person you are, and realizing how much you taught me about being a dad because you are such an incredible Mom. Thinking about the incredible tapestry of the family you made possible, woven with loving hands and patient heart. All this I see, all this I know, hoping you know it too, lying there in the warm embrace of God's love and the love of the family you created and shaped...

Thinking about what I want you kids to know, the trials and treasures of being a dad, things I might have done differently, or not at all, and things I should have done but didn't. Proud and humble at the same time, because God let me be your knight in shining armor, the guy who made it all ok, who ran beside you and finally let go of the bike the first time you actually rode it without training wheels, the guy who will always be here as long as I have breath in my body to push you to try, to cheer when you win, to pick you up when you fall, and to love you no matter what...

With all the love in my heart, I thank you, Chrissy, and Joseph, and Lauren, and Stephanie, and grandson Hunter.

I am the luckiest man in the world, because God gave you to me, and me to you.

Dad

. . . . . .

June 24, 2017

"I cry aloud to God, aloud to God, that he may hear me. In the day of my trouble I seek the Lord; in the night my hand is stretched out without wearying; my soul refuses to be comforted..." (Psalm 77)

There continues to be no material change to Chrissy's condition, and Spaulding has shared with us that it's time to move on to the next phase of her life. We are now engaging fundamental questions of life and faith, and will soon be making decisions appropriate to the situation we face. Please keep us in your prayers. We need them.

I'm awake very early, sitting in the dark and thinking about the many small ways Chrissy said "I love you" every day without ever saying a word. It was the way she "shrugged" into my arms when I walked up behind her and put my arms around her in the kitchen. It was her feigned protest when, hot and sweaty from an early morning workout, I would pretend I was going to hug her. It was her saving me the mixing bowl with the remains of the chocolate cake batter — "the lick" — rather than putting it in the dishwasher. It was our "going to work" ritual, established over decades of leaving home to fly my trips; looks and gestures that sent the message, "I love you," without every saying a word.

As love matures, the rigors of everyday life can diminish the brightness of its flame. Little things we do in the early stages of our marriage fade into a collage of daily activities. Work, children, school, chores, and "the business of life" can lead us to overlook making these small manifestations of love for one another, or to not see them in the course of everyday living.

But it's these small things that elevate the nature, deepen the meaning, and provide much-needed nurturing of our relationships. Though unspoken, they refresh and enhance the physical, emotional and spiritual communication that silently convey the message, "I love you."

Repeated actions become habits, and habits do not require conscious thought. Manifesting your love should never become a habit, because God didn't give you a habit, he gave you a unique life partner and joined you together under the sacred seal of matrimony. He picked the two of you to spend life on Earth together as husband and wife, to bear and rear children, and thereby to affirm the structure He ordained as the model for mankind. Your spouse and your family are gifts from God.

Chrissy can't do those little things any more. But her love isn't diminished, only silent. For who she is and how she loves me will never change. I carry these incredible gifts with me for life, contained in part in the many cards, notes and treasures she created from the love in her heart, and etched forever in the countless memories of our shared time together.

Live your life together so that the tears you shed when it ends are tears of remembrance, not tears of regret. Pay attention to those "little things" and don't ever let a day go by that you don't do something conscious and concrete to manifest your love to your partner. Don't forget to give thanks to the God who gave you to each other.

From the 1960's movie Love Story, "Love means never having to say you're sorry."

Bob

. . . . . .

June 27, 2017

"...Strength and dignity are her clothing, and she laughs at the time to come. She opens her mouth with wisdom, and the teaching of kindness is on her tongue. She looks well to the ways of her household, and does not eat the bread of idleness. Her children rise up and call her blessed; her husband also, and he praises her: "Many women have done excellently, but you surpass them all." Charm is deceitful, and beauty is vain, but a woman who fears the Lord is to be praised. Give her the fruit of her hands, and let her works praise her in the gates." (Psalm 31)

I spent Sunday afternoon, night, and Monday morning at Spaulding with Chris. The team has discontinued PT and OT because they are not seeing any results from the therapy. They continue to administer range of motion exercises to combat the results of 5+ months of paralysis. Her face is as beautiful as ever, her eyes as blue as the day I fell in love with her. A sense of calm surrounds her.

For the past month, I've had a knot in my stomach as we face the next phase of our journey. The issues of life, quality of life, the definition of life, and whether to sustain or end life are now front and center. And they are now inescapable.

We are faced with the requirement, driven by Chrissy's lack of further progress in rehab, to move her out of Spaulding to an assisted living facility, a nursing home, or a hospice house.

For over a month, we've hoped that a bed would come open at an assisted living facility which serves acquired brain injury patients. I visited the facility, and it is perfectly suited to Chrissy's condition, but they have no beds available, and no idea when one might come open.

I visited several nursing homes, and they are not capable of delivering the level or quality of care that Chris requires. In the opinion of every case manager and elder care professional with whom I've spoken, it's almost a certainty that she would not survive a stay in a nursing home.

I visited a hospice house, and though beautifully appointed and furnished, and with very caring staff specializing in end-of-life care, placing her there would require that we stop artificial nutrition and hydration (food and water), causing her death within two weeks.

Hence the knot in my stomach.

Last Saturday, I called and spoke with my Pastor about life and death and faith and love and vows and family and church law and the conflicting emotions, facts and options confronting us. That night, we had a family conference call to discuss our options and their associated consequences. After two-and-a-half hours on the phone, we agreed to end the call, to think and to pray, and to conference again in a day or so.

Underlying our inability to reach consensus is our shared sense that it hasn't been long enough, that brain injuries require exceptionally long recovery times, that the neurologists had said it takes 3-6 months to even establish a "trajectory" — a projection of how long it might take, and how far her recovery might go. Accordingly, we are not in a rush to enact an irreversible decision to allow Chris to die. But neither are we going to senselessly prolong her life, within the constraints of her end-of-life wishes, hoping that something that just isn't happening might occur, despite opinions to the contrary from every medical professional involved in her treatment. Ultimately, it is up to me to decide when it's time to allow the process of dying to continue without interference, allowing our beloved wife, Momma, Yaya, and friend to join God and His angels in Heaven.

Sleep was very elusive Saturday night.

Driving to Mass Sunday morning, deep in thought about what we're facing, I neared our church and, out of the blue, a question popped into my head: "Why don't you bring her home?" After Communion, in a departure from the regular music program, again out of the blue, a young lady came forward, uncased her violin, and performed a breathtaking rendition of Pachelbel's Canon, accompanied by the church pianist. This piece of music holds a very special meaning for our family, and I saw it as spiritual affirmation of the decision to bring Chrissy home. There is no such thing as coincidence in matters of faith.

When Jesus left this world, He promised to send the Holy Spirit to guide us until He comes again in glory. Our faith cannot be complete unless we accept and believe that the Holy Spirit is alive, moving and working in the world today, and speaking to us if we have ears to hear. Sometimes it's a whisper, and sometimes it's a hurricane. Sunday, it was both.

When I got home, I called the kids and shared what had happened. They concurred with the decision to bring Chris home. I called Chrissy's Mom and next-youngest sister and shared the decision with them. Chris was a daughter and sister long before I came into her life.

We want to afford Chris some more time to allow us to know with certainty that her recovery isn't going to happen. In her present state, her skin and other organs will begin to break down, and her muscles, tendons and ligaments will atrophy. It's already happening. And because we know that absent a miracle, there is no good physiological outcome for a person in a persistent vegetative state, we continue to pray that God will restore her life.

I struggle every minute of every day with the gradually increasing likelihood that we will have to honor the provision of her living will. I have been blessed with 37+ years of incredible memories of our courtship and our marriage. I see the slender slip of a girl with a beautiful heart and ready smile who gave me her life, and said "Yes, I will," as I knelt on bended knee at Portofino's Restaurant in Coupeville, WA. I see her standing with me on the cliffs of Whidbey Island, marveling at the roiled waters of Deception Pass hundreds of feet below. I see the mother of our children, the heart of our family, the nurse who served Vietnam's wounded soldiers and Marines, who also wept for the babies and kids who didn't make it at Children's Hospital in Seattle. I see her in the delivery room, her face a picture of relief, joy and awe, holding the children she brought into the world. I see her homeschooling our kids, teaching Lamaze classes, weeping at the loss of a pet, agape at the surprise First Class seat from Dulles to Paris for a Valentine Day dinner in the Eiffel Tower. I see her quietly smiling as she shows me her latest Stampin' Up creation, each a beautiful tribute to her creativity and her generosity. I see her gazing at the Pacific sunset as we walk hand-in-hand on the beach in Kauai on our first trip to her favorite place in the world.

And I see her unbridled happiness during the family reunion at which we celebrated her birthday in Maui last summer.

This has so far been a struggle of enormous proportions, and every successive step in the journey brings more and deeper challenges to our lives, physically, emotionally, and spiritually. But the avalanche of prayer lifting us up and holding us close — your prayers from all over the world, and ours here at home — are helping us discern the path ahead, guided by our faith in God and sustained by our love for Christine and one another, and for every one of you who keep us in prayer.

And so, it is very fitting that today, I rededicate my life to that slender, beautiful slip of a girl who walked down the aisle with her Dad and gave her life to me in marriage 36 years ago, on June 27, 1981.

Christine Michele, you never stopped loving me, no matter what. And I'll never stop loving you.

Happy anniversary, Mrs. G.

Always and forever,

Bob

. . . . . .

July 5, 2017

"Now Moses was keeping the flock of his father-in-law, Jethro, the priest of Midian; and he led his flock to the west side of the wilderness, and came to Horeb, the mountain of God. And the angel of the Lord appeared to him in a flame of fire out of the midst of a bush; and he looked, and lo, the bush was burning yet it was not consumed. And Moses said, "I will turn aside and see this great sight, why the bush

is not burnt." When the Lord saw that he turned aside to see, God called to him out of the bush, "Moses, Moses!" And he said, "Here am I." (Exodus 3:1-7)

Chris is coming home on Friday. We've been busy setting up the home health care services (personal care service providers, visiting nurses, primary care physician, etc.) and purchasing as many of the supplies (pillows, linens, sterile wipes, towels, etc.) and prescription drugs that Medicare and our supplemental insurance won't cover. The cost of supplies is manageable, but the cost of the medications needed to keep her body healthy (while her brain finds its way) will be a challenge. God will provide.

We've cleaned and mopped and scrubbed and dusted and vacuumed her soon-to-be room, and are trying to catch up on our rest before she arrives, as we (our daughter Stephanie, grandson Hunter, and I) will be providing daily care as well. It will be a life-changing commitment.

During the past 4+ months, we've brought pictures, cards (many of them yours — thank you), and other items to Spaulding to decorate Chrissy's room so it feels more like home. This weekend we started boxing them up and bringing them home, as we prepare for the end of her hospital stay. We had gotten home late Monday night, and had decided to wait until yesterday (Tuesday) to unload the car.

Yesterday, I walked out to the garage to unload the car. It was a spectacular 4th of July morning, cool, crisp and clear, not a cloud in the sky, birds singing, and a very light breeze blowing. It was truly a perfect day, the kind we all love, the kind that would prompt Chris to comment on how beautiful it was outside. As I thought about what she would say on a day like this, I opened the back of the CR-V, and was bathed in the scent of her unique combination of lotions and perfume. It was very strong, and it literally stopped me in my tracks, because she hasn't used those lotions or that perfume since Jan. 18th, the day she suffered the brain aneurysm, and we've driven the car several thousand miles since then. I picked up several items to bring into the house, and as I turned away from the car, on our front porch was a chipmunk, perfectly silhouetted in the morning sun. Chris loves "chippies."

At that precise moment, I felt a sudden deep sense of peace about our choice to bring Christine home. And given what I had just experienced, within the context of current circumstances, I believe this was a sign that we're going where God wants us to go.

Signs and wonders are a part of the repertoire that God uses to reinforce our faith, to let us know He is present, to ask us to work with Him, or to help settle us on a course of action. How many times do we read in Scripture that He appeared in person or sent His angels to deliver a message? And by the way, He doesn't only communicate with believers. Think about the apostle Paul, persecuting Christ's followers, then struck by lightning and blinded, but given back his sight to preach the Word of God for the rest of his life.

Whether we have eyes to see and ears to hear (and noses to smell!) God's signs and wonders, and whether we choose to attribute them to God's purpose or to dismiss them as mere coincidence, depends on the depth of our faith. Next time something strikes you as decidedly out of the ordinary, you might ask yourself if God is sending a sign within the context of your life and its present circumstances. In an increasingly secular world, the signs and wonders God performs to guide and strengthen us are very often dismissed because they don't pass muster with our intellect or our senses.

"Now faith is the substance of things hoped for, the evidence of things unseen."

Jesus told Thomas, after providing intellectual and sensory proof that He had indeed risen and triumphed over death, "Do not persist in your unbelief, but believe."

In our lives, I'm sure that God speaks to us more often than we realize. It's up to us to listen for the whisper of His voice.

You'll be glad you did. ☺

Bob

. . . . . .

July 16, 2017

> "Because he cleaves to me in love, I will deliver him; I will protect him, because he knows my name. When he calls to me, I will answer him; I will be with him in trouble, I will rescue him and honor him. With long life I will satisfy him, and show him my salvation." (Psalm 91)

Dear friends, the past 10 days have been an extreme challenge for Christine, me and our entire family. Chrissy has faced and weathered some very significant hurdles, and we continue to ask you to pray for her. We also continue to see signs of God's presence, but we cannot be certain of their meaning. Every day brings a new set of such uncertainties as we enter the realm of spirit, setting aside (but respectful of) the expressed limits of medical science.

Your prayers are needed now more than ever, as we come face to face with truly fundamental questions of life and death. This is real. It is a contest between our faith and (state-of-the-art) science. It is about soul and spirit and will to live, things that science by its own admission cannot measure. It is about decisions that begin to encroach on the authority of God as the author of all life. It is about our feeble attempts to comprehend the incomprehensible, to approach the threshold that divides our humanity from God's eternity. It is fundamentally and unavoidably about whether we truly believe in life after death, and Heaven and hell, and Calvary and the Resurrection and salvation and eternity and, ultimately, God. Remember, "You have the watch. God has the time."

Since bringing Chris home, I haven't yet had sufficient time to develop my thoughts as I have in the past, but will continue to share insights that this journey continues to provide every day. As an example...

Yesterday (Saturday), Fr. Leo came and administered the sacrament we call "Anointing of the Sick" to Chrissy. He gave Communion to several of us, and at my request he and I went outside alone to talk about the spiritual and moral issues we are facing. As we stood outside, very near the same spot where I had smelled Chrissy's perfume and seen the chippie last week, there suddenly appeared the most spectacular rainbow I have ever seen, both in size and in brilliance of color. It originated from a hillside across the Baker River valley. Even Fr. Leo was amazed. It was truly incredible, and another indication (I believe) that the road we are traveling is the road God wants us to take. But we do not presume that we know God's will, only that he gives signs if we are seeking Him.

Life is precious. As I've confronted circumstances and decisions in the past 10 days that force me to be the arbiter of life and death for someone with whom I've been united in the sacrament of matrimony for almost 4 decades, I've reached a level of exhaustion that exceeds anything I've ever experienced before.

THE POSTS

At times I rail, shaking my fist, because it's not supposed to be this way. But at the end of each day, as I say my prayers and collapse into bed or recliner for very brief catnaps which sustain me hour-to-hour, I thank God for the chance to BE exhausted in my love for Chris.

Make it your goal to reach the finish line - today, tomorrow, and at the end of your life - completely and utterly exhausted from loving your spouse. You will sleep well, if briefly, because you will know, and he or she will know, that your love exceeds any rational measure. Love your spouse every minute of every day, down to the last full measure of your devotion. Until death do you part.

After all, Jesus did it for us.

Love to you all,

Bob

. . . . . .

August 1, 2017

> "...When Martha heard that Jesus was coming, she went and met him, while Mary sat in the house. Martha said to Jesus, "Lord, if you had been here, my brother would not have died. And even now I know that whatever you ask from God, God will give you." Jesus said to her, "Your brother will rise again." Martha said to Him, "I know that he will rise again in the resurrection at the last day." Jesus said to her, "I am the resurrection and the life; he who believes in me, though he dies, yet shall he live, and whosoever lives and believes in me shall never die. Do you believe this?" She said to him, "Yes,

THE POSTS

> *Lord; I believe that you are the Christ, the Son of God, he who is coming into the world." (John 11:20-27)*

Yesterday was Chrissy's worst day since coming home three-plus weeks ago. Since she came, we've been engulfed in a physical, emotional, intellectual and spiritual maelstrom. I rebel against the reality of her condition and refuse to give up. I reject that she has been deemed by science to be "unfixable." But my opinion doesn't matter, and my vote doesn't count. Several days ago, and again yesterday, I had to give Chris morphine to alleviate severe respiratory distress and an irregular heartbeat. A battle rages within me, as I fight for her life while trying to comply with her expressed wishes not to be kept alive with extraordinary measures if unconscious.

Is she unconscious? This question dogs my footsteps every waking minute. "She" is flesh of my flesh and bone of my bone. "She" is part of me. And though she is by-and-large unresponsive, at times she shows signs of increasing awareness, moving her limbs slightly and making sounds that indicate contentment, discomfort or distress. She mouths words and makes soft sounds as she tries to speak. She sometimes moves her head in the direction of our voices, and I believe she can sometimes see shapes and shadows. Her periods of apparent sensory awakening come and go, unpredictably. About a week after she came home, after a violent bout of vomiting, she had some mucous dripping from her nose. I grabbed a sterile wipe, held it to her nose, and said, "Chris, blow your nose." She did so. I did it again about 10 seconds later, and she blew her nose again. This was a conscious response to a verbal command — one of the indicators of minimal consciousness. So — is "she" unconscious?

THE POSTS

We shift back and forth in our duty of care, from treating her medical issues to keeping her comfortable when we can't resolve them. This is our entrée into the world of hospice. I am now the arbiter of whether to treat her ailments so she continues to live, or to ease her pain and suffering so she can conclude her life's journey with dignity. As I look at her resting peacefully in our home, my heart breaks from the sorrows I brought her during our life together. I can't begin to imagine the agony of Jesus on the Cross as He bore the weight of every sin ever committed, past present and future, for every one of us.

Palliative care can be a spiritual minefield. Uncertainty and self-doubt can erode faith, but they can also strengthen it. When I gave Chrissy her first dose of morphine, I felt as if I was killing her. Yet it brought quick relief to her obvious suffering. Questions with grave moral implications arose. Is this act of mercy contrary to God's law? Jesus relieved the pain and suffering of those who came to Him, but He used His divine authority, not morphine, to do it. Is easing Chrissy's pain and suffering as she draws closer to "the other side" an act of mercy? Or am I encroaching on God's "turf" by interposing myself in her end-of-life experience? Someday, I'll know.

Conditioned for my entire lifetime to fighting with everything at my disposal to keep her alive, I am at war with myself as I knowingly allow her to continue toward the end of her life without extraordinary intervention. I know her life still has a purpose, because God gives every one of our lives purpose, from point of conception to time of natural death. Am I thwarting God's purpose by alleviating the suffering of the person I love most in the world?

As I'm being pulled down by the maelstrom, I realize that fighting to keep Chris alive is actually keeping her from the peace and joy of Heaven and the presence of Almighty God. And I have no doubt, after spending 36+ years with her, that Heaven is where she is headed.

How do we manage the temptations and tribulations of this life? Our job as believers in Jesus Christ and His promise of eternal life is to reframe everything we face in this life in the context of God's plan of salvation. We cannot let ourselves be distracted or diverted from our primary objective: earning the peace that transcends all human understanding, in Heaven in the presence of Almighty God, for all eternity.

A very dear friend (Thank you, John) has a bumper sticker on his pickup: "No Jesus, no peace. Know Jesus, know peace." Everyone who sees that truck knows the message and the messenger. Life gets an awful lot easier when we have Jesus as a friend and companion. And to have Him as a friend and companion, we have to become a friend and companion.

If you met Jesus on the street today, would you know Him? Perhaps the better question is, "If Jesus saw you on the street today, would He know you?" I fervently pray that God will know us when He sees us.

This day, and every day, be quietly conspicuous in your faith. And thank you for continuing to pray for the love of my life.

Bob

. . . . . .

August 9, 2017

"Oh God, thou art my God, I seek thee, my soul thirsts for thee; my flesh faints for thee, as in a dry and weary land where no water is. I have looked upon thee in the sanctuary, beholding thy power and glory.

> *Because thy steadfast love is better than life, my lips will praise thee. I will bless thee as long as I live; I will lift up my hands and call on thy name..." (Psalm 63)*

Yesterday, August 8, 2017, we began hospice for Christine. While this sounds grim, in fact she is in good health; but after almost 7 months, her "trajectory" is very, very shallow, and her intake of food and water is declining, possibly to reach equilibrium with her much-reduced level of activity, or possibly because her body is beginning to shut down.

Our focus has shifted from doing everything possible to keep Chris alive, to doing everything possible to make her comfortable as she nears the end of this life. There aren't words to describe the emotional, psychological and spiritual surrender required to cede the life of our beloved wife and mother to its natural end. It's not as if we ever really had any control over the outcome anyway, but within the context of my life, I feel as though "the right thing to do" is to continue the fight to keep her alive. Except it's not my wishes or my priorities that matter, because Chrissy isn't mine. She is a child of God, as all of us are. We belong to Him. She is His gift to me "until death do us part." I never really stopped to think about that part of our vows. Now, those words are my constant companion.

As Christians, we believe that the purpose of this life is to prepare for eternity. And in the deepest recesses of my heart, I know that Chrissy is ready. She is a gentle soul — the quiet girl to whom injured animals always come — and she spent her entire life serving and giving to others: as the oldest of eight children, helping her Mom care for her siblings; as an RN, caring for the sick, the injured and the dying; as a Navy Nurse, caring for wounded veterans coming home from Vietnam; as a loyal wife, encouraging me to press on even when she knew in her heart that it would take time away from "us;" as a devoted mother, loving and homeschooling our children, encouraging them, and never missing an opportunity to point out the wonders of life and the beauty of God's handiwork; as a Eucharistic Minister taking communion to the sick and the dying; as a Stampin' Up demonstrator, sharing her amazing creativity and her happiness in her craft; as a friend of the lonely and the outcasts she met along her journey; and as a firm believer in the sanctity of life from the moment of conception to the point of natural death.

We now begin the final stage of Chrissy's earthly journey, preparing ourselves for her passage into eternal life. There is no way of knowing how long she'll be with us, but we know that eventually, in God's time, present tense will fade to past and the creation of new memories will end. It is at precisely this point that we remind ourselves that the central theme of our Christian faith is the Resurrection, and that death is a necessary part of gaining a share in its glory.

As Chrissy begins this final chapter in her life, there is no escaping the reality of her suffering or the depth of our sorrow. But there is every bit of solace in the words of Our Savior: "Come to me, all you who labor and are burdened, and I will give you rest." We know what awaits her, and we rejoice in the certainty of her salvation.

If we live with pure and humble hearts, loving God and neighbor as Jesus taught us to do, we too will have a seat at the banquet, an eternity of indescribable peace and joy in the presence of the Father, Son and Holy Spirit, reunited with those we love in the midst of the angels and the saints.

We are always called to seek a deeper understanding of the profound mystery of salvation, as we continue to prepare each day for our own death and resurrection. Because Jesus himself told us that heaven and earth shall pass away, but the Word of God and the promise it contains shall never pass away.

I'm not a gambler, but I'm betting my life on it.

Bob

. . . . . .

August 11, 2017

"What shall we say then? Are we to continue in sin that grace may abound? By no means! How can we who died to sin still live in it? Do you not know that all of us who have been baptized into Christ Jesus were baptized into his death? We were buried therefore with him by baptism into death, so that as Christ was raised from the dead by the glory of the Father, we too might walk in newness of life. For if we have been united with him in a death like his, we shall certainly be united with him in a resurrection like his. We know that our old self was crucified with him so that the sinful body might be destroyed, and we might no longer be enslaved to sin. For he who has died is freed from sin. But if we have died with Christ, we believe that we shall also live with him. For we know that Christ being raised from the dead will never die again; death no longer has dominion over him. The death he died he died to sin, once for all, but the life he lives he lives to God. So you also must consider yourselves dead to sin and alive to God in Christ Jesus..." (Romans 6:1-11)

After several days without incident, Chrissy's allergies have begun to cause bouts of severe vomiting because of her difficulty swallowing as a result of the damage to her brain. It's a threat we face every day of the journey, and we've begun to use morphine to grant her relief from the distress she suffers almost every morning. It is difficult to watch, yet we are deeply thankful for the privilege of shepherding her into the arms of Jesus.

Chris and I love lemon lavender. It produces a unique delicate fragrance like no other, and we've grown small patches of it in our garden for several years. Yesterday morning, after helping her through a particularly bad bout of vomiting, I went out to our garden to "de-stress." Knowing how much she enjoys the scent of lavender, I picked several sprigs and brought them inside to put beside her pillow so she could smell the fragrance she loves.

But when simply placed next to her, the lavender had no scent. Why? Because releasing its fragrance requires crushing its leaves and stems. Put another way, to fulfill its purpose, it must give up its life.

How similar this is to our Christian faith! If we are to achieve our true purpose in life — the attainment of everlasting life in Heaven — we have to drop everything we're doing and follow Christ's example as we wend our way along the byways of this world. If we don't "crush the leaves" in our life, we cannot enjoy the fragrance of God's plan for us.

"Crushing the leaves" is simple, but it's not easy. It entails letting go of self and "putting on Christ" in everything we do. And that means doing it in all areas of our lives: physical, mental, moral, spiritual and financial. If we're doing something that is not consistent with God's laws or His intended purpose for us, we are called on to stop engaging in that behavior.

For example, as Christians we believe that our body is the "temple of the Holy Spirit." That's a pretty powerful statement. If in fact we believe that our bodies were created by God for us to accomplish His purposes in this life, then aren't we bound by our belief to treat the body with respect and dignity?

"Crushing the leaves" might mean breaking an addiction to nicotine, alcohol or narcotics. It might mean rethinking our position on the sanctity of human life. It might mean reprioritizing our finances to more meaningfully support our church. It could mean reading more books about God and theology to strengthen our knowledge and deepen our understanding of our Christian faith. But without any question, it means changing who we are and what we do to align ourselves with God's intended purpose for bringing us into this world to begin with.

Jesus told us, "He who saves his life will lose it; and he who loses his life will save it." So crush the leaves. Cultivate Christ in your life.

You'll love the fragrance, and so will everyone around you. ☺

In faith,

Bob

. . . . . .

August 17, 2017

> "He said to the man who had invited him, 'When you give a dinner or a banquet, do not invite your friends or your brothers or your kinsmen or rich neighbors, lest they also invite you in return, and you be repaid. But when you give a feast, invite the poor, the maimed, the lame, the blind, and you will be

blessed, because they cannot repay you. You will be repaid at the resurrection of the just." (Luke 14:12-14)

You and I normally dispose of saliva, phlegm and other oral secretions without even thinking about it, as a function of our autonomous nervous system. On Tuesday morning, Chrissy's mouth had a lot of phlegm which posed a real threat of asphyxiation. For more than a day, she had resisted our attempts to do "mouth care" — a necessary function, but one she does not like. She closed her mouth and clenched her jaw shut every time the special toothbrush we use touched her lips. (Is she unconscious?) After about 10 minutes of fruitless attempts to get her to open her mouth, I looked up at the Crucifix hanging on the wall and said aloud, "You know, you could help us with this."

About 30 seconds later, Chris opened her mouth and let us clear the secretions and apply the two prescription rinses we use for her oral health. I looked back up at the Cross and said aloud, "Thank you, Lord."

For almost two days, Chris had refused to open her mouth. Yet seconds after I asked God for help, she did just that, and she kept it open until I was finished with her mouth care. I believe God intervened directly in our situation and granted our prayer.

Miracles come in all sizes and shapes. We're inclined not to believe in the direct intervention of God in our lives, so we don't "tune up" our senses to be looking for them, and many of us don't really believe and thus don't expect them to happen, and they don't. But miracles happen around us every day of our lives if we have "eyes to see and ears to hear."

I believe what happened Tuesday was a miracle. Life itself is a miracle, as is our awakening every morning. The order of the universe, evident every day of our lives if we choose to be aware of it, is a miracle. The exquisitely engineered intimacy between every living thing is a miracle, because we believe it's not the chance outcome of some cosmic accident.

God is about simplicity. The Son of God came down from Heaven, born in a manger and laid in a cradle amidst beasts of burden, to fulfill the law and the Messianic prophecy. Jesus Christ was born in simple, austere surroundings, and He performed miracles such as the wedding feast at Cana and the feeding of the five thousand, to address simple needs of ordinary people. He did it then; why would He not do it now?

We are each an individual miracle — a specially-designed piece of God's plan for mankind, in which every human being ever created plays a part. Think about that. Every single human being that ever lived, or ever will, has a purpose assigned by the Author of Life. Finding and fulfilling that purpose is the key to peace and joy in this life, and it is the key to winning Heaven in the next.

Today, be someone else's miracle. Buy breakfast for a homeless person. Help an elderly person to cross a street. Mow the lawn for an ailing neighbor. But do SOMETHING. Make it your business to be a miracle today. Because "in as much as you do it for one of the least of these, my brothers, you do it for me."

Have a SPECTACULAR day.

Bob

· · · · · ·

August 31, 2017

"Hear my prayer, O Lord; let my cry come unto thee! Do not hide thy face from me in the day of my

THE POSTS

> *distress! Incline thy ear to me; answer me speedily in the day when I call! For my days pass away like smoke, and my bones burn like a furnace. My heart is smitten like grass and withered; I forget to eat my bread. Because of my loud groaning my bones cleave to my flesh. I am like a vulture of the wilderness, like an owl of the waste places; I lie awake, I am like a lonely bird on the housetop..." (Psalm 102)*

It is 1:45AM, and Stephanie and I have just finished repositioning and cleaning Chris. Our home health aide company called and said they have no people to cover her tonight, so Stephanie (and Hunter) and I are "on the job."

Today I became angry at a God who neither lets Chris go home to Heaven, nor returns her to some semblance of conscious living. She lives in limbo, neither here nor there, and we tend to her diligently as we are called to do both by love and by Christian principles. But it is exhausting, and frustrating, and terrible to watch her suffering.

Questions come fast and furious: What kind of God allows such suffering to continue month after month, by a person who lived a virtuous life, loved her husband and family, helped those less fortunate than herself, and brought joy with her wherever she went? Is this what God is all about? Do the prayers of thousands of people count for nothing? Where is this "merciful" God we're told exists? What about, "Ask and you shall receive?" What about, "If you have faith the size of a mustard seed, you can command that mountain to move," and it will?

Would that I had the patience and faith of Job. Watching this wonderful woman suffer day after day tortures the intellect and challenges the spirit. My anger will subside, and God will do whatever He will do. But underneath it all, I am still human, and subject to human emotions.

O God, do what you will to me; but either bring Chris home to Heaven or make her whole again. You can do it; it just appears that it's not your will to do so.

So I submit. "Not my will, but thine be done."

Bob

. . . . . .

October 1, 2017

"...E'lo-i, E'lo-i, la'ma sabach-tha'ni?..." (Mark 15:33)

"Be merciful to me, O God, be merciful to me, for in thee my soul takes refuge; in the shadow of thy wings I will take refuge, till the storms of destruction pass by..." (Psalm 57)

Last Thursday, September 29th, we placed Chrissy in an assisted living facility for patients with acquired brain injuries. It is comforting to know that she is in the hands of people who are specially trained and who have a world-class facility and the best of equipment to care for her. There is great comfort in knowing this. God has provided. That said, we thank you for your continued prayers for Christine and for our family.

There is another side of this that manifested itself since I left her side Friday morning — the human side, the side that bears the anguish of her empty room, her silenced voice, her vanished presence, her missing smile. There is a diminished awareness of the world around us, a dampened zest for life — if she can't be with me, the who/what/when/where/why of my life resembles Hiroshima after the bomb.

THE POSTS

How do I chart a course that honors Chris and respects her and includes her as an integral part of my life going forward, when "here" no longer means "present?" How often should I visit her? How much of my remaining life do I physically share with her? We are not in a "critical care" or "rehab" situation now. There is no urgency to be at her bedside, other than the overwhelming need I feel to be with her. We are in limbo, told that there is nothing more we can do, and that Chrissy will be in her present state for the rest of her life. She is gone, even though she is here. And life goes on, even though it doesn't.

Desolation of spirit is real. Christ himself experienced it near the end of His Passion. But He also gave us the antidote with his dying words: "Father, into thy hands I commend my spirit." I don't believe we have to be near death to offer our spirit to the Father.

No matter how dark the hour, I know that God has chosen me, and you, and every human being, all created in His image and likeness, to fulfill a specific purpose in this life. He speaks to each of us as He spoke to Jacob:

"But now thus says the Lord, he who created you, O Jacob, he who formed you, O Israel:

Fear not, for I have redeemed you; I have called you by name, you are mine. When you pass through the waters I will be with you; and through the rivers, they shall not overwhelm you; when you walk through fire you shall not be burned, and the flame shall not consume you. For I am the Lord your God, the Holy One of Israel, your Savior..."

God created each of us for a reason. It's up to us to seek His purpose, and then to accept it as our own.

Believe.

Surrender.

THE POSTS

See.
Grow.
Witness.
Rejoice.
God has incredible things in store for us.
Bob

. . . . . .

October 5, 2017

> *"...He maketh me to lie down in green pastures.*
> *He leadeth me beside the still waters. He*
> *restoreth my soul..." (Psalm 23)*

I'm awake suddenly, but not abruptly. Is that You, God? Something woke me up, and it wasn't a sound, and nothing's moving. The digital clock shows 4:20AM, and everything is perfectly still. The light from the moon, shining through the windows of our bedroom, paints the world outside with a ghostly white glow in the pre-dawn fog.

Thanks, God, for another day. I wonder if Chrissy can thank You. For too long, Lord, I've looked at all that has happened through my eyes. I wonder what it looks like through her eyes. Does she "know" she's alive? Is she still the Chris we know? Or is she someone else now? Does she have a personality, or is she just a body without the ability to think or feel emotions? Here come the questions, the relentless questions that wear me out. So I'm going to let you deal with them. All I have to do is Believe and Surrender. My hands are up, God. As high as I can raise them.

You know, Lord, she's been gone from our home for a week now. She's doing well, we're told, and my two overnight visits have confirmed it. Stephanie and Hunter and I worked hard for the last 3 months, loving her with our lives, literally. We just couldn't keep it up, Lord. I know you understand — You told your apostles at Gethsemane, "The spirit is willing, but the flesh is weak." We really tried, Father. Can you help us get past feeling guilty because we couldn't go on loving her that way? That we had to love her by putting her in the hands of people who can care for her all day, every day, better than we can? Can you help us understand that we didn't quit on her, that we didn't give up, that taking her away from home is better for her, and better for us?

I know the sorrow and guilt I'm feeling because we took her to a place of compassion and care with people who know what she needs, and what we need. I can't imagine the magnitude of the Love you have for me and for the world — so much that you sent your Son here, not into a compassionate and loving world, but into a world that didn't want to hear what He had to say, a world that ultimately tortured and killed Him. I don't know if You can feel pain, but your Word says we are made in your image and likeness, and if that includes emotions, I can't imagine the agony You must have felt as Jesus suffered, or the Love You have for me. But I'm ok just knowing it's there, even if I can't measure it.

We're beginning to adjust, Lord — almost grudgingly — to our release from the 24-hour-a-day vigil, the multiple-times-each-night runs to her room because she had hiccupped or coughed and we knew the dangers she faced — and still faces — when that happens. But you already know all that, Lord. And you already have her in your Hands — just like You have us because we accepted your Promise of Salvation.

You've got this, Lord. What I don't know is so much more than what I do. My human nature wants answers, but they only lead to more questions, in a relentless cycle of uncertainty. So

I'm letting it go, and giving it to You. There is certainty in you, Lord, even when the storms of life afflict us, on the brightest of days, and in the darkest of nights. You're here, and I'm glad You're here, Lord. Really, truly glad.

Anyway, it's time to say my morning prayers. Just wanted you to know I'm glad You're "on the job."

But then, You always were, and are, and will be.

Bob

. . . . . .

October 7, 2017

"How lovely is thy dwelling place, O Lord of hosts! My soul longs, yea, faints for the courts of the Lord; my heart and flesh sing for joy to the living God. Even the sparrow finds a home, and the swallow a nest for herself, where she may lay her young, at thy altars, O Lord of hosts, my King and my God. Blessed are those who dwell in thy house, ever singing thy praise!..." (Psalm 84)

On the way to spend the night with Chris last night, I decided to stop for dinner at a restaurant in Mont Vernon. It's a lovely restaurant, rustic, and beautifully decorated. I had a very stylish chair as my dinner companion. It was polite, and kept its silence; eloquent, mindful of its manners, and with excellent posture. The meal was wonderful, the waitstaff courteous and caring, the atmosphere pleasant, if bustling.

I was by myself, but I was not alone. I had several companions: the heartache of Chrissy's absence, and the joy I knew I would feel when I was with her again. They fought a pitched battle for my state of mind. Though the struggle was titanic, ultimately the loneliness of the present moment yielded to the future joy I knew was coming when I was with her.

"Infinite" means without limit, unmeasurable, and things that we call "infinite" are beyond our capacity to quantify or comprehend. Whenever the consequences of adversity threaten to overwhelm, I "fast-forward" to the end of the journey, and steep my spirit in the "infinity-ness" of the joy we will know in the presence of Almighty God if we live our lives according to His laws.

Sooner or later, we're all faced with the fruits of adversity — sorrow, loneliness, anger, bitterness, depression, etc. No matter the intensity of the sorrows that pierce our hearts, or the sins for which we repent, never, ever forget "infinity." When we cross over into eternity, so long as we have been faithful to God's word, infinite joy will be our reward, in the presence of God forever. By definition, that's more joy than we can even comprehend. Add to that "the peace that surpasses all human understanding," and I'm betting it's worth living for.

When life serves you up tragedy, and you're alone for dinner, go ahead and talk to the chair. Because God is sitting in that chair, if you invite him to the table.

See you at dinner! ☺

Bob

. . . . . .

October 18, 2017

"Do not let your hearts be troubled. You believe in God; believe also in me. My Father's house has many rooms; if that were not so, would I have told you that I am going there to prepare a place for you? And if I go and

THE POSTS

prepare a place for you, I will come back and take you to be with me that you also may be where I am. You know the way to the place where I am going." Thomas said to him, "Lord, we don't know where you are going, so how can we know the way?" Jesus answered, "I am the way and the truth and the life. No one comes to the Father except through me... " (John 14:1-6)

Nine months ago today, our family suffered a crushing blow, and life went in a very different direction than that which Chris and I had planned. We don't search for a reason for what happened, because there isn't one. God doesn't cause these storms; they are a natural consequence of having a physical body. We remember that before their fall, God had placed Adam and Eve into Paradise, but because of their sin, every person ever born must earn their place in Heaven. And the process of doing so includes pain, and suffering, and sorrow and death.

The wood of the Cross frames the doorway to Heaven. The blood of Christ opened that door, and we triumph over sin and death not by looking AT the Cross, but by looking THROUGH it. We don't focus on our pain and suffering. As believers in Christ, we instead contemplate the incredible eternity that awaits us. We keep our eye on the Prize, not on the suffering we endure to gain it. We transcend sorrow and pain with faith. We find peace amidst our tears because we know what awaits us.

As Chrissy and I and our family carry our cross, your love and your prayers continue to ease our burden. God holds us in His loving embrace even when we are angry, lonely or afraid.

When life throws you an inside curve ball, don't look AT the Cross; look THROUGH the Cross. Look through the Door that was opened by the blood of the Redeemer. Then re-purpose your suffering to delivering Christ's message of salvation to the world. See the beautiful eternity that awaits when you "take up your cross and follow Me."

Believe — that He is God.
Surrender — to His Authority.
See — the Table He has prepared for you.
Grow — in Wisdom drawn from His Word.
Witness — that He is King of Kings.
Rejoice — in His Promise of eternal salvation.

"...Fear not, for I have redeemed you. I have called you by name. You are Mine..." (Isaiah 43)

Don't take my word for it. Ask Him. He's been waiting forever to hear from you. ☺

Have a blessed day.
Bob

. . . . . .

October 25, 2017

> *"Thus says God, the Lord, who created the heavens and stretched them out, who spread forth the earth and what comes from it, who gives breath to the people upon it and spirit to those who walk in it: "I am the Lord, I have called you in righteousness, I have taken you by the hand and kept you; I have given you as a covenant to the people, a light to the nations, to open the eyes that are blind..." (Isaiah 42: 5-7)*

The RNs at Chrissy's facility have said she seems to be showing some small signs of neurological improvement — some new reflex responses, eyes open more and for longer periods, blinking in response to questions. These aren't consistent, but they are happening. We are cautious in our joy, because at the end of the day, she is still in a persistent vegetative state.

We have a new concern. Chris has begun a medical condition called "wasting." She's losing weight because she's not able to take in enough nourishment to provide the calories and protein needed to sustain her. Her medical team is working hard to devise a solution, and we are praying hard for their success.

Letting go of caring for Chris at home and surrendering her care to a facility, even though dedicated to those with acquired brain injury, continues to be a challenge. I felt that loving her meant being her primary caregiver, even if the price of doing so was my health and living my own life. I'm trying to let go, but not finding much success. Love isn't always rational...

Speaking of love, Jesus summed up the entirety of the law in His admonition to "Love the Lord thy God with thy whole heart, and thy whole soul, and thy whole mind, and thy whole strength; and thy neighbor as thyself." His entire existence was dedicated to bringing God's message of salvation to everyone He encountered during His time on Earth. He set the ultimate example as to what we should be doing with our lives.

Loving our neighbor isn't only about their physical care. It includes looking out for their spiritual welfare as well. It means working to help them get to Heaven even while we're working to get there ourselves. And as with many other things in life, how we share our message is as important as what we're trying to say. In a nation once guided by "E Pluribus Unum" and "In God We Trust," we see division and violence becoming an integral part of our social fabric. (What did we expect when we accepted laws that made it illegal to allow the open expression of faith in our public institutions?)

Jesus was only angry to the point of violence once that I can think of — at the moneychangers in the temple. "It is written my house is a house of prayer; but you have made it a den of thieves." He physically overturned their tables and drove them out of the building. They had violated the sanctity of the temple — God's sanctuary on Earth. When we lose respect and reverence for God, we lose our souls. (And nations die.)

Jesus was especially critical of scribes and Pharisees — priests and church lawyers — who outwardly complied with every aspect of the law, though their hearts were full of iniquity. He decried their hypocrisy. "You serpents, you brood of vipers, how are you to escape being sentenced to hell?" They made a mockery of the very law they professed. They made a great show of being righteous, even though their hearts were not.

For everyday people, Jesus used parables — stories that point out behaviors, told in such a way that people, after thinking about what He said, could realize the need to change their lives. He asked the question, and allowed the sinner to provide the answer. Or not. He was the Teacher, but He left it up to them to choose, just like He leaves it up to us. Those who choose Christ, chose life.

Again: Those who choose Christ, choose life.

We need to act as Jesus did on Earth so we can earn our way to Heaven. We don't look for the reason that tragedy befalls us. We look for the way we can turn it to God's purposes. We look TO the Cross so see the Price, and THROUGH the Cross to see the Prize.

We must become Jesus Christ to all we meet. We must teach by example, and we must love by example. No matter what it costs.

When the loving gets tough, the tough get loving.

(Or something like that...)
Bob

. . . . . .

November 4, 2017

> *"How precious is thy steadfast love, O God! The children of men take refuge in the shadow of thy wings. They feast on the abundance of thy house, and thou givest them drink from the river of thy delights. For with thee is the fountain of life; in thy light do we see light..."* (Psalm 36)

The text message from the Director of Nursing came at around 8pm last night. It was unexpected and ominously nondescript: "Hi Bob, are you headed this way tonight?" I texted back, "No, but I can be there tomorrow morning early." My heart was suddenly pounding. I had no idea what had happened that he might want me to come. Fearing the news, I sent a follow-up message: "Call me now."

Our faith faces challenges of varying severity as we head towards eternity. No matter what rains down upon us, no matter the tribulation, whether physical pain or emotional anguish, injustice or injury, rejection or betrayal, turning to God in prayer is the universal palliative. God doesn't always speak in ways we can understand. But He always listens, and if we lift up our sorrows to Him, He will shoulder our burdens and grant us respite.

Do we truly believe that our faith can move a mountain? Do we really comprehend the power at our disposal if we invoke the name of Almighty God when faced with adversity? Believing in

God is not a lukewarm proposition. It is not for the spiritually faint of heart. We believe in the power of prayer, (but...)

That subconscious "but..." is there more often than we realize. It happens because we aren't quite sure, we aren't quite committed to hurling ourselves over the cliff of rationality and freefalling with trust in God's plan for us. We believe in the power of prayer and the love of God, (but...)

"Now faith is the substance of things hoped for, the evidence of things unseen."

The world's negatives constantly bombard us. Cynicism and pragmatism undermine the power of our faith. They steal the joy of walking with God as we make our way towards eternity.

Joy is the result of unbounded faith. The unspoken "but" that tries to interject itself in our belief comes straight from the gates of Hell. If we are true to our Christian faith, we radiate the joy of knowing that no matter what happens to us, if we die with Christ to sin, we will rise with Him to eternal life. The only thing that can take that away from us is the choices we make in our lives.

So how about this as a reason to believe in the power of your prayers? What if I told you that last night, the Director of Nursing, did call. What if I told you that he wanted to make sure I wasn't driving before he delivered the news he had to bring, that last night, just before he called, Christine had a major medical event? Would your heart immediately leap for joy without hesitation because your faith was solid, or would you know a moment of fear as I did ("but...") before you picked up the phone?

Here's what he shared:

Last night, when he asked her to, Chris wiggled the toes on both her feet, pushed the bottoms of both her feet against his hands, and raised one of her legs towards her chest.

Not once.
Not twice.
Three times.

Last night, a woman who was supposed to be dead 9 months ago consciously responded to requests to move her legs and feet.

Today, I hope you're certain in the knowledge that prayer works; that YOUR prayers are working; that you and I and anyone who chooses Christ can make real things happen with the power of our prayers. Know it. Live it. And share it. Faith and joy are ours for the asking.

Eat. Pray. Smile. ☺
Bob

. . . . . .

November 13, 2017

> *"...Now there was a man in Jerusalem called Simeon, who was righteous and devout. He was waiting for the consolation of Israel, and the Holy Spirit was on him. It had been revealed to him by the Holy Spirit that he would not die before he had seen the Lord's Messiah. Moved by the Spirit, he went into the temple courts. When the parents brought in the child Jesus to do for him what the custom of the Law required, Simeon took him in his arms and praised God, saying: "Sovereign Lord, as you have promised, you may now dismiss your servant in peace. For my eyes have seen your salvation, which you have prepared in the sight of all nations: a light for revelation to the Gentiles, and the glory of your people*

> *Israel." And the child's father and mother marveled at what was said about him...." (Luke 2:22-33)*

Late last night, I watched Chris wiggle the toes on both her feet when I asked her to. It wasn't the "twitching" of reflex. It was a definite wiggle. Though she's still in a vegetative state, she is definitely rising towards the next level, minimally conscious. And here's some some more good news: after asking a fellow parishioner and friend who happens to be a doctor to intervene, we just received orders from her PCP to increase the volume of food she is receiving so we can address the ongoing "wasting" that has cost 15% of her body weight. We've begun the new regimen, and so far, so good.

PLEASE KEEP PRAYING!

This morning, I was thinking about what happened to Simeon. He was a virtuous man, and had been promised that he would live long enough to see the Messiah. One day, out of the blue, a couple named Mary and Joseph came to him in the temple to present their child, Jesus, for consecration. And somehow, some way, Simeon knew. Something told him, "This is the one!"

Can you imagine the awe of knowing that you are holding the Savior of the world in your arms? What would you say? What would you do?

Truth is, we DO hold the Savior in our arms, and we SHOULD be in awe! We hold Him in our arms every minute of every day, until we sin. When we sin, we consciously push Christ away and embrace Satan. When we sin, we turn away from God, who loves us so much that He sent His only Son to suffer and die a terrible death to reopen the gates of Heaven for us.

When we sin, we consciously reject God's love and His grace and His peace and His promise of eternal salvation.

Thankfully, God never rejects us. He loves us. Think about that. God loves us.

Do we truly comprehend what that means? Do I truly "get" that the Creator of the Universe, the Author of All Life, loves ME?

Every day we awaken is another chance to grow in the love of God. Every day, God gives us another chance to earn the grace we need to get to Heaven. And every day, we can choose to take the infant Jesus in our arms and love Him.

If we're holding the infant Jesus in our arms, Satan doesn't have a prayer.

Have a beautiful day.

Bob

. . . . . .

November 26, 2017

> "...The Lord knows the days of the blameless, and their heritage will abide for ever; they are not put to shame in evil times; in the days of famine they have abundance. But the wicked perish; the enemies of the Lord are like the glory of the pastures, they vanish — like smoke they vanish away..." (Psalm 37)

Chris, remains in PVS. That said, she is responding occasionally to some verbal requests to move her toes, and once in a while she moves her limbs or does what I call a "shrug stretch." I have absolutely no doubt that our prayers are being heard, at a time and in a way that suits God's purposes. Small miracles are miracles nonetheless!

Please continue your prayers, not only for Christine, but also for all those who suffer or mourn, because everyone has had or will have a cross to carry at some point in their lives. I pray for each of you, that God will bless your lives and families with abundant grace and peace.

Marines fight wars. We study war. We continuously adapt strategy and tactics to meet the threat of a constantly evolving enemy. We seek to discern his objective(s), ascertain his strategy and tactics, and then figure out how to defeat them. We use terms like Asymmetric Warfare, Net-centric Warfare, Collateral Damage, Forward Edge of the Battle Area, Listening Posts, Fields of Fire, and many more that enable us to apply hard science to the chaos of the battlefield. We know our capabilities, and we study the enemy's. We learn everything we can about him in the time available to prepare for battle. We train constantly, so as to be ready to engage and defeat him unconditionally, at a moment's notice, wherever and whenever he appears. And we're good at it.

We use supporting arms — artillery, mortars, air strikes, electronic warfare, drone strikes, naval gunfire, etc. — to support our fundamental fighting unit — the individual combat Marine. Because when all is said and done, it is the individual Marine rifleman on the ground who will repel the enemy's attack.

We know that when the battle begins, if we haven't trained properly or hard enough, we afford the enemy a greater likelihood of victory, and that is not an acceptable outcome. Everyone doesn't get a trophy on the battlefield. There is victor, and there is vanquished. A winner and a loser.

Our daily lives are also a battlefield. We face a cunning and relentless enemy whose objective is to steal our souls from Almighty God. He lures us with all manner of temptations in hopes that we will eventually take the bait and turn away from God. His total attention is focused on defeating us, one at a time, by exploiting our weaknesses, one temptation at a time. We each enjoy the privilege of Satan's individualized attention.

To win the battle for our souls, we must be "spiritual Marines," training hard every day so we're prepared for whatever may confront us on the battlefield of life. We must define and commit to the mission, know our own strengths and weaknesses, and understand the enemy. If you doubt the treachery and desire of Satan to take you to Hell, remember that he tried to trick the Son of God by tempting Him with all manner of worldly rewards. Do you really think he isn't coming after you?

Remember, too, though, that Jesus rebuked Satan by quoting Scripture, and sent him packing.

So can we.

The enemy loves our ignorance, because it causes confusion and uncertainty in the fog of war. For us to win, we must develop the will to win, increase our knowledge, build up our strength and reinforce our sense of purpose, so when the battle is joined, we are clear-headed and strong in repelling his attacks. That means frequent prayer, daily study of Scripture, joining with other Christians, and keeping sight of our ultimate objective: eternity in Heaven.

We also need to be humble enough to call in reinforcements if we're in danger of being overrun by evil. Offering prayer, speaking the name of Jesus, phoning a fellow Christian — in other words, taking some definitive action to bring in spiritual reinforcements must be an integral part of our battlefield strategy.

At the end of the day, each of us is a combat Marine in the war for our souls. It is our actions on the battlefield of life that will determine whether we hold our position or fall to defeat. It is our choices that will determine whether we accept the love of God or fall prey to the lure of evil.

Ignorance of Scripture and moral confusion have predictable spiritual outcomes. So do knowledge of God's word and its resultant moral clarity.

So train the way you're going to fight — to win. Because in this case, in the immortal words of Vince Lombardi, "Winning is everything, it's the ONLY thing."

God loves you. Time to love Him back. Give Satan the boot. ☺

Semper Fidelis,

Bob

. . . . . .

December 8, 2017

"...Likewise you wives, be submissive to your husbands, so that some, though they do not obey the word, may be won without a word by the behavior of their wives, when they see your reverent and chaste behavior. Let not yours be the outward adorning with braiding of hair, decoration of gold, and wearing of fine clothing, but let it be the hidden person of the heart with the imperishable jewel of a gentle and quiet spirit, which in God's sight is very precious..." (1 Peter 3:1-4)

Days have turned into weeks, and weeks into months, as the journey continues. "Normal" is redefined, along with the struggle to accept it. Our lives go on, even as Chrissy remains in PVS. We don't know who she is or what she knows or understands. But don't for a moment think that God isn't using her to accomplish His purposes.

Every day, we pray for God's direct intervention and healing for Chris. Most days, we don't see any changes — but that doesn't mean they're not taking place. Recovering from brain injuries takes an awfully long time, and even at that, we never know what the end state will be. But we continue to pray and to believe. Over the past 10-1/2 months, I've shared some of our victories with you — victories, I'm certain, that were won because of your continued prayers. God works in ways we don't understand, but from time to time He does provide us with signs that He hasn't forgotten us...

Last night, after a 4-day visit with Chris and the family, Lauren (our daughter) and her husband Derry left to fly back to their home in Seattle. On the way to the airport, they stopped to visit Chrissy once more before leaving, and as they were saying good-bye, something unbelievable happened.

Chris wept.

She has no eye infection, nor any other physical condition that would cause her to cry. But she did. And so we saw yet another manifestation of the fruits of our faith, and of God's work. We're pretty sure she can hear us from time to time, and it now seems, at least in this one instance, that she actually reacted to Lauren's sadness at having to leave. Two tears from one of her eyes trickled down her cheek.

Anyone who ever met Chris knew "the hidden person of the heart with the imperishable jewel of a gentle and quiet spirit, which in God's sight is very precious." I was so lucky that she chose to spend her life with me. And I openly admit I wasn't always the person she hoped I'd be, but she prayed for me and believed in me and trusted her life to me. And she "won me without a word" every single day because of how she lived her life. I continue to learn more about her incredible love for our family every day. And I continue to learn more about the depth of God's love for us as well.

As we look around us at a very confused world, we need to stay focused on what's important. Advent has begun, the time of preparation before the coming of the Savior at Christmas. "Make straight the way of the Lord..." John the Baptist told the people, because we know not the day nor the hour.

God is always at work in our lives, even though we may not immediately see or accept the fruits of that work. We need to make certain that we, too, are at work in our lives — preparing to receive the Messiah at Christmas, and to meet Him when we die.

If God was coming to dinner tonight, wouldn't you want your house to be in order? Would He find "the hidden person of the heart with the imperishable jewel of a gentle and quiet spirit?" Or would He find something else? And by the way, I'm not just talking about wives.

Dear friends, God IS coming to your house. It might not be tonight, but He is going to be paying you a visit. He might even visit you more than once. But when the time comes for His last visit, will you be ready?

Be spectacular in your love of God, today and every day.

All this, from two tiny tears...

Bob

. . . . . .

December 25, 2017

> "....Be not afraid; for behold, I bring you good news of a great joy which will come to all the people; for to you is born this day in the city of David a Savior, who is Christ the Lord..." (Luke 2:10-11)

THE POSTS

Because of the (now happening) forecast snowstorm, I decided to visit Chrissy yesterday, on Christmas Eve day. Joe and Naomi went in the morning, and I went in the afternoon, staying until around 9pm last night. Hunter has a cold, and we didn't want to risk exposing Chris to it, so he and Stephanie remained at home, sad that they couldn't visit Mom/Yaya for Christmas. I prayed a Rosary and several other prayers with her, on my knees at her bedside, and read all the Christmas Eve and Christmas Day readings to her. She is so beautiful, at peace as she always is when I pray with her or read Scripture. And so am I. What better evidence is there of the peace that's to be found when we read and reflect on God's word? Chris rests at times, and is awake at times, though not really aware of her surroundings. Her skin is flawless, and she is gaining back some of the weight she lost. However, she has developed a deep cough and some bronchial congestion. Please pray that this does not become pneumonia.

This month has been a raging conflict between our earthly sadness and the spiritual joy of Christmas. Regardless of our sorrow, we embrace the birth of Jesus and humbly thank God for His love and mercy. In one sense, this past year provided a compelling backdrop for us to truly understand the radiance and warmth of that love and mercy. For every one of us, each day of our lives is a battleground for our souls. No matter the intensity of the battle, we must keep our eyes on the prize, seeking constancy in faith and acceptance of God's will. We know that the sorrows of this life are temporary if we accept Christ as Lord and Savior. We know that our journey becomes easier if we actively seek Him in everything we do. We know that Christ died for us, so that He could live through us. It all began on a cold winter night, in the humblest of surroundings, with the simplest of witnesses, through the trust of Mary and Joseph in our God.

Today we celebrate the beginning of Christ's life on earth, the profound manifestation of God's love for us. Born in a stable among beasts of burden, Jesus Christ will confound the haughty, forgive the sinful, heal the sick, raise the dead, give hope to the downtrodden, and show us the Way, the Truth and the Life. His love and salvation are there for the asking. "Come to me all ye who labor and are heavy burdened, and I will give you rest."

Believe. Surrender. See. Grow. Witness. Rejoice.

These words bring a faith perspective to the terrible injury to Christine. The order in which they appear enables me to stay in the fight whenever things start to overwhelm me. They remind me that my mission in life is to commit Chrissy's tragedy to God's purposes: to share His message and bring Him to those who are searching for meaning in their own lives.

How lucky I am to have my faith.

How grateful I am that you hold me in your prayers.

How amazed I am that God loves me.

How blessed I am to have a Savior, Jesus Christ, born this day.

I pray that each of you will have a joy-filled, blessed Christmas, and that the loving gaze of the newborn Christ child will fall gentle upon you this day and every day of your lives.

Gloria in excelsis Deo!

Bob

. . . . . .

January 8, 2018

"...Now when Jesus was born in Bethlehem of Judea in the days of Herod the king, behold, wise men

> *from the East came to Jerusalem, saying, "Where is he who has been born king of the Jews? For we have seen his star in the East, and have come to worship him..." (Matthew 2:1-2)*

Chrissy's condition is largely unchanged, though she continues to gradually show increased wakefulness during the day and more consistent response to light flashed in her eyes. With the arrival of the New Year comes renewed hope that we can begin proactively working to restore her to consciousness, as we prepare to take her off hospice. She had a complete physical exam last week, and remains stable, but fragile. We stopped her weight loss by increasing her intake, and she is managing the change without any difficulty and actually gaining back weight. Please keep praying for her.

The story of the wise men's visit to the Christ child signals the end of the season of Christmas. These men spent their lives studying the word of God and saw the signs indicating that the Messiah had been born. They acted on their faith and set out to honor Him, traveling a great distance to find Him, braving winter weather, bandits, and Herod's political treachery. They brought precious gifts of gold, frankincense and myrrh — highly symbolic in our Christian faith — and "fell down and worshipped Him."

Our journey through life is an opportunity to do as the Maji did: to study the word of God, to see and understand the signs around us, and to follow the star of our faith to the abode of Jesus Christ. Scripture calls the Maji "wise men" — men imbued with wisdom. We know from Proverbs that "the beginning of wisdom is fear of the Lord." The word "fear" as used here doesn't actually mean "to be afraid." It means to exercise appropriate respect and reverence for God. Without this reverence and respect for His omnipotence and His laws, we lose the ability to know good from evil. The "scales on our eyes" remain, deceiving and confusing us, keeping us vulnerable to the wiles of the evil one.

What makes a person "wise?" Knowledge is part of it. But knowledge only makes a person smart. It is the use of knowledge enlightened by faith that makes a person wise. And that wisdom is the source of the critical gift of discernment so lacking in today's world. Wisdom and discernment enable us to recognize sin and see it for what it really is: rejecting God and embracing evil. We don't have to look very far to see manifest evidence of the loss of discernment in today's world.

The wise men brought the infant Messiah precious treasures. They braved perils known and unknown because they wanted to see and pay homage to the Son of God. They weren't born wise; they became wise. We are called to do no less. They studied God's word and incorporated it into their lives. They physically journeyed to be with Christ, regardless of the dangers that journey encompassed. And though they were kings in their own right, they prostrated themselves in the presence of the infant Christ child because they knew He was the Messiah.

Are we seeking wisdom? Have we planned for our journey to Heaven, including the detours that happen along the way? And what treasure will we present on the day we finally meet Almighty God?

We all know the old Chinese proverb, "A journey of a thousand miles begins with a single step."

Here's wishing you safe travels. ☺

Bob

. . . . . .

January 18, 2018 — One Year...

> *"...For ever, O Lord, they word is firmly fixed in the heavens. Thy faithfulness endures to all generations; thou has established the earth, and it stands fast. By thy appointment they stand this day; for all things are they servants..." (Psalm 119)*

On a small bureau in our bedroom is the note I received from my Senate assistant during caucus one year ago today. It says simply, "Senator — your wife has fallen. Your daughter called and wants you to call her ASAP."

I used to say that life changed forever that day. But I was wrong. Yes - the heart of our family was stricken, but she was not taken. Yes - she was silenced, but she speaks more clearly now than ever.

The only thing that really changed was life in this world. Our ultimate destiny remains exactly the same.

Suffering and adversity are powerful forces in our lives. Over the past year, I've learned as never before to see life through the eyes of my faith. I've learned that each day is a precious gift, another opportunity to see, touch, hear, smell, and taste life. But most importantly, each day is an investment that God makes in me, and my job is to generate a return on that investment. I think about parable of the servants who were given coins by the Master, and who were each rewarded or punished according to the increase they produced...

I've learned that despite all we see, read and hear about anger and hatred in the world today, there are many more people with love and kindness in their hearts. These are those of you who cared for our pets, left hot meals on our stove, baked chocolate chip cookies to make us smile, plowed our driveway when we were away, and relieved us of the burden of everyday tasks when our lives were in chaos. You did it without asking, and though we can only say, "Thank you," nothing can or will ever suffice to express how much your caring and your acts of kindness helped during the dark days early on when we weren't sure if Chris was going to beat the odds that were stacked so high against her.

Even as there were those who helped us with our worldly tasks, literally thousands of you have opened your hearts and lifted us up in prayer. And though we have no idea of where our earthly journey will take us, good things are happening, little things that we see from time to time that indicate that Chrissy is very slowly making progress towards consciousness. We also know that our short time on Earth, our suffering and our sorrow, will end, and that a wonderful eternity awaits us if we repent of our sins and follow the Way, the Truth and the Life.

I am sad in some ways today, but I'm also grateful that God gave me this day — to honor Him, to love my family, and to share His love with you. I'm thankful that Christine remains in my life, a constant inspiration to believe, surrender, see, grow, witness and rejoice.

Thank you for drying my tears, easing my heartache and reinforcing my faith. Thank you for your prayers, which were light in times of crushing darkness. Thank you for your love — for God, for Chris, for me, for our family.

Have a SPECTACULAR day today. Find a reason to rejoice. And then thank God for it.

God bless you.

Bob

· · · · · ·

January 27, 2018

> *"When the Son of Man comes in his glory, and all the angels with him, he will sit on his glorious throne. All the nations will be gathered before him, and he will separate the people one from another as a shepherd separates the sheep from the goats. He will put the sheep on his right and the goats on his left. Then the King will say to those on his right, 'Come, you who are blessed by my Father; take your inheritance, the kingdom prepared for you since the creation of the world. For I was hungry and you gave me something to eat, I was thirsty and you gave me something to drink, I was a stranger and you invited me in, I needed clothes and you clothed me, I was sick and you looked after me, I was in prison and you came to visit me.' Then the righteous will answer him, 'Lord, when did we see you hungry and feed you, or thirsty and give you something to drink? When did we see you a stranger and invite you in, or needing clothes and clothe you? When did we see you sick or in prison and go to visit you?' The King will reply, 'Truly I tell you, whatever you did for one of the least of these brothers and sisters of mine, you did for me.'" (Matthew 25:30-40)*

In brain injury patients, respiratory issues can arise very quickly, and when coupled with the ever-present risk of pneumonia due to being bed-ridden for long periods of time, are a cause for serious concern. Add to this the wintertime danger of influenza, and you have the potential for a deadly "perfect storm." About two weeks ago, Chris developed a cough — clearly cause for concern. She began generating lots of phlegm, which brings with it the increased risk of aspiration (inhaling it into her lungs) and elevated risk of suffocation. I'm happy to share that she weathered this episode and the immediate danger has passed. In another small sign of progress, it appears that her periods of wakefulness and sleep are beginning to align with the normal diurnal cycle: she is mostly asleep at night, and most of her periods of wakefulness are happening during the day. We're seeing a slow progression of what I call "small miracles." But small miracles are miracles nonetheless. Her eyes now blink in response to a bright light about 80% of the time — another sign that her brain is finding new ways to transmit and process information. I am absolutely convinced that prayer is making the difference. She is still definitely in PVS, but is very slowly moving towards "minimally conscious." God is answering our prayers for her in His own time. ("You have a watch, but God has the time.")

When we go on vacation, we pack the things we think we'll need both for the journey and when we get to the resort. Toothbrush and toothpaste, deodorant, shaving cream and razor, and other personal hygiene items go into the "dob kit," and appropriate clothing goes into the suitcase as well — footwear, bathing suits, underwear, shorts, t-shirts, ball cap — you get the idea.

Faith and Scripture tell us that our life in this world is a journey, and I our destination should be the wonderful place we call "Heaven." Like any other trip, it brings the potential for unexpected detours and disasters. Like any other trip, we make choices along the way that determine whether we'll reach our destination. And like any other trip, we'll need the proper ID to gain entry to the resort.

Unlike any earthly resort, however, Jesus has already paid the price of our admission into Heaven. But we can't forget that

His death and Resurrection do not guarantee that we'll find the gates of Heaven, or that we'll get in when we get there. We have to pay the cost of the journey, and we need the right ID card to check in.

That ID card is formed partly from sacraments, and partly from living a life committed to the love of God and neighbor. It's imprinted with the decisions we make during our lives. God knew before we were ever born that we were going to fail, and that we were bound for eternal damnation unless He did something to intervene. Because He loves us, He sent his Son to suffer a terrible death, expiating our sins and reopening to us the gates of Heaven. So we all fail, but It's how we fight back from those failures that gives us access to the kingdom of Heaven: with repentance, atonement, and the active practice of our faith. It's up to us to make the right choices along the way, and to store up the grace we'll need to find favor on the Last Day.

Because when we get to the gates of Heaven, I'm willing to bet that God's going to ask,

"What's in YOUR wallet?" ☺

And of all the places I've ever been, this is the one place I really don't want to be caught short.

Thank you for loving Chris and continuing to pray for her.

Bob

. . . . . .

January 28, 2018

> *"Unless the Lord builds the house,*
> *the builders labor in vain.*
> *Unless the Lord watches over the city,*
> *the guards stand watch in vain.*

THE POSTS

> *In vain you rise early*
> *and stay up late,*
> *toiling for food to eat—*
> *for he grants sleep to those he loves..." (Psalm 127)*

I spent yesterday (Saturday) afternoon and night and this morning (Sunday) with Chrissy. It was a very difficult night - very labored breathing, short gasping breaths when inhaling, and forced exhalation. O2 level was at 93-97%, so she's getting the oxygen she needs, but was really struggling with the physical act of breathing. We gave her morphine (I hate it) and turned her on her side, which brought relief. She is unable to breathe normally when on her back. She has kyphosis, and I wonder if it has progressed more rapidly because of her loss of muscle mass and tone. The curvature of her spine may put pressure on her lungs when she is laying on her back. I will discuss it with the Director of Nursing and Doctor ASAP. It is all in God's hands, but we do what we can to keep things headed in the right direction.

This morning, I held her face in my hands and kissed her lips, her forehead, her cheeks. I prayed a Rosary, and I'm sitting still with her, a Chopin Polonaise in the background, looking at the person who built my life with me, and in many ways, for me. Her eyes open from time to time, though she is quiet and still. The stillness is both reassuring and maddening. I want her to get out of that bed, to walk, to talk, to sing, to laugh; for her eyes to light up when she sees Hunter, for her to be there for Lauren and Stephanie and Joseph when they have things they can only discuss with Mom; for her gifted hands to continue crafting the beautiful things only she can conceptualize and create.

But not today. Maybe never again. But at least I have the gift of being WITH her. I hope she knows how much I love her, we love her, the world loves her, and most of all, how much God loves her. How can she not know? She lived a life of loving others, and in so doing, deepened her love of God. She loved/loves me, and that makes me the luckiest man on Earth. She showed me the way, every day of our life together. She shows me the way today.

Never doubt that God loves you, no matter how desperate your situation or how crushing the burden of your sins. If you're ever inclined to stop thinking that God loves you, start with this:

> *"Do not fear, for I have redeemed you;*
> *I have summoned you by name; you are mine.*
> *When you pass through the waters, I will be with you;*
> *And when you pass through the rivers,*
> *they will not sweep over you.*
> *When you walk through the fire, you will not be burned;*
> *the flames will not set you ablaze.*
> *For I am the Lord your God, the Holy One*
> *of Israel, your Savior; (Isaiah 43:)*

Think about this: Jesus Christ was created by the Father to save you, and me, and every human being who has been or ever will be born. The Holy Spirit is here right this very minute, looking for the opening in your heart that will let Him lead you to Jesus Christ and, through Jesus, to the Father. Stop fighting, and come to Christ, because you are His. We are His. And He is ours, if we humble ourselves to ask.

So what are you waiting for?

Bob

· · · · · ·

February 11, 2018

> *"...Trust in the Lord with all your heart, and do not rely on your own insight. In all your ways acknowledge Him, and he will make straight your paths..." (Proverbs 3: 5-6)*

Chrissy has had several respiratory and stimulus response setbacks during the past month, but seems to be recovering. She seems somewhat more lethargic and a bit less awake as I sit with her today. But I refuse to entertain the possibility that she's not recovering, and I rely on my faith, because it's the only way to make sense of the past 13 months, to convert the devastation visited on our wife and mother into seeking and proclaiming God's purpose for our lives. I humbly thank each of you for your continued prayers.

As the months wear on, I feel a growing sense of distance from Chrissy's body, though I'm as close as I ever was to the essence of who she is. I am slowly surrendering her to God — as if she was ever not His anyway. It is very difficult to accept that I'm slowly beginning to engage life without her, because I desperately don't want to. But in fact, that's exactly what's happening.

Though she's 104 miles away, many vestiges of her presence in our home remind me of the way she loved us, was always there when we needed her, was always doing for us and for others. I'm fighting the gradual but inexorable change of status, from Chrissy as the active centerpiece of our family, to Chrissy as completely dependent on others for every aspect of her life.

No matter the battle that rages over accepting her as an invalid, our ultimate comfort lies in the fact that it's what she believed, the way she lived, and how she loved that must inspire our lives going forward. Her faith, quiet but solid, manifested itself in everything she ever did, and I don't doubt for a second that that very same faith sustains her in this world as God uses her and us to accomplish His purposes.

Do we see our spouses, children, families, friends, and yes, strangers as God's creations, brought into our lives to help us achieve the purpose for which He gave us life? Do we see ourselves as God's creations, placed in this world to help others achieve the purpose for which He gave them life? Imagine the world if we looked at everyone we ever met — and never met — in that way.

Every morning when you wake up, think about how to live to inspire others. After all, we're called on to use God's gifts — body, mind and spirit — to be the light of the world. Maybe

I'm wearing rose colored glasses. That said, do you think God will accept the excuse that we chose to wear blindfolds?

Inspire someone today. For that matter, inspire EVERYONE today.

I dare you. ☺

Bob

. . . . . .

February 14, 2018

Then he poured water into a basin, and began to wash the disciples' feet and to wipe them with the towel with which he was girded. He came to Simon Peter; and Peter said to him, "Lord, do you wash my feet?" Jesus answered him, "What I am doing you do not know now, but afterward you will understand." Peter said to him, "You shall never wash my feet." Jesus answered him, If I do not wash you, you have no part

THE POSTS

> *in me." Simon Peter said to him, "Lord, not my feet only but also my hands and my head!" (John 13:5-9)*

Today is St. Valentine's Day. Chrissy is comfortable, but has started "wasting." She is unable to take in the volume of calories and protein she needs to sustain her life, so her body is slowly drawing them from her muscle tissue. Her once beautiful legs are getting thin, melting away to skin and bones. I don't know what she is or may be feeling or thinking. Darkness.

I could take her off hospice to do the things she needs to keep her alive. But then I ask myself, "What is the purpose?" If we can't repair the damage to her brain, what sense is there in working to keep her body alive? Do I "let nature take its course," or do I fight for her life, knowing there is very little likelihood of ever hearing her beautiful voice again?

Would I be keeping her alive for her sake, or for mine? And what does "alive" mean? There are no easy answers. There is very little, if any, black-and-white in this place in which I find myself.

But there is always "lumen Christi" — the light of Christ.

Sadness is watching her slowly waste away and die; joy is knowing where she is going. It's selfish to want to keep her physically here, to love her for me, rather than to commend her to God, loving her for her.

Choose for myself, or choose for her? Hobson lives. For 36 years we have been one, and together. Now we're facing the part where it ends, except that it's not ending. "Until death do us part" is under serious review. I'm not sure I can fully understand it. But I don't have a choice. The process of "parting" has become a slow dance with death, and I'm holding her up as she dances.

A friend with whom I sometimes share my thoughts told me last week, "Reality only wins a hundred percent of the time." I'm working to make my reality what God wants for Christine. But I don't know how God wants me to care for her. I've reached the point, finally, that I want her to find peace, and it isn't here. So do I follow my belief and my religion and continue to keep her "alive?" Prolonging her vegetative "life" will extend her suffering, if in fact she is suffering. I don't want to let her go, but she's really not mine to keep.

Will I spend eternity in Hell for my decisions? They are mine, and I own them. Or maybe it's better said that "they own me."

Sometimes it seems as if God is tearing her out of my life one cell at a time...

I'm trying hard to look through the Cross and not at it. The Cross is ugly, bloodstained, violent, the ultimate battleground of good vs. evil. And evil won the battle on that terrible, wonderful day.

The Ultimate Contradiction. Until the Resurrection.

When the darkness threatens to overwhelm, get down on your knees and pray.

Before the darkness threatens to overwhelm, get down on your knees and pray.

Every day of your life, get down on your knees and pray.

Bob

· · · · · ·

March 10, 2018

"...I am the Lord, and there is no other, besides me there is no God; I gird you, though you do not know me, that men may know, from the rising of the sun and from the west, that there is none besides me; I am the Lord and there is no other. I form light and

THE POSTS

create darkness, I make weal and create woe, I am the Lord, who do all these things..." (Isaiah 45: 5-7)

Chris continues with little change to her condition, now almost 14 months into our journey. The nature of our challenge has changed significantly. Where once we were dealing with neurological and physical crises which focused our attention on the immediate present, we now struggle with the absence of significant change and the prospect of PVS for the rest of her life. This new struggle is largely psychological, driven by the indelible image of Chrissy spending the rest of her life in a bed, unable to move and being fed through a tube, as we go about our lives blessed with all our faculties. Our burden hasn't lessened, it's only changed. If anything, it's heavier, and its attendant consequences to faith and health are potentially deadlier. We now have more than enough time to visualize her future in vivid, inescapable, tormenting detail.

Each day underscores her physical absence from our lives; every night is a battle to push back the avalanche of uninvited questions: Should we accept her present condition, or should we try to awaken her? Does loving her mean I should accept her condition and go on with my life, or does it mean I should do everything possible to restore her life? Isn't accepting her present condition just waiting for her to die? Knowing that her brain's centers for personality and memory were severely damaged, exactly who is inside the body in the bed? What is the meaning of "mercy?" Is it more merciful to end her life, or to keep her alive? For how long? You say you love her, but does love mean you keep her alive in a bed unable to move, or do you turn off nutrition and hydration and allow her to die and be with the God she loves?

The constant battle to push back against these questions wears on mind, body and soul. Intellect and will become the adversaries of our faith. But no matter our incredible advances in science and technology; no matter our skill in planning for the future; no matter all of mankind's achievements in every field of human endeavor, we are forced to accept that the future remains contingent on things beyond our control.

In this or any other situation that could ever arise, the only true remedy for the war between our intellect and our faith lies in Scripture and prayer. If we seek to live up to what God expects of us, we immerse ourselves in prayer and surrender the outcome to Him.

"Let go, let God." Some might call this an escape from reality. I call it an escape TO reality.

Make your escape today — to the heart and home of Almighty God. After all, it IS the Lord's day... 😊

Bob

. . . . . .

March 24, 2018

"...And behold, a Canaanite woman from the region came out and cried, "Have mercy on me, O Lord, Son of David: my daughter is severely possessed by a demon." But he did not answer her a word. And his disciples came and begged him, saying, "Send her away, for she is crying after us." He answered, "I was sent only to the lost sheep of the house of Israel." But she came and knelt before him, saying, "Lord, help me." And he answered, "It is not fair to take the children's bread and throw it to the dogs." She said, Yes Lord, yet even

THE POSTS

> *the dogs eat the crumbs that fall from their masters' table." Then Jesus answered her, "O woman, great is your faith! Be it done for you as you desire." And her daughter was healed instantly..." (Matthew 15:22-28)*

I've thought about writing this post for an entire week. After 14 months and 6 days on this journey, mindful of and grateful for the love and prayers you lavish on me and Christine, I am not inclined to raise false hope about her condition. She is still in PVS, and of late is at increased risk of suffocation from the large volume of secretions that gather in her larynx which block her airway when she coughs from time to time. But something happened last Sunday night that you deserve to know.

Last Sunday, the 4th Sunday of Lent, I went to Mass and then drove down to be with Chris for the rest of the day and through the night. I love our time together, as I pray with her, and I read to her, and hold her hands in mine, and talk to her. Her muscle mass is almost entirely gone, and she is turned every two hours to keep her skin intact and her circulation as robust as possible. No matter the challenges, she is as beautiful as ever.

I was sleeping in my cot near the foot of her bed when I heard her cough hard, and then the sound of her breathing stopped. I jumped up and ran to her. Her eyes were wide open in abject terror, because her airway was blocked and she couldn't breathe. I turned on the suction machine and cleared her throat. It took about 5 or 6 seconds, and as I was clearing the obstruction to her airway, I spoke to her, told her she was going to be okay, and the fear left her face. Her eyes, though, stayed wide open, and she looked directly at me for about 30 seconds. I don't know whether she actually SAW me, but there is no question that she was looking AT me, steadily, for half a minute.

The realization of what I had just seen rendered me speechless. Think about this: for Chrissy to show fear, she must have understood that she was in danger. And recognizing this, her brain was then able to signal the muscles in her face to show fear, to communicate what she was experiencing, just like any of us would.

Then she looked directly at me, into my eyes, for half a minute, before her expression returned to "normal."

I spoke during the week with the Director of Nursing, and he told me that he has felt for some time that Chrissy is becoming more conscious, and that they are occasionally able to communicate with her by asking her to blink once for yes, twice for no, and three times for maybe.

Also last week, I received news I had been praying for: the facility has contracted with one of the doctors I had asked to care for Chrissy as her primary care physician. This opens the door to taking her off of hospice and beginning to work proactively to restore her physical condition. It also means we can look into trying to assist her brain to heal and recover as much of her faculties as is possible. I don't believe it's a coincidence that this all happened the week before Palm Sunday, one week before Holy Week — the culmination of every prophesy in the Bible about our Redemption through the mercy of God in the blood of Jesus Christ poured out through His sacrifice at Calvary.

Matthew 15: 22-28 is about two things: Christ's invitation to those once thought to be excluded from God's plan of salvation, and the importance of persistence in prayer. We've been praying now for 14 months, and those prayers are bearing fruit, slowly but surely. With this incident last Sunday night, I believe God has shown me two things: first, that we can share in the Redemption; and second, that He is ever-present, and He hears our prayers.

God does not give up on us. Ever. So let's not give up on Him. Persist in prayer, and remain steadfast in faith.
Bob

. . . . . .

April 1, 2018

> "And very early on the first day of the week they went to the tomb when the sun had risen. And they were saying to one another, "Who will roll away the stone for us from the door of the tomb?" And looking up, they saw that the stone was rolled back — it was very large. And entering the tomb, they saw a young man sitting on the right side, dressed in a white robe; and they were amazed. And he said to them, "Do not be amazed; you seek Jesus of Nazareth, who was crucified. He has risen, he is not here; see the place where they laid him. But go, tell his disciples and Peter that he is going before you to Galilee; there you will see him, as he told you." And they went out and fled from the tomb; for trembling and astonishment had come upon them; and they said nothing to any one, for they were afraid." (Mark 16: 3-8)

March 28, Chrissy was discharged from hospice. We're no longer prohibited from working to improve her condition. She is still in PVS, but at times is more awake and more aware. She occasionally moves her extremities, and I've seen her "stretch" her entire body on numerous occasions. We move ahead cautiously, with full trust and confidence in God's plan. We remain deeply grateful for your continued prayers. If you could see the difference in her from a year ago, you would know that your prayers are working. Our God is an awesome God.

Today, Easter Sunday, we commemorate the Resurrection of Jesus Christ from the dead and the fulfillment of God's promise of salvation. This day, God's love for us is manifested in all its glory. This day, sin and death are vanquished forever. This day, the gates of Heaven are thrown open to mankind.

Good Friday was a day of horror for Christ's followers. They watched as the Son of God, bearer of the New Covenant, was betrayed, humiliated, tormented, tortured and killed. They didn't yet understand the meaning of His promise to "rebuild this house in three days," because they couldn't.

When Jesus delivered up His spirit and died, their faith was crushed. They only saw the Cross, because they were unable to see beyond it. They couldn't comprehend the sequel to Calvary because until Christ died to free us from sin and death, there was no sequel to life. They couldn't understand the Resurrection until its physical reality was visited upon them, when the women arrived at the tomb and the angel told them, "...You seek Jesus of Nazareth, who was crucified. He has risen, he is not here; see the place where they laid him..."

Today we celebrate The Greatest Love Story Ever Told. Christ's crucifixion and death paid the price of our salvation. Think about that. He took upon himself every sin ever committed and washed us clean with His blood. Then He rose from the dead to teach us not only to look at the Cross, but to see beyond it.

"And entering the tomb...they were amazed."

"And they went out and fled from the tomb, for trembling and astonishment had come upon them; and they said nothing to anyone, for they were afraid."

If trembling and astonishment aren't our reaction to The Greatest Love Story Ever Told, perhaps we don't truly comprehend the incredible act of love it represents. Maybe we're "comfortable" with it because we haven't really thought about it. Today, especially, we must sit down and truly contemplate what Almighty God has done for us. On this day especially, we must ask ourselves, "Do we flee from the tomb? Are trembling and astonishment upon us? Do we refrain from proclaiming the Cross and Resurrection because we are afraid of what the world might think?"

Tremble today, because we know God found us worthy enough to pay the Ultimate Ransom for our souls.

Be amazed, because the stone that closed the gates of Heaven to us has been moved out of the way.

Be in awe, because "...I have redeemed you; I have called you by name, you are mine..." (Isaiah 43: 1-2)

Have an astonishing day. ☺

Bob

. . . . . .

April 14, 2018

"Now there is in Jerusalem by the heep Gate a pool, in Hebrew called Beth-za-tha, which has five porticoes. In these lay a multitude of invalids, blind, lame, paralyzed. One man was there, who had been ill for thirty-eight years. When Jesus saw him and knew that he had been lying here a long time, he said to him, "Do you want to be healed?" The sick man answered him, "Sir I have no man to put me into the pool when the water

is troubled, and while I am going another steps down before me." Jesus said to him, "Rise, take up your pallet, and walk." And at once the man was healed, and he took up his pallet and walked." (John 5: 2-9)

In 2010, I met a person who has since become a good friend. We've been in touch off and on for the last 8 years, including occasional lunches and political activities. About a month ago, he called me at home. He, a friend, and his cousin and his cousin's wife were in Warren having lunch and he invited me to join them. I took my grandson, and we headed to the restaurant.

During lunch, our conversation migrated to Chrissy's condition, and his cousin's wife cautiously asked what had happened. I shared the events of the past 15 months, and she asked if I believed that physical infirmities could be healed by faith, and she then told us her story.

She was born with spina bifida, a congenital deformity of the spine. In 1974, she was healed after a Christian minister prayed over her. She has been completely normal ever since. The man who healed her has healed hundreds of others around the world, including children with autism, people with cancer, and many with all kinds of afflictions.

She related that the man who had healed her was going to be at a service in Goffstown on April 11-12 and asked if I would be open to having him pray over Christine.

Without hesitation, I agreed.

Jesus healed people from every walk of life who suffered physical afflictions of every kind. Holy men and women in the ensuing 2000 years have continued to heal the sick, performing miracles that defy every tenet of modern medicine.

The element of faith is vital to living our lives as God would have us do, and to healing us, whether our ailments be physical, mental, or moral. Jesus Christ gave us numerous examples of God's power, manifested in helping those who were "ill" in body, mind, and spirit. He went on to give his life for us at Calvary, because he knew that none of us could heal ourselves and find redemption on our own.

Look into your life, and diagnose your ailments. Then put yourself in the hands of Jesus Christ to seek the healing and peace that only He can bring.

Get well soon! ☺

Bob

. . . . . .

May 6, 2018

"Surely he has borne our griefs and carried our sorrows; yet we esteemed him stricken, smitten by God, and afflicted. But he was wounded for our transgressions, he was bruised for our iniquities; upon him was the chastisement that made us whole, and with his stripes we are healed. All we like sheep have gone astray; we have turned every one to his own way; and the Lord has laid on him the iniquity of us all." (Isaiah 53: 4-6)

Chrissy continues in PVS, and we continue praying for her with open minds and loving hearts. About a month ago, I asked you to pray with increased fervor because (now you'll understand) I asked a Christian minister who has healed people around the world and was visiting a local faith community, to pray over Chris. A group of us prayed at her bedside for about half an hour.

Though no immediate result was forthcoming, last Sunday afternoon, during my visit with her, shortly after she had been turned (she's turned every two hours around the clock), I reached over the bed rail and gently grasped her upper right arm, letting her know I was with her.

She then did something she's never done before: she moved her entire right leg, from hip to foot — not a muscle spasm, but movement such as you or I would do to change position. And I've recently noticed that she will occasionally move her head in the direction of my voice - only about an inch, but it's definitely a neural response that's producing intentional movement.

I believe God is continuing His healing work with Chrissy.

For the last month or so, "missing Chris" has permeated my life. The arrival of Spring should inspire a celebration of new life; but Chrissy's condition made its arrival poignant. The silence at home is a stark counterpoint to the sounds of new life all around us. I miss her physical presence, the music of her voice, the twinkle in her eyes, the magic of her smile. Caught up and wandering in a spiritual desert focused on myself, it finally dawned on me that I had lost sight of the centerpiece of Christian salvation: Jesus Christ.

Ironically, I've told friends and strangers many times, "It is during periods of silence in our lives that God whispers most clearly to us." I stopped embracing the adversity, and instead, I embraced my personal sense of loss. Didn't God understand that I was suffering? But when we actualize God's message of love, suffering and adversity only serve to purify and sanctify us, in turn rendering us more receptive to understanding God's purpose for us, more aware of the promptings of the Holy Spirit, and more pleasing to God more completely.

Sensory deprivation and silence were used with devastating effectiveness against spies during the Cold War. Extended periods of such treatment led to insanity and death. Spiritual deprivation can paralyze us, or it can compel us to deepen our relationship with God. Mystics (Christian and other) seek such perfect silence as a means to enter into total communion with God while still here on Earth.

In seeing only that which was missing from my life, I lost sight of that which is present in it: God the Father, the Alpha and the Omega; God the Son, Jesus Christ, the Way, the Truth and the Life; and God the Holy Spirit, the active enabler of God's work in this world. And I lost sight of the incredible spiritual power of the prayers thousands of you are offering for Christine.

At Calvary, in His moment of deepest anguish and spiritual desolation, when those He loved most had disavowed even knowing Him, Christ's last prayer was, "Father, into thy hands I commend my spirit." With that utterance, He gave himself over completely to our Father's will.

Likewise, when we're facing desolation and silence, we, too, must put ourselves completely in God's hands. Whether pauper or king, sinner or saint, we must keep sight of the message of salvation: Jesus Christ was sent by a loving Father to wash away our sins with His blood. The incomprehensible anguish of bearing the burden of that expiation dwarfs any suffering any human being will ever encounter.

In our suffering, we must commend ourselves into our Father's hands and conjoin our anguish to that of His beloved Son.

In the movie, "The Bucket List," Morgan Freeman and Jack Nicholson, cast as two terminally ill men, assembled a list of things they wanted to do before they died. On that list were two items that are particularly relevant: (1) Help a complete stranger; and (2) find the joy in your life.

We don't need to wait until we're dying to accomplish these two items. Today, and every day, we can help a complete stranger, and we can find the joy in our lives.

And it's quite possible we're able to do both at the same time. ☺

Bob

. . . . . .

May 20, 2018

> *"The Lord is my shepherd, I shall not want. He maketh me to lie down in green pastures. He leadeth me beside the still waters. He restoreth my soul. He leadeth me in paths of righteousness for His name's sake. Yea, though I walk through the valley of the shadow of death, I will fear no evil, for thou art with me; thy rod and thy staff, they comfort me. Thou preparest a table before me in the presence of my enemies; thou anointest my head with oil, my cup runneth over. Surely goodness and mercy shall follow me all the days of my life, and I will dwell in the house of the Lord forever." (Psalm 23)*

There's been no substantial change since our last update, but Chrissy's g-tube (the latex rubber tube through her abdominal wall into her stomach, by which she receives all her nutrition and hydration) is going to need replacement in the not-too-distant future. It was surgically installed 16 months ago and is beginning to break down. Rather than waiting for it to fail and precipitate an emergency, we'd like to be proactive and make the change under controlled conditions. The transport to and from the hospital is a significant threat to her; the anesthesia is a much bigger threat, because we don't know how her badly injured brain will respond to it. I'm grateful beyond words for your continued prayers for Chris and for our family.

I keep a picture of Chrissy as the "wallpaper" on my cellphone. It's the first picture I took with the then-new phone, totally spontaneous, and it captured the smile she shared with everyone whose life she touched. Her eyes show the gentle wonder with which she approached life, and which made her so easy to love. She is the "giving-est" person I ever met, and her love, her laughter, and her generosity were pure, and selfless, and genuine. Thank you, God, for bringing her to me. Forgive me for the hurts I caused her, for the time I didn't share with her, for the love I sometimes didn't see. She enabled everything I've done for 35+ years, and then suddenly she couldn't give any more — at least not the way she used to. But she does continue to give.

Our lives changed drastically one month before we retired and would begin to enjoy all she had waited for 35 years. We talked about our specific plans for the remainder of 2017 the day before she was stricken. She was elated, and laughing, and full of excitement and joy at the prospect of our being together. Now she lays in a bed, unable to eat, move, speak or see, with no way for us to know her state of mind, and little for us to do except remember how, and how much, she loved us. And to pray, fervently and unceasingly, for God's will to bring healing.

Over the past sixteen months, I've yelled at God quite a bit. He hasn't yelled back, and that's probably a good thing. God didn't cause her affliction. In fact, the world God gave us was free of sin and death and sorrow until our original parents screwed it up. I continue searching for how to turn our tragedy to God's purposes. Maybe I'm looking too hard. Maybe I need to lay down for a while in that green pasture, to rest for a bit beside those still waters.

We're trapped by the terms of her living will. Her request to not continue life if unconscious is in direct conflict with her request to maintain hydration and nutrition — a fundamental principle of our faith. Honoring the one means keeping her alive indefinitely. Honoring the other sentences her to die of thirst and starvation. I have chosen life, because I know how strong her faith was, and is. And I know that God calls on us to respect Him as the Author of Life. No matter what the world says, it's His exclusive domain.

Some have challenged whether Chrissy's life has value given her current condition. I believe her life DOES have value, and here's why. I know there are thousands of you praying for us, and that your faith and ours is stronger because of it. Some have shared that these posts have brought you closer to God, or strengthened your faith, or saved your marriage, or helped you cope with tragedy. There IS value — infinite value — in Chrissy's life, because God created her and me and every one of us with a specific role in His plan of salvation. It's not our place to know that plan, or to know why certain things happen, only that He promised us that if we follow Him, we will one day be with Him in Paradise.

Some shake their heads at what they consider blind obedience. But following the dictates of conscience is not "blind obedience." It is "informed obedience" to the inviolable sanctity of human life. We ignore this truth at the eternal peril of our immortal souls. I relearn, day after day, the meaning of "surrender." There are aspects of this situation I will never get my arms or my head around. So I have to let them go, because wrestling them will ultimately steal my health, my mind, my soul and my life.

Making the Lord our shepherd requires a conscious act, reaffirmed every single day of our lives. It requires combating the complacency that sets in during the ordinary times and rejecting the doubt and fear that assail us when tragedy comes our way. If we make that conscious choice, if "the Lord is my shepherd," God will show us green pastures and still waters, and He will restore our souls. But if we heed anything other than the call of the Shepherd, we will eventually become lost in the wilderness of the world.

When beset by uncertainty, anger, fear or despair, stop, look and listen for the Shepherd.

Because He and His angels are actively looking and listening for you. ☺

Bob

. . . . . .

June 6, 2018

> "Thus says God, the Lord, who created the heavens and stretched them out, who spread forth the earth and what comes from it, who gives breath to the people upon it and spirit to those who walk in it: "I am the Lord, I have called you in righteousness, I have taken you by the hand and kept you; I have given you as a covenant to the people, a light to the nations, to open the eyes that are blind, to bring out the prisoners from the dungeon, from the prison those who sit in darkness. I am the Lord, that is my name; my glory I give to no other, nor my praise to

> graven images. Behold, the former things have come to pass, and new things I now declare; before they spring forth I tell you of them." (Isaiah 42:5-9)

On June 2nd Chrissy turned 70. Stephanie, Hunter and I visited her and spent the afternoon celebrating with her. She had a wonderfully quiet day, no respiratory issues, no vomiting, and lots of rest between her "awake" periods. I decided to wait until today to share my thoughts because several things have happened in the past week, one of which I wanted to confirm before sharing them with you.

Since September 28 last year, we've needed a Primary Care Physician (PCP) for Chris. We've had three pending arrangements fall through at the last minute, meaning that we weren't able to get doctor's orders (required) for physical, occupational or speech therapy. A very gracious doctor who was Chrissy's PCP when we were caring for her at home did help when things were deteriorating rapidly, but she is 90 miles from Chrissy's facility and couldn't physically visit as needed to meet the legal requirements for the level of care Chris needs. We've prayed hard that a PCP would come forth, and I'm asking you to thank God with me because tomorrow morning, Tuesday, June 5, Chrissy's new PCP will examine her in her bed. Not only does Chris have a new PCP, but so do all the residents of the assisted living home, because a particular doctors' group has agreed to take on the whole facility as a client. For so long we have waited, and God has provided in even greater measure than we ever expected. I fully expect that orders for Physical and Occupational Therapy will be forthcoming almost immediately, and I'll be able to discuss other measures that we might consider to improve Chrissy's condition.

On Memorial Day weekend, I spent (as I usually do) Sunday afternoon and night with Chris. I keep a cot in her spacious room and have to believe she knows I'm there. It's beautiful to watch her face become peaceful as I pray with and for her. As I was getting ready to leave her on that Monday morning, standing on the left side of her bed, I kissed her forehead, told her that I love her and that I'd be back soon.

What happened next stopped me in my tracks.

She partially turned her head and raised her right shoulder and upper arm towards me, lifting them completely off the wedges and pillows supporting her. It is the single most deliberate and expansive movement she has made since January 18, 2017. I have no doubt whatsoever that she was communicating. This was not a convulsion or spasm. It was a deliberate movement.

I've spent the intervening week thinking about Chrissy's incredible courage. I've thought a lot about the purpose and meaning of suffering, because as much as our family struggles, I cannot even begin to imagine the suffering she is enduring. Though at times horribly difficult, we believe that suffering enables us to participate in a very small way in Christ's suffering and death for our sins. There is no way to comprehend the scope and depth of what He went through at Calvary: expiation of every sin ever committed by mankind. Our individual suffering provides a means to greater sanctification in our own lives as we participate in a small way in Christ's agony on the Cross.

If we hold true to our commitment to the sanctity of life, we are compelled to see suffering as something that enriches our lives, both when we help alleviate the suffering of others, and by accepting our own suffering as a share in the redemptive power of Christ's crucifixion.

I want to share a recent personal story that has provided me with some perspective on suffering.

After reconnecting with a Marine Corps friend with whom I flew many years ago, he emailed me that he was suffering from an illness that causes tendons and ligaments to harden. It will ultimately, slowly, kill him. Several weeks ago, he called me, and shared that his wife of many years had just been diagnosed with ALS — Lou Gehrig's disease. It will ultimately, slowly, kill her. They will enjoy the privilege of watching one another die, day by day, eventually being unable to do anything for one another except to watch, and to pray.

I am humbled by the magnitude of the suffering they will endure alone, together.

Please pray for them, as we reaffirm our belief in the sanctity of human life and the redemptive power of suffering. God doesn't cause tragedies. But He knows them, and His love for us is only the greater because by enduring them to the end, we live out our obligation to respect Him as the Author of Life.

"I am the Alpha and the Omega, the First and the Last, the Beginning and the End." (Revelations 22:13)

God bless each of you, and all of you. Now please go practice your Greek. ☺

Bob

. . . . . .

June 15, 2018

"Now there was a man in Jerusalem called Simeon, who was righteous and devout. He was waiting for the consolation of Israel, and the Holy Spirit was on him. It had been revealed to him by the Holy Spirit that he

> *would not die before he had seen the Lords' messiah. Moved by the Spirit, he went into the temple courts. When the parents brought in the child Jesus to do for him what the custom of the Law required, Simeon took him in his arms and praised God, saying, "Sovereign Lord, as you have promise, you may now dismiss your servant in peace. For my eyes have seen your salvation, which you have prepared in the sight of all nations, a light for revelation to the Gentiles, and the glory of your people Israel." (Luke 2, 25-32)*

I stayed with Chris Thursday night through Friday morning, and she's doing well. She was breathing almost no problems with phlegm, and she slept through the night very comfortably. I do range of motion exercises and massage her arms, wrists and hands to fight the contracture that threatens her flexibility. Interestingly, her right hand was perfectly relaxed. Her left hand, however, was curled up into a tight fist. I set to work to loosen it up, and in so doing I pushed my index finger down between her palm and clenched fingers to massage her finger joints. As I was doing so, she pulled my hand towards her. This was not a spasm, but another indication that her brain is finding alternative ways to communicate with her extremities. We continue to pray, and to trust in God and His plan for Christine and for each of us.

"Luck" has sometimes been defined as opportunity meeting preparedness.

I used to wonder how Simeon figured out that Jesus was the Messiah, but no longer. It was luck. He was "...righteous and devout, and waiting..."

Righteousness grows out of being grounded in God's law and living a life of virtue — without fanfare or expectation of acclaim or personal benefit. It means avoiding and rejecting evil. And it requires humility, as we remind ourselves it was God's love for us — and only His love for us — that moved Him to send His Son to die for us and thereby reopen the Gates of Heaven.

Devotion comes from loving Jesus Christ and His message. It inspires gratitude for that which was consummated and perfected on the Cross at Calvary.

Can you imagine the amazement Simeon felt when He held the Christ child and knew in his heart that this was The One?

Would our lives be different if we treated every person we ever met as if they were "The One?"

And how much better would our world be if we "turned the other cheek" and forgave those who offended us "seventy times seven times" or went the extra mile for those in need, physically or spiritually?

> *Then the righteous will answer him, "Lord, when did we see thee hungry and feed thee, or thirsty and give thee drink? And when did we see thee a stranger and welcome thee, or naked and clothe thee? And when did we see thee sick or in prison and visit thee?" And the King will answer them, "Truly, I say to you, as you did it to one of the least of these my brethren, you did it to me." (Matthew 25: 37-40)*

There is no shortage of opportunity to treat others as if they were "The One," or to minister to those in need physically or spiritually. The question is, have you made it your business to recognize them?

Here's to us having 20/20 vision. ☺

Bob

June 27, 2018 — 37th Anniversary

"...The Lord loves those who hate evil; He preserves the lives of his saints; He delivers them from the hand of the wicked. Light dawns for the righteous, and joy for the upright in heart. Rejoice in the Lord, O you righteous, and give thanks to His holy name." (Psalm 97)

Chrissy seems to have plateaued for the time being. Some days we see things that give us cause for optimism, some days bring reason to fear. Change is definitely happening, though. She now occasionally slightly moves her head, moves her legs, moves her arms; though small movements, they are definitely an improvement. She sometimes opens her eyes in response to noises. In every case, we turn to God, in thanksgiving or in supplication, because her life, and our lives, are His.

Because God gave us free will, we don't have to accept or acknowledge His supremacy. We can choose to put ourselves first. And when we do, the world begins to fall apart. Just look around to see the manifestations and consequences of disrespect for God as the author of all life. They are everywhere, as every sinner who has felt the terrible desolation of spiritual alienation from God, knows.

Dear Chris,

Today we celebrate and **remember** the people, places, memories and events — some happy, some sad — that wove the tapestry of our life together. Today we celebrate our story — the story that began the day we said, "I do," 37 years ago.

Today is the day I **regret** the things I said and did and wish I hadn't, and the things I didn't do that I wish I had, because of the sorrow they caused the person I love most in this world.

Today is the day I **reflect** on our life together, because laughter and joy are what God wanted me to bring to you, but that's not always what I did.

Today is the day I **rejoice** in the **redemptive** power of the Crucifixion and the **restorative** power of the **Resurrection**. Our marriage survived because of your faith when my love of self was washing the world out from under you, and the thought of tomorrow brought pangs of dread instead of peals of laughter, and you prayed out of love, and fear, and hope, and you saved me.

Today is the day I **reaffirm** with my heart, mind, body and soul that marrying you is the best thing I ever did. Thank you for seeing in me the person you believed would love, honor and cherish you during our journey. Forgive me for the times I didn't deserve that love.

That you married me was a gift; that you stayed with me was a miracle. I wish I had always remembered that, and that I had always respected and loved you the way God intended. But I sometimes didn't, and that's why God sent His Son — to redeem me from the jaws of Hell, and to give me the chance to earn Heaven.

I miss you, Chrissy. You're here, but you're not. I miss the sound of your voice, the music of your laughter, the warmth of your embrace, the twinkle in your eyes, your beautiful smile, your selfless heart, your abundant kindness, your gentle encouragement, and the million other things that you brought to me, to our children, to our families, to our friends, and to everyone whose life you touched.

And though you're not able to do the things you used to do, to say the things we want to hear, to care for us as we wish you could, you are as beautiful today as ever, because no earthly affliction can diminish the light and the love you bring to the world and to the lives of all who know you.

Happy 37th anniversary, Mrs. G. I love you.

Please come home soon. I need you.

Our kids need you.

The world needs you.

Always and forever,

Bob

. . . . . .

July 16, 2018

'"Yet even now," says the Lord, "return to me with all your heart, with fasting, with weeping, and with mourning; and rend your hearts and not your garments." Return to the Lord, your God, for he is gracious and merciful, slow to anger, and abounding in steadfast love, and repents of evil.' (Joel 2: 12-13)

Christine continues as she has been, with very small changes indicating that her neuro-muscular system may slowly be finding new pathways within her brain. She moves her head an inch or two, her right shoulder and upper arm do a slight "shrug" motion, and her right arm occasionally pulls upward and inward towards her upper torso. We continue to pray, fully trusting in God's purposes. We recommit ourselves to eagerly believing that God is at work here. Thank you for loving Christine and our family with your prayers.

For the past 18 months, we've fought against despair and resignation as we push back against the relentless image of a helpless, bedridden, motionless, Christine. Tragedy and the limits of our understanding can cause us to question God's purposes, and it can undermine our zest for the Lord.

The mind, heart and body, in the absence of God's redeeming grace, will experience spiritual starvation, leading us away from God and into desolation. The numbness and paralysis caused by life's protracted struggles can cause us to relax or even abandon the practice of our faith.

Nothing in life is static: not our love of God, not God's love for us, and not our faith. If we're not gaining ground, we're falling behind. God's love and His power are omnipresent, but we have to take hold of them of our own free will. We must push the envelope of our faith to grow our love of God. We must nurture our body, mind and soul every single day with the grace we receive through prayer, fasting, and studying God's word.

There is an insidious trap is becoming comfortable with our faith. Prayer becomes more of a habit than a conscious, deliberate outreach to grasp God's hand and let Him lead us. Ultimately, anything less than total commitment to seeking God's purpose for us denies us the fullness of His love because we aren't doing our part to earn it. Being satisfied with the status quo means we accept the distance that exists between where we are and where God wants us to be.

Being saved doesn't just happen on its own. Every day of our lives, we must consciously choose to GO TO HIM. The joy we seek is not of this world; it is the joy that only a vibrant relationship with Father, Son and Holy Spirit can bring. And it's the work of building that vibrant relationship that should exhaust us, not the trials and tribulations of this imperfect world.

As Christians, we are called to grow, to deepen our finite relationship with an Infinite God, to remove the "basket" that hides the light of our faith from a world that desperately needs it. We are called to faithfully and actively seek God. "...rend your hearts, and not your garments..."

We have to actively keep moving towards God. It's not good to keep the Master of Creation waiting. ☺

Because He loves you.

Bob

. . . . . .

August 28, 2018

"Fear not, for I have redeemed you; I have called you by name, you are mine..." (Isaiah 43:1)

I wish I had more to share with you about Chris, but she remains stable with some indications that she may be gradually improving. This is totally consistent with the v e r y s l o w progress that's associated with the severity of her brain injury. We think she may occasionally be trying to speak, as she sometimes makes "throat noises" when we're talking with her over the phone or in person; she sometimes wiggles the toes on her left foot when asked to do so, and sometimes she'll stop when asked to stop. Every glimmer of hope is welcome. Please keep us all in your prayers as our journey continues.

We are now in for the "long pull," and that's what prompted me to write today. My updates are coming less frequently, as life is acquiring a "new normal." The "emotional adrenaline" that drove us when she was fighting for her life and we were doing everything possible to keep her alive is no longer surging through our hearts and minds. We are settling into a different "normal." Things are stable. Calm prevails.

An average person today can expect to live to age 85. In those 31,000+ days, our sense of wonder about creation, about life, and about those God places in our lives, is often dulled by life's routine. Unless we consciously and continuously refresh and reinforce our sense of wonder at the magnificence of God's creation, the routine of daily life gradually erodes our spiritual awareness of the unique and beautiful gift that each day and each person in our life represents. Complacency replaces enthusiasm, and the world slowly steals away the joy God intended for us.

I've felt the approaching onset of complacency — especially spiritually now that God has delivered us from the storm. So I remind myself of Isaiah (above) and the fact that God specifically created me in His image and likeness for a reason.

Calling ourselves "followers of Christ" is, in one sense, a manifestation of complacency. We should not be "following" Christ; we should be chasing Him. That means exertion and effort, working to discern and then accomplish God's plan for us.

At the beginning of each day, and at its end, I've started asking myself, "Am I worth the investment God made in me with the death and Resurrection of His Son?" Generating a return on that investment means actively investing the capital God has given us — our lives — in growing our faith and sharing this investment opportunity with others.

Spiritual growth requires active exertion of mind and body. We Marines say that "Pain is weakness leaving the body" and "No pain, no gain." If we're not having aches and pains, we're not growing spiritually. We are compelled to reject worldly temptations and live lives of virtue.

We can make ourselves more pleasing to God through our suffering. No matter how hard it is, we must seek out God's priorities and share his message of salvation by living it — in our thoughts, words and deeds.

So don't just follow Jesus Christ. Chase Him.

And please let us know if you ever catch Him. ☺

Bob

. . . . . .

September 2, 2018

"Or do you presume upon the riches of his kindness and forbearance and patience? Do you not know that God's kindness is meant to lead you to repentance?" (Romans 2: 4)

Chrissy remains where God needs her to be to accomplish His purposes. I am certain that among them is greater sanctification for me, and I am grateful to Him as He uses the people in my life to lead me closer to Him. Christine is one of God's messengers to me. So are you.

I'm slowly sorting through the things we've acquired during 37 years of marriage. They continue to provide wonderful insights into Chrissy's faith and love of God, me, our family, and our friends. I'm learning things I never knew about her, often amazed at what she accomplished and the lives she touched. After almost 20 months, I'm just beginning to dig out from under the emotional turmoil and spiritual tempest we've endured with God's help and your prayers. I owe each of you more than my words can ever convey. Please keep praying.

Early this morning, as I was sifting through some of Chrissy's "stuff" from her craft room, I came upon an index-card-sized lithograph that shows Christ suspended from a rope as He's being taken down from the Cross after His crucifixion. Inscribed on the back side of this card was the following message:

> *Abandoned to death*
> *you descended into the deep*
> *where the longing*
> *of our poor soul's memory cries out;*
> *and there, in raw silence*
> *at the roots of our illusions,*
> *you rescued us.*

I find this description of salvation profoundly powerful.

In the same Epistle to the Romans quoted at the start of this message, Paul wrote:

"Therefore God gave them up in the lusts of their hearts to impurity, to the dishonoring of their bodies among themselves, because they exchanged the truth about God for a lie and worshiped and served the creature rather than the Creator, who is blessed forever! Amen!

"For this reason God gave them up to dishonorable passions. Their women exchanged natural relations for unnatural, and the men likewise gave up natural relations with women and were consumed with passion for one another, men committing shameless acts with men and receiving in their own persons the due penalty for their error.

And since they did not see fit to acknowledge God, God gave them up to a base mind and to improper conduct. They were filled with all manner of wickedness, evil, covetousness, malice. Full of envy, murder, strife, deceit, malignity, they are gossips, slanderers, haters of God, insolent, haughty, boastful, inventors of evil, disobedient to parents, foolish, faithless, heartless, ruthless. Though they know God's decree that those who do such things deserve to die, they not only do them but approve those who practice them."

Our nation's Founders, without exception, expounded repeatedly that a nation that loses its basis in faith does not long remain a free people. History bears this out time and time again. Re-reading the verse from Chrissy's room raises the question of whether our nation is being confounded and deceived by illusion. Are we confusing "freedom" with "license" and exchanging "liberty" for "libertine?"

Jesus Christ told those whose sins he forgave, "Go and sin no more," and "Go your way, your faith has saved you." But it's not just rejecting sin that God wants from us. He wants the complete transformation of our hearts. Ending sinful behavior out of fear of judgment is only a reaction to the Truth. It is not embracing or loving the Truth. God has so much more in mind for us if we complete the transaction by not only rejecting sin but pursuing Truth — chasing after Christ — and transforming our hearts so we can truly live joyful, meaningful lives.

Banks require you to use a teller or ATM to access your wealth. The Father requires us to use Jesus to receive His riches: forgiveness of our sins and receipt of the grace to enter the Kingdom of Heaven. It is Christ alone, through the workings of the Holy Spirit, who can transform our hearts, and He'll do it if we let Him. "I am the Way, the Truth, and the Life. No one comes to the Father but through me," isn't a maybe. It's a pronouncement of theological fact by the Son of God.

When Jesus was working with everyday people, He frequently taught by using parables. But He went after those with treachery in their hearts directly. Remember the scribes and pharisees? "...you brood of vipers..." Remember the money-changers in the temple? He drove them out with whips and knocked over their tables because they were defiling the house of God. When a nation rebels against the Word of God and enshrines in its law things that contradict God's law, it's future is in peril.

In the last moments of His agony on the Cross, Jesus forgave those who killed Him: "Father, forgive them, for they know not what they do." But what will happen to those who continue to sin and DO know what they do?

God's love is not unconditional. We have to do our part, not only by rejecting Satan and all his allurements, but by committing our hearts, minds and bodies to the Son of God because we love Him.

See you at the ATM. ☺
Bob

. . . . . .

September 13, 2018

"Come to me, all ye who labor and are heavy laden, and I will give you rest. Take my yoke upon you, and learn from me; for I am gentle and lowly in heart, and you will find rest for your souls. For my yoke is easy, and my burden is light." (Matthew 11:28-30)

The phone rang yesterday afternoon, and the voice at the other end of the line asked quietly, "Is this Bob?" I replied that it was, and in a soft voice, Matt (Chrissy's speech therapist) delivered the message we didn't want to hear. Like her physical and occupational therapists, he too was ending his work with Chris because over the past two months of regular visits, she had not responded to treatment. I could feel the regret and sorrow in his voice, because he knew what his message would mean to us. I quietly thanked him for all he had done, and for his compassion, and for the hope he had brought to us and to Chris and to so many others during his years of practice.

We've been living in hope for 20 months. For the past 3 months, we've been waiting with fingers crossed as courses of therapy intended to raise her to a higher level of consciousness were administered. But one by one, they were withdrawn, and our hoped-for outcomes didn't happen. We're left with the stark reality of her condition and a sense of futility at our inability to improve it. I sensed his feeling of defeat as Matt hung up the phone, and I exhaled slowly. My shoulders slumped and I looked down at the floor by my feet.

Matt's phone call brought back the stone around my heart. It's real, so much so that I actually have to lean forward to accommodate its presence. It's about the size of my hands if I clasp them together.

This morning, I awakened early and walked through the house and out into the barn in the pre-dawn darkness. Some years ago, I had built a kneeler large enough so that Chris and I could kneel and pray together; I wish I had used it more, but that's a story for another time. I knelt and prayed briefly, but suddenly realized I don't even know what to pray for anymore. And maybe that's the point that God is trying to make: that sometimes, our prayer has to be simply giving up the emptiness in our lives and the stone around our hearts to His loving care.

THE POSTS

Hope based upon the works of man is a false hope. Only hope derived from complete trust in God can deliver what our hearts and minds yearn for, and our souls truly need.

You know, it's kind of interesting that the stone around my heart is about the same size as my hands when I clasp them together...

Bring hope to someone who needs it today. It'll make your heart sing. ☺

Bob

. . . . . .

October 7, 2018

"I remember the days of long ago; I meditate on all your works and consider what your hands have done. I spread out my hands to you; I thirst for you like a parched land. Answer me quickly, Lord; my spirit fails. Do not hide your face from me or I will be like those who go down to the pit. Let the morning bring me word of your unfailing love, for I have put my trust in you. Show me the way I should go, for to you I entrust my life. Rescue me from my enemies, Lord, for I hide myself in you. Teach me to do your will, for you are my God; may your good Spirit lead me on level ground. For your name's sake, Lord, preserve my life; in your righteousness, bring me out of trouble. In your unfailing love, silence my enemies; destroy all my foes, for I am your servant." (Psalm 143: 5-12)

I started this post several weeks ago when I was with Chris. I need to finish it now.

She's sound asleep this morning, as I sit next to her after a fairly uneventful night, the noise of the portable air filtration unit giving texture to the predawn darkness. Over the past 21 months, some (not at her current facility) have hinted that we are prolonging a life that has little or no value, and that perhaps the best thing to do is to turn off the machine that provides her food and water and let her die. Life would be so much easier. Flip the switch and cure the inconvenience.

How do we assign value to a life? Jesus admonished rich and poor alike that the things of this world will not be the metrics of our fitness for Heaven. In essence, Chrissy in her vegetative state is living in complete poverty. But though she lies motionless in a bed, she is having a profound effect on my life and on lives all over the world. Some have shared privately that they've regained their faith because we've told her story. So how do you value saving a soul?

We know that the Cross is only part of the story of salvation. The Resurrection tells us the rest. And at the end of the day, no matter our crosses during the journey of life, they are actually the pathway to sharing in the Resurrection.

Watching her sleep, I realize that there's something beautiful and sacred here. It's the opportunity to see the hand of God in all that we encounter in life, and to seek His purpose in determining our response. Chrissy trusted me with her life, and God entrusted me with her care. I'll let Him decide when it's time for her to come home.

> *"For what will it profit a man, if he gains the whole world, and forfeits his life?..." (Matthew 16:26)*

Sit down today and give part of your life to someone — your husband, wife, child, brother, sister, friend, or stranger. Help them with their crosses, and yours will truly become lighter.

God will hear your sighs of relief. ☺
Have a loving day.
Bob

. . . . . .

October 14, 2018

"Fret not yourself because of the wicked, be not envious of wrongdoers! For they will soon fade like the grass, and wither like the green herb. Trust in the Lord, and do good; so you will dwell in the land, and enjoy security. Take delight in the Lord, and he will give you the desires of your heart. Commit your way to the Lord; trust in him, and he will act. He will bring forth your vindication as the light, and your right as the noonday. Be still before the Lord, and wait patiently for him; fret not yourself over him who prospers in his way, over the man who carries out evil devices! Refrain from anger, and forsake wrath! Fret not yourself; it tends only to evil. For the wicked shall be cut off, but those who wait for the Lord shall possess the land." (Psalm 37:1-9)

Under our economic system and our form of government, while all are created equal and endowed by our Creator with certain inalienable rights, the outcome of our lives spans the entire gamut of human achievement: from stunning victories to crushing defeats; from opulent prosperity to utter poverty; and from lives based on Christian principles to lives dedicated to hedonism.

The removal of God from our schools and our public institutions is wreaking havoc on families and the structural institutions that are essential to perpetuating our civilization. Every metric and statistic point unambiguously to the devolution of what was once a God-fearing (and God-protected) nation. We see example after example of evil winning out over goodness, of dishonesty and treachery overcoming virtue and principle. It's easy to get distracted by the success of the ungodly; but at the end of the day — at the end of OUR days — we will be held to account for everything we've done — or failed to do — with our lives.

The Ten Commandments are fundamental to our (rapidly deteriorating) system of law and order; without them as a framework, knowledge will not be transformed into wisdom. Proverbs tells us that "the beginning of wisdom is fear of the Lord." Removal of any mention of God or Scripture from the formal education of our children is (as planned) destroying the moral fabric of our nation. The prognosis is certain if we don't reverse this disastrous course. Our children are being given knowledge without the benefit of a moral framework within which to use it — the equivalent of giving a child a loaded gun to play with, with no idea how to use it. The result? Substance abuse is epidemic, as is the proliferation of STDs, pornography, sex slavery, divorce, domestic violence, and disrespect for lawful authority.

As Christians, we're called to share the Truth with those whose lives we touch. That's a tall order because most of us are reluctant to engage in discussions about faith, religion, and politics. But if we don't overcome our distaste for talking about "that stuff," Christ among us is silenced, and the resulting moral cacophony is deafening.

President Teddy Roosevelt is often cited for his well-known quote: "Speak softly and carry a big stick."

That's not an invitation to stay silent when conflict arises, be it physical, emotional, or spiritual. It's an exhortation to, "Speak, softly."

Who knows? Your thoughtful words may wake the dead.
Bob

. . . . . .

November 11, 2018
> *"Thy steadfast love, O Lord, extends to the heavens, they faithfulness to the clouds. Thy righteousness is like the mountains of God, thy judgments are like the great deep; man and beast thou savest, O Lord. How precious is thy steadfast love, O God! The children of men take refuge in the shadow of thy wings. They feast on the abundance of thy house, and thou givest them drink from the river of thy delights. For with thee is the fountain of life; in thy light do we see light. O continue thy steadfast love to those who know thee, and thy salvation to the upright of heart!" (Psalm 36)*

Chrissy's condition remains unchanged. She does spend about 3 hours each day sitting up in a Broda chair, "socializing" with other residents or "watching" a movie. She also gets a whirlpool bath three times each week. We visit, we pray with her, read to her, watch movies with her, talk to her, make sure she knows our love for her has only grown stronger. She doesn't respond, but I know she knows how much we love her, and I know she knows God's love for her.

Each of us formulates a foundation upon which we build our lives. Sometimes we use the wrong materials in that foundation, or we build it on flawed footings, or we don't maintain it, and the house we should be building for God teeters with spiritual uncertainty or collapses into sin.

During the 22+ months of this journey, I've struggled to find God's purpose in Christine's condition. I've spent almost two years looking for some intricate or complicated secret that God would disclose in an "Aha!" moment. God let me continue to flail around within my human limitations, and it was only when I finally became still that I found what I'd been seeking. It's been visible all along, but I couldn't see it.

The purpose for Chrissy's life going forward was actually revealed to me the day after she was stricken. Just a few days ago, I finally stopped looking for what I thought it should be, and there it was, right in front of me. It's been in plain sight since January 18, 2017 but I couldn't see it because I was so intent on trying to fit God's purpose into the context of my life. But that's exactly the opposite of what God wants us to do.

God wants us to fit OUR purpose into the context of HIS life.

Christine's affliction opened the door to sharing God's word and His love and spreading the beautiful message of salvation in a way I could never have done before. That's God's purpose for me, and it's His purpose for every person ever born. I've spent almost two years looking behind spiritual doors and pawing through emotional closets for something that's been obvious since Day 1. It was only when I stopped looking for what I thought God should provide that I found what He had already given me.

When things are upside down and the barbarians are at the gate, we are wise to take stock of that which we already have, rather than pursuing that which we may never obtain. It's almost certain that what we need is in plain sight.

Stop struggling! Don't fight your burden, embrace it! And you'll find God standing right there with you, showing you the way if only you have eyes to see, and ears to hear.

Stop! Look! Listen! He's waiting for you. 😊
Bob

. . . . . .

November 25, 2018

> *"There are many who say, 'O that we might see some good! Lift up the light of thy countenance upon us, O Lord!' Thou has put more joy in my heart than they have when their grain and wine abound. In peace I will both lie down and sleep; for thou alone, O Lord, makest me dwell in safety." (Psalm 4: 6-8)*

Last night, at dinner with my son and daughter-in-law in Florida, the phone rang. I glanced at the incoming caller ID and steeled myself to answer the call: it was the Director of Nursing at Chrissy's assisted living facility — not a good sign at that time of night. The news wasn't good: Chrissy's gastric tube had failed in two places, and they weren't able to repair it. Her means of receiving food, water and medications was finally breaking down. Designed to last 12-18 months, it has been her means of receiving nourishment for 22 months and is finally wearing out.

We knew this was going to happen at some point, so though alarming, it's something we discussed and prepared for. Gastric tube failure is life-threatening, and our only options are either to put her in hospice care and keep her comfortable as she dies, or to take her to the ER and admit her for surgery to replace the failed tube. I told him I needed some time to contact our children and reaffirm the decision we had made months ago knowing that the tube was eventually going to fail.

Replacing a g-tube is normally a fairly routine procedure, but it does require general anesthesia. Because of the damage to her brain, and because her immune and respiratory systems are compromised, there is no way of knowing which anesthesia to use, how much to administer, or what unintended or unforeseen consequences might ensue. Death is a very real possibility.

After two hours on the phone with our children, Chrissy's 7 siblings and her Mom, I texted our decision to the Director of Nursing: please admit her to the hospital ER, schedule the surgery, and I'll be on the first flight home Friday morning (today).

I know that many of you pray for Chris and for our family; and I also know that you utter those prayers with full faith in God, and full acceptance of His answer. I can tell you with certainty that your prayers work. I've been strengthened by them when Chrissy's condition threatens to overwhelm me. I've learned to surrender my helplessness to God, to hand Him the heartache and the uncertainty.

I know God heard your prayers last night, because no sooner had I texted our decision to proceed with the surgery to the Director of Nursing and turned on my computer to change my airline reservations, I received the following text message:

"All set. No emergency. Able to cut tube and apply Lopez valve. No leaks. Working tube. Can address after return home. Thank you for answer. Will update Marcy (Nurse Practitioner) in the AM. All is well for the moment. Deep breath. Exhale. All set."

I did take a deep breath and exhaled slowly. And today my day is one of humble thanksgiving — to you for your prayers, and to God for His intervention. He has given us more time: time to love, time to grow, time to prepare for the next steps in our journey, whatever they may be and wherever they may lead us.

At the end of the day, we all deal with tragedy and sorrow, because they're an integral part of life. But tragedy is only a means to an end: Life provides the means, and God provides the end. But none of this works if we're not willing to embrace His message.

So reach out and put your arms around Him. After all, He's had His arms around you since forever. Go ahead - He's waiting. ☺

Have a blessed and beautiful day.
Bob

. . . . . .

December 19, 2018

> *"Yea, though I walk through the valley*
> *of the shadow of death, I will fear no evil.*
> *For thou art with me..." (Psalm 23: 4)*

It's the evening before the surgery to replace Chrissy's G-tube — the lifeline that's been providing her hydration and nutrition for 23 months. The quiet of her room is broken only by the rasp of her breathing and the rhythmic cycling of the electric pump that pushes liquid nourishment and water through her abdominal wall and into her stomach. Somewhere in the building, Christmas carols are playing.

Myriad thoughts compete for my attention. Random and jangled, they offer fear, love, hope, uncertainty, weariness, and optimism. Each is briefly victorious before being ousted by another. Will angels guide the doctors' hands or is tonight the last time I'll cradle her hands in mine? She looks very peaceful now that I've raised the head of her bed and rearranged her pillows so she won't choke and aspirate saliva and phlegm. She's still the most beautiful woman I've ever seen.

Tonight I noticed something. The stand holding the food and water that nourishes her body is shaped like the Cross that delivers spiritual nourishment for our souls. Stop nourishment from one and you risk life. Stop nourishment from the other and you risk eternity...

It should count for something that God sent His Son to die for us. How many times do we disregard that Sacrifice? How many times do we disrespect His incredible act of love? Can we even comprehend the agony of Christ, who took on Himself the expiation of every sin ever committed in the history of the world? It's not the Ten Suggestions; it's the Ten Commandments, and following them must be a priority in our lives. When we fall — and we all do — God is looking for repentance, atonement and a firm resolution not to fall again. Remember — a Covenant is signed by two parties, and there is a penalty for breach of contract.

When we are discouraged or mired in sin, repentance and prayer bring peace and forgiveness. Faith, diligently applied to life, always conquers despair. Prayer lifts and strengthen us. The Light will conquer the darkness. That's God's promise to us if we are faithful to Him.

Make the Lord your shepherd, today and every day of your life, so you'll be ready when it's your turn to enter that valley.

Bob

. . . . . .

January 6, 2019

"*...Now the word of the Lord came to me saying,*
'Before I formed you in the womb I knew you, and

before you were born I consecrated you; I appointed you a prophet to the nations...'" (Jeremiah 1: 4-5)

Chrissy's condition is stable, though I occasionally notice slight movements of her legs and head. We're buying a computer and software to set up a music therapy program using her favorite songs and composers interspersed with stories of our family adventures and individual messages telling her to keep working to heal her brain and wake up. With prayer, we give witness to our belief in God's power to heal her if He wills it. And we thank you from the bottom of our hearts for your continued prayers.

Christ is the fulfillment of all the prophesies in the Old Testament, the manifestation (Epiphany) of God's love for us, the Lamb of God killed to accomplish our redemption. His life, death and resurrection were prophesied, and enabled "those who have eyes to see and ears to hear" to change their lives and embrace His New Covenant.

God has a plan, and we are each, individually, a part of it. We are wise to stop and consider what specific contributions our all-knowing God, in creating us, had in mind for us as part of His plan. I sometimes wonder what the prophets would have said each of us would accomplish on God's behalf if we were the object of their visions. Do we actively seek God's plan for our lives, or do we live day by day, distracted by the temptations and rigors of this life?

If the prophets of old had envisioned our individual lives, what would they have written about us? What feats of faith would they have foretold? What part of God's ordained plan for mankind would they have said we were going to fulfill?

When planning major projects, we visualize the final product and then design a process to achieve it. We start with the finished product and work our way backwards, establishing milestones, deadlines, goals and objectives, ultimately producing a master plan.

Isn't life a "major project," and doesn't it deserve a "master plan?" Ultimately, we are the product of the choices we make during our life on Earth. What will that product look like when we walk through death's door and stand before Almighty God to give an accounting of our lives?

Why did God create you? What are you here to accomplish as part of His divine plan? If you're not sure, pray carefully and constantly that He will show you. *"Ask and you shall receive, seek and you shall find, knock and it shall be opened to you." (Matthew 7:7)*

A life is a terrible thing to waste. So don't. Visualize your entry to Heaven, discern the purpose for which God created you, and build a master plan to get it done. ☺

Wishing you a blessed and joy-filled 2019,
Bob

. . . . . .

January 19, 2019

"Blessed be the God and Father of our Lord Jesus Christ!
By his great mercy we have been born anew to a living
hope through the resurrection of Jesus Christ from
the dead, and to an inheritance which is imperishable,
undefiled, and unfading, kept in heaven for you, who by
God's power are guarded through faith for a salvation
ready to be revealed in the last time. In this you rejoice,
though now for a little while you may have to suffer
various trials, so that the genuineness of your faith,

> *more precious than gold which though perishable is tested by fire, may redound to praise and glory and honor at the revelation of Jesus Christ. Without having seen Him you love him; though you do not now see him you believe in him and rejoice with unutterable and exalted joy. As the outcome of your faith you obtain the salvation of your souls." (1 Peter: 3-9)*

Today begins the third year of the journey. Chrissy is stable and unchanged, and we continue to hope that she will recover, fully knowing that recovery may not be what God has in mind. We believe God can work a miracle here, but we don't know whether He will. We wander in the desert, waiting, watching, and hoping, in many ways prevented from moving forward with our lives because she is unable to move forward with hers. Still and silent, her love and goodness nevertheless remain an integral part of our lives. She continues to touch us every day.

Though we're being "tested by fire" we remain resolute in our faith and rejoice, albeit sometimes through our tears, that "as the outcome of your faith you obtain the salvation of your souls."

Do not for an instant believe that my faith doesn't waver. There are days when it requires a major effort just to get out of bed. When that happens, I go back to basics, and find reasons to rejoice: God has given me another day to share His message, and the freedom to decide how to do it — whether by writing a post or performing a random act of kindness to bring a smile to someone in need.

When we focus on our own sorrows, we lose sight of the good things in our lives and our potential to live out Christ's message by bringing good things to others.

A philosopher once said that "Music is the language of the soul." Years ago, the rock group "America" wrote a song called "I Need You." Please close your eyes, click on the link, and take the time to really listen to it.

https://www.youtube.com/watch?v=UkrdwDB9J_M

The words of this song are intriguing. They could be me singing to Chris; they could be me praying to Christ; or they could be Christ calling to me. All three are equally valid; but how we hear and interpret the words depends on our outlook on life and their relevance to the circumstances in which we find ourselves.

Our lives are driven by our perspective. And our perspective depends on our faith. So when we're faced with devastation and sorrow — in fact, ESPECIALLY when faced with devastation and sorrow — don't forget that "as the outcome of your faith you obtain the salvation of your souls."

Whether it be our loved ones, our friends, our God, or His Son, the message is the same:

"I Need You." ☺

Bob

. . . . . .

March 3, 2019

"You have been born anew, not of perishable seed but of imperishable, through the living and abiding word of God; for 'All flesh is like grass and all its glory like the flower of grass. The grass withers, and the flower falls, but the word of the Lord abides fore ever.'" (1 Peter 1:23-25)

THE POSTS

Please forgive my failure to post for the past two months. It has been a proverbial "forty days in the desert" for us. While Chrissy's condition remains stable, her ability to digest is slightly diminishing, and we have reduced her rate of food intake, but increased the time she receives it, so her level of nutrition remains about the same. She suffered a serious setback about 6 weeks ago which brought me to a standstill. She had been diagnosed with osteoporosis several years before her aneurysm, but it wasn't severe, and she was being treated for it. However, when a person is unable to move, as she has been for the past 26 months, and can't engage even in normal exertions, their bones leach out calcium and become increasingly brittle. In early February one of the LNAs at the facility, while performing range-of-motion exercises on Chrissy's left arm, heard a "pop" and immediately called the duty RN to her room. Nothing seemed out of the ordinary until several days later when a large area of bruising (indicating internal bleeding) appeared around the entire lower half of her upper left arm, down to her elbow. She started showing signs of pain and distress, and while performing the every-two-hour repositioning necessary to keep her from developing skin ulcerations, she began making sounds and showing facial expressions indicating she was in pain, even in her vegetative state. A portable x-ray unit was quickly dispatched to the facility, and it revealed that her upper left arm had broken about 2 inches below the shoulder.

Medications were prescribed to manage her pain, and her arm was immobilized using a special sling to (hopefully) enable the ends of broken bone (humerus) to knit. This seems to be working, and another x-ray will soon show if it's healing. Our priority is to ensure that Chris is comfortable and safely pain-free, and her medical team works constantly to ensure that this is the case.

It's not easy to watch the person you love most in the world break one piece at a time. Anger, despair, guilt, blame, horror and fear rage within, and can potentially lead us in directions that are at least counterproductive, if not in fact harmful. At the end of the day, faith and prayer — yours and mine — saved me again.

Faith and prayer enable us to transcend our human nature and lay at the foot of the Cross those things that are beyond our comprehension, no matter how grotesque or horrifying. How powerless we really are over so much of life, despite all the worldly trappings and contrivances we construct to deliver the illusion that we are in control. How much our lives must change when we truly comprehend that we only really control our own eternal destiny, and that only by virtue of the choices we make every day.

Gaining entry to the kingdom of Heaven is simple, but it's not easy. It requires applying the letter and spirit of the Ten Commandments to our every thought, word and deed. It requires the conscious discipline of becoming Christ to everyone we encounter until worldly habits and propensities are washed away by the blood of Christ through the exercise of our free will. Free will is a gift — but it's fraught with spiritual, emotional and physical danger if not exercised within the discipline of Christian virtue.

I don't know which of the LNAs was administering the range of motion therapy when Chrissy's arm fractured, and I don't need to know. I was told that she wept for the rest of the day, and that it has deprived her of peace of mind ever since. So I've decided to write a letter to her letting her know I understand her sorrow, that I know she did not intentionally cause harm, that Chris and I forgive her, and that I want her to forgive herself as well. It's what Chrissy would do, and it's the right thing to do. It's another small way I find myself becoming a better person because of the struggle of the past two years. I believe this is part of God's purpose for the road on which we find ourselves.

I'm becoming a better person because of the suffering of the person I love most in this world. No matter the enormity of our suffering or the severity of our pain, we must present it as a gift at the foot of the Cross, our small share of the incomprehensible agony of Jesus Christ as He suffered to expiate the guilt of mankind for every sin ever committed. We can share in His suffering in a small way by virtue of our own.

When viewed through the eyes of faith, Christine is a gift from God — a gift that keeps on giving. I thank God, for bringing her into my life and allowing me to love her. And I thank Him for letting me be part of her life and allowing me the gift of her love for me.

Live today, and every day, as if each moment is your last. Bind your free will with love of God and neighbor. Offer your trials as a gift at the foot of the Cross. It will change the way you live for the rest of your life.

Have a beautiful day.
Bob

. . . . . .

March 30, 2019

"Then the disciples came to him privately and said, 'Why could we not cast it out?' He said to them, 'Because of

THE POSTS

> *your little faith. For truly, I say to you, if you have faith as a grain of mustard seed, you will say to this mountain, 'Move from here to there,' and it will move; and nothing will be impossible to you.'" (Matthew 17:19-21)*

About two months ago, as we began the third year of this journey, questions lurking in my subconscious began to surface. I had always managed to push them back down and lock them away. But we've been dealing with this now for over two years, and the questions were becoming more insistent: Does Chris want to continue to live in her present condition? How would I feel if I was in her condition? Does love include making a conscious decision to end someone's life?

I started researching ways to communicate with her, things such as a "functional MRI" or using a medium who communicates with those in a vegetative state. As I pursued this line of thinking, I ultimately arrived at the question of what to do if she wants to die. It's a question with a terrible answer, because our only option would be stopping nutrition and hydration and causing death by thirst and starvation.

Last Sunday, while I was visiting Chris, the staff came to reposition her — something they do every 2 hours around the clock. They finished up and left the room, and shortly thereafter, Chrissy's face indicated that something was very wrong. I asked her if her arm was hurting her. What happened next took my breath away.

She turned her head slightly towards me, making throat noises and moving her lips. She was trying to talk. I turned her body slightly to her left, repositioned the pillow under her arm to change the angle at which her arm was resting, and her "talking" stopped.

THE POSTS

When I'm with Chris, I pray with her, read her favorite Nicholas Sparks novels aloud to her, talk to her, and occasionally watch DVDs of movies and TV shows we enjoyed. This Sunday, it was "China Beach," a story about an Army nurse serving in a field hospital in Vietnam. As a Navy nurse, Chris had taken care of grievously wounded Marines coming home from Vietnam, so the series was one of her favorites. Watching the DVD with her, I held her right hand as it rested against her right thigh. Suddenly her hand started trembling, and her thigh began a pronounced twitch every four or five seconds. I stopped the DVD and asked her if she was trying to tell me she loved me.

Her lips started moving, and I told her I took that as a yes. Her hand stopped trembling, her thigh stopped twitching, her lips stopped moving, and a look of peace came over her face.

I was stunned, but I shouldn't have been, because "our God is an awesome God." But God and Christine weren't finished with me quite yet.

People who have recovered from a coma or vegetative state describe it as being underwater, at times down deep and at times coming up near the surface. I have no doubt that Chris was near the surface, so I decided to tell her about my constant struggle with the question of whether she wanted to continue to live in her present condition. As I continued talking, her face became very peaceful, but I didn't feel as if I'd gotten an answer.

Late that night, while setting up the cot I sleep on when I stay with Chris overnight, I glanced at her sleeping form, silent testimony to a life of loving and caring for others, and it struck me like a bolt of lightning that emotion and intellect were leading me towards rationalizing ending the life of the person I love most.

When we're faced with a protracted struggle, our intellect often works at crossed purposes to our faith. Intellect and emotion can produce "logic" that undermines and contradicts our faith in God. Following our human inclinations, no matter how well-intentioned, can lead us to spiritual suicide as we attempt to "solve" problems whose outcomes belong solely in the hands of God. Instead of reinforcing our faith, intellect and emotion can render us capable of rationalizing sin and evil and committing violence against our most sacred beliefs.

Anxiety and doubt wear on us, hour after hour, day after day, year after year, working to undermine the single most important tenet of our faith: our acknowledgement of almighty God as the author of all life and the sole judge of when it should end. Rule Number One: "I am the Lord, thy God. Thou shalt not have strange gods before me." We make ourselves false gods when we take upon ourselves decisions that belong to God alone — as in the decision to end life.

And now, the rest of the story.

Monday morning, after the first good night's sleep I'd had in weeks, I shared with the Director of Nursing the struggle I was having as to whether Chris might want to end her suffering. He smiled knowingly and told me that not long after her arm had been broken, he had asked her, during one of her "near surface" episodes, if she wanted to continue working to recover. When she's "near the surface," she responds to questions with blinks of her eyes (one means yes, two means no). Her answer was, in his words, "a very strong yes."

I believe Christine's love of God and her family prompted her to blink the only answer her faith could allow: life is God's to give, and His alone to take. Lying in a bed, unable to see, speak, move, or eat, my wife continues loving me and teaching me every day of her life.

Jesus told us, "Render unto Caesar the things that are Caesar's, and unto God the things that are God's." That includes not meddling in areas that are the purview of the Almighty. When we follow this advice, we sleep a whole lot better at night. Believe me, I know.

Pleasant dreams. ☺

Bob

. . . . . .

July 18, 2019 (Begun May 21, 2019)

"Bless the Lord, O my soul; and all that is within me bless His holy name! Bless the Lord, O my soul, and forget not all His benefits, who forgives all your iniquity, who heals all your diseases, who redeems your life from the Pit, who crowns you with steadfast love and mercy, who satisfies you with good as long as you live so that your youth is renewed like the eagle's." (Psalm 103)

Chris is as physically healthy as is possible in her condition. Her skin condition is flawless, and her body is functioning as it should. She'll occasionally sigh or make a gentle musical sound with her voice. I've seen her turn her body an inch or two to the right, and occasionally she'll move her legs an inch or two. She sleeps through the night, and is awake during the day, with occasional naps from time to time. She spends about 3 hours each day in her Broda chair among the other residents at the facility and enjoys a whirlpool bath every other day.

As I prayed with her in the wee hours this morning, I felt a profound sense of gratitude. The arrival of Spring, especially after this unusually harsh winter, signals new life and new beginnings. No matter our travails or our suffering, most of us have a great deal for which to be thankful.

We take for granted things that much of the rest of the world has never had: hot and cold running water and electricity in our homes, mobility, opportunity, employment, liberty — the list is very very long. Our quality of life should engender gratitude from the moment we open our eyes in the morning until the moment we close them at night.

Being thankful means knowing that the good things in our lives come from a God who loves us. It means understanding the order of creation, with God as King and us as His ambassadors. Truly understanding the vastness of God's love requires a concerted effort because we tend to lose sight of the myriad details that reflect His beneficence in every nook and cranny of our lives.

Imagine what the world would be if every human being started the day with thanksgiving to God for our incredible blessings and maintained that frame of mind all day long. Things we consider of monumental importance, and for which we sometimes abandon our call to godliness, would be relegated to their rightful lower priority in our lives. Frustration and anger would decrease as we choose to stay focused on God's love and the blessings He has bestowed on us instead of the trials of daily life and the sometimes-extraordinary burdens with which we are laden.

It's possible to immerse ourselves in worldly pursuits and priorities to the point that we lose sight of our real purpose in life and ultimately lose our souls. It doesn't happen all at once; it's a gradual process, as pressures of daily living squeeze out precious time needed to spend with God and family without distractions. And if we don't invest that time into God and family, we eventually lose both. Oh, we might still be going through the motions, but just like our bodies, if we don't maintain our spiritual "core," things will slowly deteriorate with serious eternal consequences.

Today, July 18, 2019, is two-and-a-half years to the day that Chris was stricken. Wide awake at 1:30am, I turned on the TV and, interestingly, the movie "An Officer and A Gentleman" was playing. I say "interestingly" since Chris and I always considered this "our movie" because it was filmed on Whidbey Island, Washington, where we met while stationed there. The rush of happy memories and the recollection of those wonderful days jarred me out of the emotional numbness that has descended as months and years continue to pass with little change in her condition.

Strange as it may sound, several weeks ago, I believe Chris came to visit me at home. She did so once before during the early weeks of this journey, and in the same way. I sensed her presence from the sudden strong scent of her perfume in our bedroom just as I was about to fall asleep. I spoke to her about what I believed was the reason she was visiting and told her I would take care of it the way that she would. A minute later, the scent was gone. The effects of her visit, however, are not.

There is deadly spiritual peril in long-term trials which can sap our strength and drain the color out of our lives. The only true antidote is to double down in prayer and to pay particular attention to the many things in our lives that give cause for thanksgiving. Tragedy and sorrow can lead us into darkness. But our proper response to adversity — prayer and gratitude for what we do have — will always lead us closer to God. There is always sunshine above the clouds.

Look around. See the beauty of God's creation even amidst your burdens. And find in everything around you a reason to thank God for His undying love for us.

See you at the cinema. ☺
Bob

. . . . . .

July 31, 2019

> Then the disciples came to Jesus privately and said, "Why could we not cast it out?" He said to them, "Because of your little faith. For truly I say to you, if you have faith the size of a mustard seed, you can say to this mountain, 'Move from here to there,' and it will move; and nothing will be impossible to you." (Matthew 17:20)

Two weeks ago when I visited her, Chrissy seemed "sleepier" than normal, so we didn't "watch" any China Beach episodes. But I did put on a CD of music from 1974-75: Neil Diamond, the Bee Gees, Billy Joel, Diana Ross, Elton John — the selection of music ran the gamut of pop songs of that era. I closed the door to her room and turned it up as loud as it would go. She went from being sleepier than normal to more alert than normal. Music therapy is a known phenomenon. Someone once said that "Music is the language of the soul." I believe it.

Shortly after I arrived for my weekly visit, one of the LNAs who cares for her looked at me and said, "You know she spoke this week." Not quite sure whether I had heard her correctly, I looked at her and asked her to repeat what she'd said. She replied, "Chris spoke to me this week, on Wednesday," and proceeded to share what had happened:

When she and her LNA partner finished repositioning Chris, (they do it every two hours, around the clock, 24/7/365) and started to leave the room, they heard Chris whisper something. Surprised, the LNA went back to the bed and asked her if she needed anything. In a very faint voice, Chrissy whispered, "Stay." The LNA asked Chris, "Why, are you lonely?" and Chris nodded her head.

I was speechless when I heard this, and carried it in my heart, uncertain as to whether it was totally factual. In other words, I doubted.

Then last Tuesday I called Chris and spoke to her as I try to do every day. I told her that one of the LNAs said she had spoken, and I asked her to say "Hi," because it only requires pushing air through her voice box. She started a guttural sound that ended a few seconds later with a squeaky, high-pitched "Hi."

It's amazing how profound an impact a single word can have on our outlook on life.

Several weeks ago cleaning up around the house, I came across a baseball cap that belongs to Chris. I really liked this particular cap because its color (fuchsia) really sets off the blue in her eyes, and I always made it a point to tell her. It's the "little things" in life that often mean the most to those we love. A word of encouragement, an unexpected little gift, a surprise bouquet of flowers, a note left under a pillow — these things show our love and bring joy to those we asked to share our life's journey.

So what is your spouse's special color? And what did you tell him or her today to put a smile on their face and joy in their heart?

By the way, that fuchsia ballcap is now front-and-center on the dresser in her room, in plain view for when those beautiful blue eyes are once again able to see. It's also my reminder not to doubt God's work, and that your prayers for Christine are bearing fruit. God is healing her in His own time and in His own

way. Thank you for your prayers for Chrissy, and for the joy those prayers are bringing to me. 😊
    Bob

. . . . . .

September 2, 2019

> *"I will tell of thy name to my brethren; in the midst of the congregation I will praise thee: "You who fear the Lord, praise him! all you sons of Jacob, glorify him, and stand in awe of him, all you sons of Israel! For he has not despised nor abhorred the affliction of the afflicted; he has not hid his face from him, but has heard, when he cried to him.""* (Psalm 22: 22-24)

Chrissy's physical health is excellent, except for a receding bout with shingles, as we continue our journey of faith. Last Thursday, while talking to her on the phone, I told her I loved her, and that I knew she would tell me the same thing if she could. For the next minute-and-a-half, in a sometimes sing-song, sometimes guttural voice that carried with it inflections and intonation, she cobbled together sounds and syllables that weren't words that I could recognize but were clearly an attempt to speak to me.

    Yesterday afternoon while in her room, I noticed that she was slightly flushed — a sign that she is too warm. I adjusted her covers and wiped some moisture from the corners of her mouth. Then I kissed her on the forehead and whispered in her ear that I loved her.

    And in a very, very soft voice, barely audible, with her beautiful blue eyes wide open, she whispered, "I love you."

I awakened very early this morning amid swirling thoughts about faith, love, and the power of prayer. At least in part, God's answer to our prayers, His promises in Scripture, and the hope that has carried us to this day was manifested yesterday afternoon. It wasn't an accident, and it wasn't wishful thinking or fanciful imagination. Simply put, because we believe, and because we are praying, God acted, and Christine spoke.

God's work of redemption is ongoing until the end of the world. As part of that work, He has a plan for each and every one of us. He uses people to achieve His purposes, and He is using Christine and me, as we share this incredible story with you. He also intends to use you if you choose to follow Him. It's up to us to discern the purpose for which God put us on this Earth, and then to pursue that purpose every day of our lives.

At the end of the day, we are called to be His disciples. "And when they saw him, they worshiped Him, but some doubted. And Jesus came and said to them, 'All authority in heaven and on earth has been given to me. Go therefore and make disciples of all nations, baptizing them in the name of the Father and of the Son and of the Holy Spirit, teaching them to observe all that I have commanded you; and lo, I am with you always, even unto the end of the world." (Matthew 28:17-20)

"When the disciples heard this, they were greatly astonished and asked, 'Who then can be saved?' Jesus looked at them and said, 'With man this is impossible, but with God all things are possible.'" (Matthew 19: 25-26)

With assurances like this from Jesus himself, our choice should be easy. With all the signs and wonders that God puts before us if we have "eyes to see and ears to hear," our choice should be easy. With the carnage being visited upon our nation because we have rejected God's laws and replaced them with our own, the choice should be easy.

So don't be difficult.

Believe. Surrender. See. Grow. Witness. Rejoice.

Because miracles really do happen. ☺

Bob

. . . . . .

October 3, 2019

> *"I will not leave you desolate; I will come to you.*
> *Yet a little while and the world will see me no more,*
> *but you will see me; because I live, you will live also.*
> *In that day you will know that I am in my Father, and*
> *you in me, and I in you. He who has my commandments*
> *and keeps them, he it is who loves me; and he who*
> *loves me will be loved by my Father, and I will love*
> *him and manifest myself to him." (John 14:18-21)*

Chris is much the same and remains completely dependent on us and others for her care. While she hasn't spoken any actual words since her "I love you" to me, she occasionally responds to comments with "voice sounds" and sometimes initiates voice sounds on her own. They range from a series of throaty rasps to beautiful sing-song sighs. I don't understand what she's trying to say, but God does. I'm profoundly grateful for the nurses (RNs and LNAs) who care for her 24/7/365, repositioning her every 2 hours around the clock, giving her whirlpool baths every other day (Chris really loves these, and is totally relaxed afterwards), and getting her out of bed and into her Broda chair every day to be in the company of other residents for several hours. Every one of the residents of her facility has suffered a severe brain injury of some sort, and all are dependent on these incredible nurses for their survival. Please say a special prayer for them today and every day.

Fall is here, and we are blessed with the beautiful splendor of God's creation. Our world is painted in spectacular colors, with cool crisp mornings and warm sunny afternoons. Nature's glorious raiment is a testimonial to God's amazing plan and the order He has given to the universe.

Just like nature, our lives also have seasons, and each has its own unique challenges and rewards.

We rejoice with the explosion of new life every Spring. This new life blossoms into the lush fullness of summer, eventually bearing fruit before dressing in the magnificent autumn colors that are a harbinger that winter is coming, and with it the end of nature's cycle of life.

We are born with original sin, baptized to cleanse us of it, and nurtured through sacraments instituted by Jesus Christ to prepare and strengthen us to meet life's challenges. That's the "Spring" of our life.

During our Summer of life we work and raise families and pursue our many interests. If we become complacent in the faith that should be the foundation of our march towards eternity, we put at risk the spiritual autumn that will dress us in our finest "fall foliage" to be judged by Jesus Christ.

We are truly blessed to live surrounded by trees wearing the brilliant colors that God has ordained. But trees don't have a choice; their colors are an act of nature. On the other hand, because we have free will, our thoughts, words and deeds will paint us with the colors we'll be wearing when our days come to an end.

For us, every day should be autumn, and we should be resplendent in the beautiful, brilliant colors of our faith.

So pay attention to the seasons of your life. Because only God knows when those seasons will end. ☺

Bob

. . . . . .

October 10, 2019

> *"Make me to know thy ways, O Lord; teach me thy paths. Lead me in thy truth, and teach me, for thou art the God of my salvation; for thee I wait all the day long." (Psalm 25: 4-5)*

Chris remains the same, occasionally making voice sounds when we speak with her (she did again last night), as we continue to pray for her recovery with full faith in God.

Trusting God is sometimes difficult because our human hearts and minds seeks visible answers to our questions and affirmative responses to our prayers. I struggle all the time with Chrissy's physical absence from our home and her non-presence in my activities, even as I fully embrace her in my heart. As I continue my activities, particularly recreation and enjoyment, guilt is a constant threat even though she would want me to remain fully engaged. My weekly visits with her are critically important to making sure she knows she is always foremost in my life; they're also critically important to me as a fulfillment of my promise to "love, honor and cherish" her.

Guilt and fear are Satan's means of assailing our faith in God. He wants us sad, even though God wants us to live joyfully. He wants us afraid even though God wants us to be confident in His plan for our lives. He wants us to doubt even as God wants us to believe.

When we are in pain or sorrow, we must trust in God, laying our anguish at the foot of the Cross. Try to comprehend the enormity of Christ's agony as he hung on the Tree, bearing the weight of every sin ever committed by humanity, past, present and future. Our pain and sorrow become much more manageable when we join them to Christ's redemptive agony at Calvary.

Salvation requires that we continuously reinforce our foundation of faith. Doubt, fear, and the entire gamut of human frailties can undermine our faith and jeopardize God's plan for us and for humanity. So does sin. When we violate God's laws, we begin to unravel the moral fabric necessary to remain a just and righteous people. Scripture reveals time and time again that when mankind substitutes its judgment for the moral creed defined by the Ten Commandments, all hell breaks loose - literally. If you think not, just look around you. Teen suicide, substance abuse, unmarried pregnancy, divorce, disrespect, violence, rebelliousness — the consequences aren't hard to see. When an individual disregards God's laws, the entire society is weakened. And when a society disregards God's laws, it winds up on the scrap heap of history.

Fear and doubt are Satan's tools, especially during life's tribulations. Don't let them steer you away from the love of God. Don't let the mystery of our faith become a liability to your salvation. No one ever said gaining Heaven would be easy. But it isn't at all complicated: "I am the Way, the Truth and the Life."

Believe!

Bob

. . . . . .

December 1, 2019
> "Seek the Lord while he may be found, call upon him while he is near; let the wicked forsake his way, and the unrighteous man his thoughts; let him return to the Lord, that he may have mercy on him, and to our God, for he will abundantly pardon. For my thoughts are not your thoughts, neither are your ways my ways, says the Lord. For as the heavens are higher than the earth, so are my ways higher than your ways and my thoughts than your thoughts. For as the rain and the snow come down from heaven and return not thither but water the earth, making it bring forth and sprout, giving seed to the sower and bread to the eater, so shall my word be that goes forth from my mouth; it shall not return to me empty, but it shall accomplish that which I purpose, and prosper in the thing for which I sent it." (Isaiah 55: 6-11)

Chris continues her journey, accompanied by our prayers, visits, cards and phone calls. She remains vegetative; but Saturday night while talking to her on the phone about our kids, she started trying to talk. It was more pronounced than ever before, rasping guttural sounds interspersed with soft singsong sighs. And yesterday (Sunday) when I asked her if she wanted to receive communion, she responded the same way. Please continue to pray for her recovery. While we hope it could be immediate, we accept God's wisdom in accomplishing all things in His time.

With every visit, Chris inspires me to persevere in seeking God's purpose for her condition. She serves as a beacon of faith, bringing me to greater awareness of God's love for us and of the need for us to remain strong in our love for Him.

Marriage provides an opportunity to inspire our life partners — not only on our wedding day but every day for the rest of our lives together. The world's worries and woes can cause us to overlook our responsibility for the spiritual welfare of our spouses and families. It doesn't help that our human nature tends to prioritize worldly concerns and cause us to neglect our relationships. Failing to provide inspiration, reassurance and spiritual leadership can have catastrophic consequences. If we don't inspire our spouses and our children to grow closer to God, we put their souls at risk and trivialize the salvation for which Christ offered himself on the Cross.

Spiritual leadership at home can inspire spouses and children to "seek Him while he can be found." Failing to provide spiritual leadership sends the message that an active spiritual life isn't really a priority. The signs of our spiritual complacency are everywhere. Substance abuse, mental illness, 40% out-of-wedlock pregnancies, the STD epidemic, and the 50% divorce rate aren't problems, they are symptoms. They evidence our rejection of God's laws and the adoption of the tempting but disastrously false premise that moral relativism can provide the guardrails needed to protect us from evil. The carnage being visited on our families and our children says otherwise.

Unless we take seriously our role as spiritual leaders at home and in the communities in which we live, secular humanism and moral relativism — already very evident in our schools and government institutions — will smother our faith and render us less able — and ultimately unable — to differentiate between good and evil. If we don't accept and carry out our obligation to lead ourselves, our spouses and our families towards the light of

God's salvation, someone or something else will lead them away from it.

Staying true to our faith requires effort. Just as athletes must train diligently to build skills, strength and stamina for their contests, so we as Christians and combatants in the war Satan wages for our souls must prepare ourselves and our loved ones every day for the spiritual battles we will face. Only through consistent prayer, worship and studying Scripture can we develop the spiritual strength to choose God — and to inspire others to do the same — when temptation arises and evil manifests itself.

So eat your spiritual Wheaties, do your spiritual workouts, and inspire your spouses and children to grow closer to God. You'll be glad you did.

Because the God who created us is watching and waiting. But He's not going to wait forever.

Bob

. . . . . .

December 23, 2019

"The true light that enlightens every man was coming into the world. He was in the world, and the world was made through him, yet the world knew him not. But to all who received Him, who believed in His name, he gave power to become children of God; who were born, not of blood or of the will of the flesh nor of the will of man, but of God." (John 1: 9-13)

I'm sitting in Chrissy's room at 2am, watching her sleep. She is the picture of peace, her breathing slow and steady, her face as beautiful as the day we first met. She continues largely as she has, but I noticed that she is beginning to move her forearms through a greater range of motion (5-6 inches) than what I've seen before. She continues to make voice noises occasionally when I'm talking with her in person or on the phone. And when I pray with her, she becomes very quiet, usually closes her eyes and a look of complete calm comes to her face. She truly brings me closer to God. What a beautiful gift she is to me...

Do we really believe Jesus Christ is the light of the world? Have we truly received him, and do we believe in his name? Do we understand the power of our faith if we choose to become children of God? Exercising that power requires a conscious decision, a carefully considered and willful commitment to act in a certain way. As we approach the end of Advent, preparing to celebrate the birth of Jesus Christ, we have before us the option of accepting the power to transform our lives, our families and the world.

We are not saved just because Christ died for us. We are saved because we choose to accept him as the Messiah, and we order our lives according to his Commandments. We have within us "the power to become children of God" but it's incumbent on us to make the choice to accept and exercise that power by living virtuous lives. It means recognizing sin in all its forms and rejecting it. It means accepting our responsibility for the salvation of family, friends and strangers, letting them know when they're acting outside God's laws in a clear but loving way.

The power to become children of God carries with it the obligation to bring the message of salvation to others, and we can't do that if we're timid in the practice of our faith. If we don't plant the seeds of faith when an opportunity presents itself, God can't nurture them.

The power offered to us is the power to reject sin and evil, to live virtuous lives, and to lead our families on our shared journey to eternity. God so loved us that he sent his only begotten Son to die for us. But that alone does not gain us Heaven. To gain Heaven, we must accept the power inherent in Christ's birth, death and resurrection and use it to clean up our lives.

John the Baptist walked the Holy Land "bearing witness to the light" and baptizing those who accepted his message presaging the arrival of the Messiah. Those "in power", both clergy and government officials, wanted to know who he was, and this was his answer: *"I am the voice of one crying in the wilderness, 'Make straight the way of the Lord,' as the prophet Isaiah said."*

If the road we're walking isn't straight, if we aren't rejecting sin in our lives, the coming celebration of the birth of Christ offers us the incredible privilege of accepting the power of God and adjusting our course to attain eternal life in Heaven.

Accept the power to triumph over sin and death. Take control of your life. Make straight the way of the Lord.

Who knows? We may bump into each other along the Way. ☺

Wishing you a blessed and joyful Christmas,

Bob

. . . . . .

January 18, 2020

> *"At that time Jesus declared, 'I thank thee, Father, Lord of heaven and earth, that thou hast hidden these things from the wise and understanding and revealed them to babes; yea, Father, for such was thy gracious will. All things have been delivered to*

> *me by my Father; and no one knows the Son except the Father, and no one knows the Father except the Son and any one to whom the Son chooses to reveal him. Come to me, all ye who labor and are heavy laden, and I will give you rest. Take my yoke upon you, and learn from me; for I am gentle and lowly in heart, and you will find rest for your souls. For my yoke is easy, and my burden is light.'" (Matthew 11: 25-30)*

Three years ago January 18th, we were at Chrissy's bedside as medical science told us she would not survive. But God had a different plan for her, and for me, and for all whose lives she has touched in the ensuing 1095 days. She remains in good health, as very tiny indications of healing continue. She inspires me, as God continues working through her for my sanctification.

A sense of emptiness has occasionally assailed me during this journey, perhaps from hundreds of one-way conversations, from saying "I love you" when I leave to come home, or at the end of every phone call, with silence as my answer. But there have been small miracles from time to time that bolster faith and sustain hope and increase my love of God. If we have "eyes to see and ears to hear," we can push back the darkness that threatens the soul as the ebb and flow of memories, of joys and sorrows, of events and circumstances, of dreams met and those that never came to be, color our existence.

In the aftermath of tragedy, you empty yourself — heart, mind, body and soul — waiting, watching, listening, and praying, hour after hour, day after day, year after year, for the miracle you believe can happen, but hasn't. And the emptiness beckons...

The Chinese symbol for "crisis" consists of two characters. One means "danger" and the other means "opportunity." Every crisis can go one of two ways. The wrong way — danger — can bring spiritual death, with substance abuse, domestic violence, teen suicide, infidelity, and the myriad of sinful diversions which ultimately devour our souls and take us to Hell.

Using the other Chinese character, we choose the "opportunity" that comes with every crisis — the opportunity to draw closer to God. With prayer, we transcend the spiritual danger, filling our emptiness with God's love for us. We begin to notice others who are empty, sharing with them the saving message of Christ's love. We turn our suffering and theirs to God's purposes.

Speaking to God in prayer and listening to him in quiet solitude are the only way to counter the consequences of adversity. Only in communion with God can we find peace and salvation. Let us drink the word of God, and strengthen us in faith.

让我们饮于神的话，使我们在信心上坚固. ☺

Bob

. . . . . .

March 7, 2020

> *"And he told them many things in parables, saying: 'A sower of seed went out to sow. And as he sowed, some seeds fell along the path, and the birds came and devoured them. Other seeds fell on rocky ground, where they had not much soil, and immediately they sprang up, since they had no depth of soil, but when the sun rose they were scorched; and since they had no root they withered away. Other seeds fell upon thorns, and the thorns grew up and choked them. Other seeds fell on good soil and brought forth*

> *grain, some a hundred-fold, some sixty, some thirty. He who has ears, let him hear.'" (Matthew 13:3-9)*

Chris continues to inspire me with her strength. We see tiny indications that she is gradually moving towards minimally conscious — the next level of consciousness above her vegetative state. Our faith yields steadfast hope that she will be restored to full health, and we continue seeking God's will, gratefully joining with you in praying for her recovery and to maintain the strength of our conviction with each passing day.

Whether by the sudden blow of an unexpected loss or the protracted burden of a long-term affliction, tragedy will at some point become our traveling companion on the journey of life. And the spiritual consequences that result from that tragedy will depend on the strength of our faith. Tragedy and sorrow can strengthen our faith, or they can weaken it; they can bring us closer to God, or they can draw us away from Him.

Tragedy's impact is determined by our relationship with God. Did our mustard seed of faith fall on rocky ground, or rich soil? Was it choked by love of the material world? Did it get scorched by the bright lights and glamour of sin, or die on the rocky ground of complacency? Or did we provide the rich soil needed for it to thrive, so it will be strong and vibrant when we encounter life's storms?

During the 3+ years of this walk with tragedy, I've spent too many hours looking back, and not enough time looking ahead. When I look back, I rebel against what happened to her. This in turn introduces doubt about God's love for us and His plan for our lives. I waste precious time, energy and grace grappling with a past that cannot be changed, instead of investing myself in the limitless possibilities that God provides for the future.

When we look ahead, each day brings the opportunity to nurture the seed of our faith — not only for our spiritual benefit but also for the benefit of all those whose lives we will touch. When we look ahead, we can construct a purpose for the life events that brought us to where we are.

When we commit ourselves to believing in God's love and His plan of salvation, understanding God's purpose for allowing tragedy in our lives will conquer the weeds of doubt that seek to choke the seedling of our faith — but only when we're looking ahead.

About two years ago, one of our daughters made a card for me. She knew I was struggling with what had happened to Chrissy. Here's what she wrote inside the card:

"That mountain you are carrying, you were only supposed to climb."

When we look back, we risk carrying the mountains of our past sins and sorrows on our backs, forcing us to lean forward and forcing us to look down. What we should be doing is standing straight, free of the burdens of the past, and looking ahead because we learned from our mistakes and truly embrace the message of salvation fulfilled in Christ's sacrifice at Calvary.

Satan wants us to despair, to lose heart and to become trapped in the treacherous quicksand of doubt. He thrives when we clutter our mind and burden our spirit with past failures and sorrows; they sap our spiritual, emotional and even our physical strength, undermining our faith and weakening our relationship with Christ and His church.

God doesn't want us carrying the burden of our past sins and tragedies. The death of his Son on the Cross has already paid the price for our transgressions, and we are thus relieved of that burden if we repent, atone and truly understand and embrace what He did for us on Good Friday. No need to look back with regret or sorrow; only look ahead to discern and avoid the pitfalls of sin and to experience the joy that God has in store for us.

We can't escape the fact that we must conquer the mountains of guilt and sorrow in our lives. But understand, too, that truly believing in Jesus Christ requires us to leave them behind. That's what God had in mind when He sent his only begotten Son to die for us. We disrespect His life, death and resurrection when we fail to accept, with humble and contrite hearts, the forgiveness paid for with His blood. God wants us looking forward towards our resurrection, not looking back at the wreckage of the sins and sorrows for which His Son has already paid the price.

So — nurture and protect the seed of faith from the choking weeds of this world, let go of the mountains of your past sins and sorrows, and embrace, if you can, the enormity of the love God has for you and for all mankind.

https://www.youtube.com/watch?v=-C_3eYj-pOM

Bob

. . . . . .

April 11, 2020

> *"When I was with you day after day in the temple, you did not lay hands on me. But this is your hour, and the power of darkness."* (Luke 22:53)

I haven't seen Christine since March 8 because of the COVID-19 pandemic. Her facility wisely and rightly ended all visits because of the vulnerability of its residents, all of whom are severely brain-injured and whose immune systems are therefore badly compromised. I speak to her every day, sometimes twice a day, and her condition remains unchanged. The inability to visit wears on me, as we are both strengthened when we're together and I can pray with her, watch movies, listen to music, play piano for her, hold her hand, touch her face, speak to her. But no matter, because I know that her love of our Lord, and her family, and all whose lives she touched remains intact. It's who she is.

"But this is your hour, and the power of darkness..."

Sin is a willful act in opposition to the laws of God. None of us is free of sin, nor immune from the darkness and spiritual desolation that comes with it. Sin prevailed the day that Jesus Christ was crucified, and it ravaged the faith of those who believed in Him.

Today, the day after the world chose darkness and crucified the Lamb of God, we now wait in darkness, our Master wrapped in a shroud in the utter darkness of the tomb. His disciples are scattered, frightened not only physically for fear of persecution, but their souls are smothered by the darkness of doubt. He was God, but He is dead. Was he a fraud? Were we deceived? How could this happen? What is to become of the hope He inspired, the love He practiced and preached, the eternal life He promised?

Our lives are darkened both by sin and by tragedy. The darkness of sin is born of rebellion; the darkness of tragedy is born of sorrow. But for both, the path back to the Light is one and the same: Jesus Christ. Whether in spiritual darkness because we deliberately broke God's law, or emotional darkness because we're devastated by tragedy, the way back to the Light is the same.

The crucifixion of Jesus Christ is the eternal stage on which was performed the salvation of mankind. Calvary was the most powerful drama ever enacted; its author is the Creator of the universe. Antagonists and protagonists were splendidly portrayed by God for the entire world to see forever.

Tragedy is portrayed through Mary, the Mother of Jesus, who saw her innocent Son crucified because a sinful world chose to pardon a murderer. The darkness of sin rings in the words of the scoffing thief to Jesus' left, who with his dying words rejected the faith that would have saved him from eternal damnation. All had profound roles to play on that magnificent, terrible stage called Calvary.

But that terrible stage also portrayed characters who showed us the essential elements of salvation. The Roman centurian Longinus, who stood watch at Golgotha with his detachment of soldiers and proclaimed, *"Truly, this was the Son of God,"* and whose detachment guarded the sepulcher in which Christ was buried, later left the Roman legions and preached the gospel in Cappadocia. He gave his life to Christ, and was ultimately beheaded by order of Pontius Pilate.

And who can forget the penitent thief, who called out, *"Jesus, remember me when you come into your kingdom,"* and the words of salvation that Jesus spoke to him in reply: *"Truly I say to you, today you will be with me in Paradise."*

So we see both sides of the drama: the sinners' choice to reject God and accept damnation, and the penitents' conversion to the promise of salvation through Jesus Christ. Each made a choice, and each lives today, either in the presence of God because they confessed their sins, proclaimed their faith and left the darkness to proclaim the gospel of Light; or in eternal darkness, separated forever from the Light because they willfully rejected salvation.

Each of us today — especially on this Holy Saturday with the body of Christ bathed in the darkness of death — has the incredible opportunity to reflect on the sacred mystery of Calvary, to consider the "players" on that terrible, wonderful stage, and to choose the role we want to play in God's ever-unfolding drama of salvation. We are called to reaffirm our faith in God's message delivered through His son, Jesus Christ.

Set aside some time today to find a quiet place and ponder the divine mystery being played out before you. With our free will, we get to choose the character we'll play on the stage of life. If you need to change sides, I pray for you to receive the courage and strength to do so. And if you're where God wants you to be, then please pray for those who have yet to choose Jesus Christ, and for those who have left this life having chosen the darkness.

Today, as our Savior lies in the grave, we weep in sorrow and tremble with doubt. But we also know what He promised as the central Actor in the drama of salvation. Tomorrow, that Promise is fulfilled.

See you in central casting. ☺
Bob

. . . . . .

September 14, 2020

"Great indeed, we confess, is the mystery of our religion: He was manifested in the flesh, vindicated in the Spirit, seen by angels, preached among the nations, believed on in the world, taken up in glory." (1 Timothy 3:16)

Chris continues in her vegetative state, in stable health and without complications. Her facility has not any COVID-19 occurrences among residents or staff. Having not seen her for almost half a year, I was concerned that her eyes seemed dull and lifeless on my first renewed visit. She was very lethargic as well. I began to talk to her about our children, her best friend, the dog, the weather, the house, and everything else I could think of. Though I call her every day, there is no substitute for the actual sound or touch of a loved one. Because of the COVID-19 protocols, touch is not allowed, and minimum 6 feet social distancing is the rule — with all meetings conducted outside the facility. I believe that being so close, but not allowed to touch, probably brings a special kind of heartache for her; I know it does for me.

Forty-one years ago today, on Sept. 14, 1979, I met a petite, blue-eyed, gentle-spirited Navy Nurse named Christine. That meeting began a journey that continues today. She tolerated my weaknesses, forgave my failures, raised our children, kept our home, nurtured our family, and made it possible for me to accomplish everything in my life. I love her more today than ever.

Do you remember the day you met your spouse? Was it love at first sight, or did it grow slowly until you realized that this person had become an indispensable part your life? Did you know right away that this was THE person you intended to spend the rest of your life with, or did you come to this realization only after a period of courtship?

Love comes to us in different ways and at different times in our lives. But when it happens, it becomes a transformative force that changes the very essence of who we are.

Do you remember the day you met Jesus Christ? Was it love at first sight, or did it grow slowly until you realized that this

Person had become an indispensable part of your life? Did you know right away that this was THE Person you intended to spend the rest of your life with, or did you come to this realization only after a period of courtship?

Our Father, through Jesus Christ and the Holy Spirit, is always waiting for us to declare our love and dedicate our lives to Him. Every day is another opportunity to reject sin and evil, and to transform our lives in pursuit of eternal life. And when we transform ourselves by putting on Christ, we also transform the person we asked to share their lives with us, and the children born of that union. Nothing compares to the love of a spouse who admires you for bringing Christ into your home and making Him an active part of your marriage and your family.

Today's world is truly "upside-down." Evil is everywhere, and rejection of God's laws and His love is in plain sight all around us. Hatred, violence, disrespect, anger, perversion — all are increasing, with very visible consequences about which we are warned in Scripture: *"The wages of sin is death."*

Now, more than ever, we need to profess our love of God, to nurture and strengthen our relationship with Christ in a very real way. By doing so, we gain the grace we need to become "a light unto all nations," repudiating the onslaught of evil in our homes, our families, our communities and our nation. The fierce spiritual war of "powers and principalities" is being waged for the soul of our nation, one person, one family, one community at a time. Now, more than ever, we need to reinforce our relationships with our spouse and our Creator. Without investing ourselves in those relationships, both become vulnerable to the ravages of life's storms and the world's cynicism.

Figure out the day you met your spouse and the day you met your Savior. If you're not sure, talk with them about it. Make them know it's important, and that they're the most important things in your life. They'll be glad you did.

So will you. ☺

Bob

. . . . . .

September 22, 2020

"Hear my prayer, O Lord; give ear to my supplications! In thy faithfulness answer me, in thy righteousness! Enter not into judgment with thy servant; for no man living is righteous before thee. For the enemy has pursued me; he has crushed my life to the ground; he has made me sit in darkness like those long dead. Therefore my spirit faints within me; my heart within me is appalled." (Psalm 143:1-4)

During a recent phone call to Christine, I asked her to intervene with God to help me with a difficult personal issue. I believe she is very close to Him. As I prayed with her, she uttered a long guttural sigh, and seconds later I smelled her perfume right here in our home. Her health remains constant. So does her love for me.

There are different types of darkness in the world. Among them are the natural darkness of the night and the spiritual darkness of evil. For the first, we have lamps and lanterns. But the only way to dispel the darkness of evil is with "lumen Christi' — the light of Christ. From the darkness of sin and spiritual death, with repentance and atonement we can return to the state of grace needed to reach Heaven. None of us is excused from accounting for our sins or God's call to repent and reform our lives.

Recognition of evil depends on a well-developed conscience that alerts us to the danger of impending sin. Temptations come our way every day, and the only way to resist them is to be constantly mindful of the presence of God. If we're not close enough to Christ to feel "the heat" of a wakened conscience when we're about to commit a sin, then our relationship with Him is merely that of an acquaintance. And that's not going to be enough.

Numerous verses in Scripture speak to the way we should pray. Among them is parable of the tax collector who stood at the back of the temple, contritely saying over and over, *"God, have mercy on me, a sinner."* Jesus tells us that he went home "justified." Another is the Penitent Thief who was crucified at Christ's right hand: *"Jesus, remember me when you come into your kingdom."* Imagine hearing the words Jesus uttered to him as he was dying: *"Amen I say to you, this day thou shalt be with me in Paradise."*

Because we don't know when we'll be called home, prayer should be an integral part of our daily lives. By frequently, if not constantly reaching out to Him in prayer, our attention is on God and He provides the grace we need to deal with life's travails and the temptations that come before us. Our conscience is strengthened, and we're no longer merely acquaintances of Jesus, we're engaging him as a close friend and partner in our lives.

I've known Christ as both a distant acquaintance and a close friend and partner at various times of my life. When I've fallen, my "prayer life" wasn't what it should have been, and my relationship with Him was distant. The suffering and sorrow which resulted were not what God had in mind for me, for those who suffered because of me, or for any of us.

Repentance and atonement are not easy. But they are the price we must pay — along with the price Jesus paid on the Cross

— to return to His fold. And when we do return, there is great joy in Heaven — and in our own hearts as well.

Please don't die with regrets, or lacking the grace you need to reach Heaven. Please don't be too proud to fall on your knees before God and confess, repent and atone. Reach out to Him. He's waiting, and His reward is the "peace beyond all human understanding."

https://www.youtube.com/watch?v=rRyOS0nZr7s

To love God, we have to know Him. And to know Him, we have to communicate with Him.

So what are you waiting for? Start talking! ☺

Bob

. . . . . .

December 24, 2020

"While they were there, the time came for her to have her child, and she gave birth to her firstborn son. She wrapped him in swaddling clothes and laid him in a manger, because there was no room for them in the inn. Now there were shepherds in that region living in the fields and keeping the night watch over their flock. The angel of the Lord appeared to them and the glory of the Lord shone around them, and they were struck with great fear. The angel said to them, "Do not be afraid; for behold, I proclaim to you good news of great joy that will be for all the people. For today in the city of David a savior has been born for you who is Messiah and Lord. And this will be a sign for you: you will find an infant wrapped in swaddling clothes and lying in a manger. And suddenly there was a multitude

THE POSTS

of the heavenly host with the angel, praising God and saying: "Glory to God in the highest, and on earth peace to those on whom his favor rests."" (Luke 2: 1-14)

It's been much too long since I've shared my thoughts with you, as the "ordinariness" and "unchangingness" of Chrissy's condition has provided no "spark" to do so. But I've come to realize that it's wrong to wait for something "important enough" to move us to do God's work. We need to be at it every day of our lives. I'm sorry for being away so long.

There's been no change in Chrissy's condition, and she remains quiet and serene — a wonderful example for the rest of us as we battle a pandemic, political upheaval, economic catastrophe, government paralysis, and increasing global strife on the Eve of Christmas. Her facility has been locked down for most of the past 9 months. We haven't been able to visit for most of that time, which makes it all that much more critical that we speak with her every day so she knows we're staying with her on the journey.

So yesterday, Chrissy "spoke" to me for about 45 seconds, as I was sharing with her the details of an earlier phone conversation with our daughter Lauren. During a momentary pause in my commentary, she began to "speak" — not words that I could understand, but beautiful, melodic sing-song phrases, her voice rising and falling like the voice of an angel, her lips articulating "words" which seemed to be an affirmation of the things I'd said to Lauren. It was the most uplifting moment I've had for the past several years — a beautiful brief cut of the soundtrack of a choir of angels. It was the perfect prologue as we pause on this Christmas Eve to prepare to receive our Savior.

THE POSTS

I can't recall the last time Chrissy "spoke," but yesterday my heart and soul leaped with the realization that she still has enough cognitive ability to try to share what is in her heart. Day after day, week after week, month after month, year after year, we call and speak to her, sharing our day's experiences, encouraging her, letting her know that our love only grows stronger. In our hearts, we're always seeking a sign that she comprehends, that she is "there." Yesterday, she let me know.

There is a common thread to Chriss's "speaking." It always happens when I'm sharing something about one of our children — a triumph, a tragedy, a conflict, an aspiration. Her love for Joe, Lauren and Stephanie, and grandson Hunter was incredibly strong, and I believe it remains strong to this day. Why wouldn't it? God gave Mothers such a special role, and provided them with a share of the very same love He holds for us.

Our world is an evolving train wreck. Natural disasters, political upheaval, war, and pestilence assail us. It's always been this way, but these days it's so much more visible, and perhaps much more prevalent and dangerous, than ever before. Thousands of years of human dissonance continue to march towards a crescendo of evil as the world cries out for Redemption, foretold by the prophets, heralded by choirs of angels, and fulfilled in the quiet innocence of a helpless Child laying on a bed of straw in a manger on a cold winter's night two thousand years ago.

Amid the turmoil around us, it is dangerously easy to become jaded and cynical, to doubt that God is truly with us, and to seek some sign that He hears us, that He is "there." When we're lost in the wilderness of sin and doubt, we are the lost sheep that Jesus came to find. The beginning of His search for us happened 2020 years ago tonight.

No matter the noise of the world, no matter the fear, the distress, the hatred, the violence, the cacophony of discord around us; tonight we hear the song of our redemption, in the tiny voice of a helpless God child whose sole purpose was and is to bring us home to our Father in Heaven.

Remember what grade school teachers taught us about how to cross a street? "Stop, look, and listen."

STOP what you are doing. Break the bad habits and toss the attitudes that lead you away from God.

LOOK for those shepherds tending their flocks. They're all around you — find one whose message touches you and follow it.

And LISTEN with every fiber of your being for those choirs of angels whose voices proclaimed the arrival of the Messiah. Those voices might just be the quiet whispers of those you love most, whose sounds have become unintelligible amid the din of a world gone amok.

Glory to God in the highest, and peace on Earth to those on whom his favor rests. I love each of you, and wish you a joyful, holy Christmas, as angel choirs proclaim the birth of Jesus Christ, our Lord and Savior.

Bob

. . . . . .

August 12, 2021

"And he said this parable: A man had a fig tree planted in his vineyard, and he came seeking fruit on it and found none. And he said to the vinedresser, "Lo these three years I have come seeking fruit on this fig tree, and I find none. Cut it down; why should it use up the ground?" And he answered him, "Let it

> *alone, sir, this year also, till I dig about it and put on manure. And if it bears fruit next year, well and good; but if not, you can cut it down." (Luke 13:6-9)*

Chrissy continues her stable existence, showing slight signs of gradual improvement. Her limbs occasionally make small movements — a sign that perhaps some neural impulses are beginning to find their way to her extremities. And she occasionally seems to be trying to talk, moving her lips, and making "voice noises" at the same time, apparently trying to respond to our questions or comments. Miracles do happen, and we continue to pray and believe. Recharging our faith is so important, as the days, weeks, and months of this chapter of our lives have become years. It's dangerously easy to become settled or complacent with our spiritual condition. Weariness, stability, and spiritual complacency tempt us to passivity, and Satan lurks for those who become weak.

The world continues its bizarre COVID contortions as government mandates collide with individual rights and freedoms. The increasing societal upheaval we're experiencing has been in the making for a very long time. It was predictable, given the trajectory of our nation and the world for the past half century.

I view the world as having three sets of laws: God's laws, Nature's laws, and Man's laws. It isn't rocket science to prioritize them in order of importance. But when Man's laws begin contradicting, and even rejecting the "laws of Nature and of Nature's God," history has repeatedly chronicled the downfall of the offending civilization.

When we place mankind at the top of the "world order," we challenge the eternal and natural order of the universe. By doing so, we rebel against the model that God provided at the dawn of creation. Fundamental definitions and societal structures begin to crumble, and moral confusion results. Societal decay and disorder begin to manifest themselves, as the moral order established by God is violated. As goes the condition of the family in a society, so goes the future of that society. Look around...

We have been given — and forgiven — so much. God is visiting our "fig orchard" at this very moment. The chaos we see around us is not the fruit that God had expected of us. He has given us many reprieves, but there will be a final harvest. What are we doing to restore order to our world — the order established in the eternal guidance of Scripture, and affirmed by the sacrifice of God made man at Calvary?

It's time to prune the trees and pull up the weeds. The Master will be returning to check the harvest.

Be bountiful!

Bob

. . . . . .

September 14, 2021

"Come to me all ye who are weary and burdened, and I will give you rest. Take my yoke upon you and learn from me, for I am gentle and humble in heart, and you will find rest for your souls. For my yoke is easy, and my burden is light." (Matthew 11: 28-30)

There are four levels of consciousness: coma, vegetative state, minimally conscious, and conscious. The "vegetative state" is likened to being underwater, sometimes very deep and sometimes near the surface. I believe that Christine is beginning to spend more time "near the surface" than she has before. The brain heals at a dreadfully slow pace; but it has an amazing capacity to find different neural pathways and to regenerate some of its capabilities. We continue to pray, and to be inspired by her will to live.

In the several years that have passed since she was stricken, dealing with the reality of her condition has periodically provided revelations about life, death, faith, family, love, marriage, joy, sorrow, sin, guilt, regret, forgiveness, and God. Some were realized with harsh rapidity; others came much more subtly. But all have helped me better understand God's love for us.

After almost five years, I have come to realize that one of the things I miss most is the emotional sustenance that comes from the quick hugs we gave each other during the course of the day; from her hand gently grasping my forearm sometimes signaling care and sometimes caution; from the unspoken "I love you" that passed between us when our eyes met, and words weren't needed.

Too often I didn't comprehend the gentleness she brought to our life together, the small acts of giving — handmade cards and Hershey kisses she'd put in my aircrew luggage to surprise me when I opened my rollaboard halfway around the world; pictures and needlepoint and knitting and Santa Clauses and dolls and teddy bears and the amazingly beautiful creations she made and happily shared, enriching my life and nurturing our family and our friends. Christine was/is a Registered Nurse; but her care for us went far beyond taking care of cuts, bruises, sprains, and head colds.

Absence of these small gestures, and failing to express gratitude for them, can gradually make us brittle, as life and the world divert our attention away from that which is truly important. Events and circumstances tempt us to look in the wrong places for the emotional and psychological fulfillment we need, opening the door for sin to enter our lives.

Chrissy's arms no longer give me hugs, her voice no longer speaks to me, her eyes no longer express her feelings, and her hands no longer create the beautiful things that underscored her love for me and for our family and friends. And no matter where we look for emotional, spiritual, and psychological sustenance, nothing in this world can provide the living water we need to sustain love or overcome grief.

When we lose a loved one, whether to death or to some other misfortune or affliction, there's only one place to find the living water that will bring us peace. It flows only from the outstretched arms of Jesus Christ on the Cross, embracing each of us and all of mankind with the love that surpasses all human understanding.

Christ's arms outstretched on the Cross are an everlasting welcome to His embrace and God's love; an eternal promise that though in this life we may not be relieved of grief or affliction, the grace and peace we need to continue our journey as He would have us live is forever present for the asking. His eyes look into our hearts and invite us to come to Him with our pains and sorrows; and His outstretched hands offer us the greatest gifts ever given to mankind: forgiveness and salvation.

Letting go of pain, sorrow, and grief becomes much easier and helps us grow in faith when we fully understand that Jesus is there to lift our burdens from us if we surrender them to Him.

Reflect on Christ's love, and then accept His embrace. If we truly accept Him, it's like no other hug we'll ever get.

Bob

· · · · · ·

Epilogue

> *"Whereof what's past is prologue; what to come, in yours and my discharge."*
> —William Shakespeare, "The Tempest"

In one way or another, everything we experience in life is preparing us for something we will encounter in the future. We study hard in school to gain the knowledge and skills to prepare for future success. We train hard too as individuals and teams to prepare for athletic contests on the field. But how many of us continue to nurture and strengthen our faith so that it may enable us to weather the storms and rejoice in the triumphs of life in preparation for eternity?

May you never stop searching for the "thread of faith" that God has woven into the tapestry of your life. I assure you it's there if you look for it hard enough.

If this book brings you closer to Almighty God, rekindles or deepens your faith, leads you to restore a broken relationship,

EPILOGUE

heals a past hurt, or simply reinforces your faith, Christine and I will have succeeded in turning her tragedy to God's purposes.

> May our Lord and Savior "raise you up on eagle's wings,
> Bear you on the breath of dawn,
> Make you to shine like the sun,
> And hold you in the palm of His hand."
> To God be the glory.

Bob and Christine

About the Author

After graduating from the United States Naval Academy in 1975, Bob Giuda was commissioned a second lieutenant in the United States Marine Corps. Upon receiving his Navy Wings of Gold he served as a carrier-based attack pilot and instructor,  training pilots to operate from our nation's aircraft carriers. While in the Marines, he met the love of his life, Christine, a Navy Nurse, to whom he remains married after forty-one years. They have three grown children.

After the Marines, Giuda served as an FBI Agent, working against major drug cartels and flying surveillance missions against domestic and international cartels and terrorist organizations. In 1986, he joined United Airlines, retiring as a Boeing 777 international captain in February 2017.

After 9/11, he won international recognition for leading the US effort to train and arm airline pilots to prevent future airline hijackings. He has served in numerous local elected offices as well as six years as a State Representative and six more as a State Senator, before retiring from political office in December 2022. He is an accomplished pianist, loves fishing, enjoys traveling, and currently resides in Warren, New Hampshire.

www.ingramcontent.com/pod-product-compliance
Lightning Source LLC
Chambersburg PA
CBHW050547160426
43199CB00015B/2562